AMONG THE
IRANIANS

A GUIDE TO IRAN'S
CULTURE AND CUSTOMS

SOFIA A. KOUTLAKI

INTERCULTURAL PRESS
A Nicholas Brealey Publishing Company

BOSTON • LONDON

To my father, Antonis Koutlakis, who always believed in me.
And to Hossein, who turned from a pen-friend
into an instrument of the Friend.

First published by Intercultural Press, an imprint of Nicholas Brealey Publishing, in 2010.

20 Park Plaza, Suite 1115A	3-5 Spafield Street, Clerkenwell
Boston, MA 02116, USA	London, EC1R 4QB, UK
Tel: + 617-523-3801	Tel: +44-(0)-207-239-0360
Fax: + 617-523-3708	Fax: +44-(0)-207-239-0370
www.interculturalpress.com	www.nicholasbrealey.com

Printed in Turkey

14 13 12 11 10   1 2 3 4 5

ISBN: 978-1-931930-90-1

Library of Congress Cataloging-in-Publication Data
[has been applied for]

CONTENTS

Contents

Contents

ACKNOWLEDGMENTS

The seed of this book lay dormant in my mind for almost ten
years until I visited the *Word Into Art* exhibition at the British
Museum in September 2006. As I stood looking at the work of an Iranian
photographer, I overheard an Iranian woman trying to explain to her non-
Iranian companion what each element in the photograph "meant" to her.
While the friend listened to the explanation and things began to make sense
to her, I had the idea: what if there were a book that contained a basic
grounding in Iranian culture, a sort of handbook?

An hour later I sat at the Café Nero in Oxford Street, scribbling bits that
eventually found their way into the present introduction of this book, and
a few weeks later, my old colleagues and friends Catherine Madinaveitia,
Alex Harvie, and Hayedeh Mashayekh met for lunch off Trafalgar Square in
central London. I sounded my idea out to them and I started writing.

People in three continents have had an input into turning the idea into
a book. In London, Alex has been the good fairy of this book: she took the
idea under her wing, sprinkled her magic dust, and turned it into a viable
proposal. She read the first chapters while the tone was establishing itself,
and has since given of her time and shared her valuable experience whenever I asked her. I cannot thank her enough.

Many thanks go to Catherine who helped with the search for a home
for this book and also read earlier drafts of the first chapters with the keen
eye of an English teacher. Sarah Arnott read and made useful comments
that improved the clarity of the first two chapters and Appendix A. London publisher Nick Brealey saw the potential of the idea and referred it to
Intercultural Press in Boston, and later met with me. His input gave firm
direction to my idea, and I thank him for everything.

In Boston, Erika Heilman and Jennifer Olsen helped the project find its feet, especially at the beginning of the writing; later on they managed the project efficiently and were very good at putting up with the inconvenience and distance in our communications. Thank you for everything you've done, even for the little things I don't know about but you must have done to make this project become reality.

Intercultural Press editor, Rebecca Greenberg, ironed out inconsistencies and, with her probing questions made significant improvements on the text. The clarity of the text owes a lot to her and I thank her profoundly.

The one person who has been with me for the long haul was Hayedeh Mashayekh. In her capacity as an experienced cook, she provided the delicious recipes included here, and checked Chapter 9 more than once. But that was not all—she read every chapter line by line with patience and the thorough and experienced eye of an editor. Her office in Tehran shared by Zohreh Hedayati Bidhendi has been a welcome space where they generously shared their deep knowledge of Iranian history and culture with me. Zohreh also lent me books and looked up facts for me. I would like to thank them both for their time and hospitality.

During writing, Soraya Javanmard and Mariam Samavati, who participated in my English class at the Noqte Atf Institute, Tehran, helped with research and lent me books. Thank you both.

Over the years many Iranians, too many to mention, have unwittingly provided material that has found its way here, and helped me learn much. Among of all these, my husband Hossein Fakhri Moghaddam's family must always occupy a very important place. Mâmân-jun, the embodiment of selfless devotion until the end of her life, and Hâj Nâsser, or Âqâ-jun as we, his children and grandchildren called him, embraced me as a daughter from the moment they met me and taught many of the things I know about Iranian culture. In my mind, Iranian everyday culture is intertwined with their memory. They are out of reach to thank now, but may their souls live on in bliss.

Thank you, Hossein, for collecting information for the business chapter, for sharing my life and putting up with my moods for these last twenty-three years (and with no end in sight).

Finally, I should add that any errors and inaccuracies, of which there must be many, as always remain my responsibility.

INTRODUCTION

In recent years Iran has been featured regularly in world news: the ongoing nuclear issue, the Iranian outlook on the Palestinian issue, and the launch of the Omid satellite into space in February 2009 to name a few. In addition, the unrest that followed the presidential election in June 2009 when Mr. Ahmadinejad was elected for a second term was beamed to every corner of the world through official news channels, on Web blogs, and on social networking sites, keeping Iran at the forefront of the news and once more heightening the world's interest in Iran.

During the post-election unrest, Greek friends and family, disturbed by the news footage shown on their TV screens, rang me to ask whether we were affected by the events. I reassured them that we were all right: apart from the streets around Tehran University and some other areas in the center of the city where shops closed early—places people avoided for a few days after the elections—life continued as normal in the rest of the city, as in the rest of Iran. People went about their daily work, visited each other's houses, shopped, held wedding celebrations, and youngsters went to their language and swimming classes. This is the image of Iran that this book presents.

I am writing this Introduction in Tehran in early August 2009, a few days after my return from a trip to my native city of Athens, Greece. Greeks generally know a little bit about ancient Iran, mostly from their school history books, but modern Iran remains, for the most part, a

mystery. Three chance encounters I had while in Greece typify common attitudes about Iran and its people outside the country.

In a street in central Athens, a young man distributing free samples of beauty products offered to sign me up for a promotional course of beauty treatments. I excused myself, saying that I live in Tehran. He paused. "Do you go there on the Metro?" My reply, "Well, first on the Metro and then by airplane," was met with a blank stare. "Tehran, you know, Iran?" I tried again.

"Oh, yes . . . Is it safe there? No bombs, no terrorists?"

In a conversation with a relative, she reported that the young son of a friend who had recently visited Iran expressed the view that, culturally, Iran is "forty years backward." For a few days afterward I was mulling this idea over, trying to work out what exactly he may have had in mind, until one day at my local bank a chance conversation with a bank employee shed some light. During her visit to Iran, the employee loved the atmosphere and the community spirit. She liked the fact that families spent time together enjoying themselves in parks. She found Iranians cultured, refined, polite, and welcoming, and was impressed by the fact that even very young children behaved with respect. These are practices and pastimes that were current in Greece and elsewhere many years ago, and conjure up images of close family relationships and traditional values.

These indicative responses and the many more I have heard over the years range from total ignorance, to negative and sometimes patronizing attitudes, to positive appreciation and a wish to know more about Iranians. To my mind, such comments highlight the need to understand the culture of this intriguing nation, now more urgently than ever. Thus this book was born.

It is late Thursday evening as I write. The notes of a violin waft through the mesh screen, accompanying a hoarse, male voice with a sad tinge, singing of Love, the aching feeling in the pit of the stomach, "the desire of the moth for the star."

I try to ignore the singing and get on with my work. The man walks up to the little park to the north of our block of flats, but he returns to stand under the eastern windows again, singing of how his heartstrings are bound inextricably with the Beloved's strands of hair.

I take a 500-tuman note out of my purse, put on a white chador, and open the mesh screen. He doesn't see me at first, but then he looks up. He is tall and thin, with tanned skin and untidy hair. The paper money, limp as a withered leaf, floats down to the pavement. He picks it up and touches his forehead with it. "May God bless you, pilgrim lady, may your table be full of His blessings." He resumes his song.

The second floor neighbor calls him from her window and throws down some money and a wrapped candy.

"May you always taste sweetness, pilgrim lady; may God reward your kindness."

The music reminds me of pre-EU Athens, where I was born and grew up, the memory vague as a dream. Tehran is in many ways similar to the Athens of my youth: the traffic and the summer heat (still the same), the smog, the pickup trucks buying metal, from old crockery to decommissioned refrigerators and discarded water boilers.

The minstrel walks down to the next street. I close the mesh screen, thinking about the time and the long distance, physical and psychological, I have covered over the years.

In October 1986, during my final year of studying English literature at the University of Athens, I received an envelope bearing a series of postage stamps featuring flowers of various colors and some writing in Arabic script. It had come all the way from Iran. Out of curiosity I slit open the envelope before I returned to our flat on the third floor. To my 23-year-old self, Iran was attractive and intriguing at the same time: an ancient nation that had waged war against my ancestors five centuries before Christ, and was now presented in the news as a land of fist-shaking mobs of unshaven men and of women wrapped in black veils from head to foot, embroiled in war with its neighbor Iraq. That was all I knew about Iran at the time.

The envelope contained a letter written in German from Hossein, an architecture student in Tehran currently working and learning German in preparation for his move to study in Germany. He talked about his family of two brothers and two sisters, and of his hobbies, drawing and reading, but the writing had nothing of the fluency and the air of European glamour that the letters from my other pen friends from Germany,

Italy, and the Canary Isles had. Unlike those letters, it ended up in the bottom of my desk drawer, unanswered.

I forgot about Hossein until the spring of 1987, when I received another letter from him accompanied by a color photo: a young man with raven-black hair and a benign smile, seated in front of a row of potted red geraniums. Hossein was coming to Athens.

This letter could not be ignored. I imagined the possibility of a tall, dark stranger arriving at our front door one day, speaking German—not something that would impress my parents. But how could I prevent it? Since he had found my address via the Goethe Institute in Tehran, where more appropriate to meet than at the Goethe Institute in Athens, where I spent the free time between my lectures every week? I wrote back that he would find me every Tuesday afternoon between 4:00 and 6:00 in the foyer of the Institute, Omirou Street, behind the Catholic Church. Tuesday, May 5, 1987, the day I met Hossein, was my first brush with Iranian culture. Less than a year later, I married him, and we settled in England, where we both worked and studied until 1997. Then we moved to Iran for three years, and then back to England until 2007, when we came back to Tehran once again.

Over the years, I have observed the lives and the practices of Iranians in Tehran and in London. This book is the distillation of these observations, and as such they are made from my vantage point and are not exhaustive or infallible. Through my marriage to Hossein, I entered a certain religious and social milieu in his native city, Tehran. This is a social circle in which the men now in their 70s and older own small shops or artisan workshops, and the women of the same age move mostly within their family circles. Their sons have either continued and expanded the family trade or entered the Tehran Bazaar, with a few of them entering tertiary education. Their daughters have had some schooling—some have finished high school—and married within their class. But the young men and women of the third generation now increasingly go to university. On the whole, the social milieu within which I move in Iran is of a traditional, religious character, affording me a specific and unique window into Iranian culture.

As we begin the analysis of Iranian culture and customs, I want to add a caveat here. Many of the practices and social rules I describe should

be seen as tendencies, not as absolutes, in the sense that they can be deviated from and broken. Some may sound unfamiliar to Iranians living abroad, or indeed to those within Iran who belong to another social class. Bear in mind that Iran is a vast country of over 70 million inhabitants belonging to various ethnic groups. The population of the capital, Tehran, now numbers about 14 million people, and just like every megalopolis, it is the home of wide cultural variations in customs and everyday practices. Nonetheless, even if some of the details I describe are specific to people I have encountered, the tendencies are universally recognized by Iranians as their own.

A long, exciting relationship with Iranian culture started on the day I met Hossein, intermittently as a student and continuously as a foreign bride. I learned many things by trial and error (lots of them!), others by observations and probing questions: How to say what you mean, how to mean it without saying it, how to negotiate the politeness maze, the concept of "dirt," folk beliefs about food, how to dress so as not to give wrong messages, along with intriguing details such as how to fill up the petrol tank according to gender. In short, I had to learn everything about Iranian culture from the basics to the subtleties of love and arguing. This book distills that experience.

This book was written for curious and discerning Western readers who want to see behind the negative images and get insight into a culture that is very little understood and appreciated in the West. I hope that the readers of this book will have the same kind of experience as my friend Alex, who came to Tehran on business in the summer of 2000. She said she enjoyed her visit to Iran because I helped her understand the whys and the wherefores of what she saw and encountered. So we will set off on a journey similar to the one I began over twenty years ago, and we will observe and analyze behaviors in which some motifs recur with regularity and blend with each other.

Given the amount of material that I could have included in this book, *Among the Iranians* is something of a sampler, much like a buffet full of tempting dishes but, alas, one can only have one plateful altogether, one bite of each dish. I had to be selective and adhered to two criteria. First, I have included lesser-known information that, in my opinion, would be of interest and practical use to readers, and second, I have tried

to focus on the many positive aspects of Iranian culture in order to paint a picture of Iran that is not often shown.

A story is told of how Jesus Christ and his disciples passed by the rotting corpse of a dog. "What a disgusting smell!" the disciples complained. "What bright, white teeth!" Christ said, because he didn't like any of God's creatures to be spoken of in a disparaging way. "Don't act like flies," he told them, "who fly around so many beautiful things but eventually settle on filth. Don't notice only people's defects."[1] In this book I have tried to follow this advice.

Having lived among Iranians in England and in Iran for the last twenty years, I have observed a decisive period for the Iranian nation. The end of the Iran-Iraq War, called by Iranians the Imposed War, in August 1988 marked the beginning of a new era of peace, reconstruction, and social change. Less than a year later, in June 1989, the leader of the Islamic Revolution, Imam Khomeini (known in the West as Ayatollah Khomeini) passed away, leaving behind a religious, political, and social legacy whose impact is still felt in Iran and in other parts of the world.

Iranian society is now in transition, and its traditional culture is undergoing change. At different points in this book I hint at practices that are changing or are on the way out. To some Iranian friends who read and commented on the text before publication, the practices and customs I write about brought back childhood memories and nostalgia for the Iran of their grandparents, while to others they are still very much a live, vibrant part of their everyday lives.

Numerous factors are at play, some similar to those in other societies, some specific to the Iranian reality. At this point in its history, the Iranian nation is young, in the sense that young people form the largest social group. In 1976 the population was 34 million, in 1989 it reached 50 million, and twenty years later it has stabilized at over 70 million.[2]

This population explosion means that more than half of the Iranian population are now in their thirties or younger and have not experienced life before the Islamic Revolution. These young Iranians formed 40 percent of the voters in the 2005 presidential election,[3] and in the June 2009 presidential elections they constituted the majority of the electoral body. According to the governmental body overseeing the June 2009 presiden-

tial elections, 46.3 million Iranians were eligible to vote. These many young people compete for limited life opportunities—admission to universities, jobs, housing, suitable marriage partners—which poses a serious challenge for the government and across society.

I hope to be able to help you discover everything you might want to know about Iran, and I hope that you will find the process as enjoyable as I have—and still do. And so the big journey continues, for Iran, for America, and for every one of us. Only God knows what's in store. So, as the Iranians say, "What must one do? *Tavakkol be Khodâ*'"—or, in other words, In God We Trust.

SAK, Tehran, August 2009

TRANSLITERATION NOTE

I have adopted a simple, accessible transliteration system that accurately represents current standard Persian pronunciation rather than spelling.

The English letters and letter combinations have approximately the same sounds as in English, e.g., **ch** as in *chair* and **sh** as in *shop*, apart from the following:

kh: voiceless velar uvular with scrape, approximating to **ch** in the *loch* and as in the German *doch*

q: voiced or voiceless uvular plosive, according to phonetic context; approximating the first sound of *quorum* but articulated deeper in the throat

gh: voiced uvular fricative, similar to the French *r*

zh: as in *leisure*

a: as in *hat*

â: as in *bath*

u: as in *zoo*

Words and names that have become standardized in English follow their established spelling, e.g., Isfahan, Ramadan, and Imam.

ONE

Getting There

The first time I visited Iran, I felt as if I had stepped into another world: it was February 1989, just six months after the end of the Iran-Iraq war. At the time I worked for an Iranian governmental company in London and was invited to Iran for the celebrations of the tenth anniversary of the Islamic Revolution. My in-laws, who couldn't wait to meet me, were at the Hotel Homa almost as soon as I was shown into my room and got my tour guide's permission to spend the night in their house.

I took a black chador I had borrowed from a friend back in London out of my suitcase. My friend had explained that Shahr-e Rey, or Shabdolazim, Hossein's home town in the south of Tehran is a pilgrimage destination because the saint Hazrat Abdol-Azim is buried there, so a black chador is to be worn in the street. I found the idea of wearing a chador exciting, just like a child dressing up. The trouble was that I was one hand short: overnight bag in one hand, bag with presents in the other, and the missing one to hold the chador in place. I must have been a ridiculous sight as I stumbled out of the lift to meet my father- and sister-in-law. Hâj Nâsser the Blacksmith, as he introduced himself, was shorter and stockier than Hossein but had the same endearing smile. Sister-in-law Mansureh, a primary school teacher, was the same age as me and single, with eyebrows still unspoilt by the beautician's hand over hazelnut-colored, almond-shaped eyes.

I n some ways Iran is similar to the elephant in the story "The Elephant in the Dark" related by Rumi (1207–1273) in *The Masnavi*. The story appears in slightly different versions in various cultures (e.g., the men are blind in some, or the elephant is in a dark room in others), but the moral remains the same. The men have never seen an elephant, and since they cannot see it, they resort to feeling the animal with their hands. When they compare notes later, they find that they are in total disagreement over what an elephant looks like. The man who touched its trunk says that it looks like a water spout; the one who touched its ear insists that it is a fan; the man who felt its leg describes it as a pillar; and another who touched its back is convinced it is a throne.

So it is with Iran. Ask ten people what they know about the country and you will most likely receive a variety of responses. Some confuse Iran with its neighbor Iraq; Americans may recall the U.S. embassy hostage crisis; others remember the war with Iraq from 1980–1988 (which Iranians refer to as the Imposed War). A couple more may remember President George W. Bush's "Axis of Evil" speech, while others will mention the nuclear issue and the "treatment" of women in Iran.

For some people, Iran is the continuation of ancient civilizations, the ancient Persia memorialized in the writings of Herodotus and Xenophon, the land of splendid mosques and majestic palaces; it is the land of art, of fine Persian carpets and luxuriously haired cats, of miniatures and verdant gardens. For others, it is a land of unspoiled natural beauty and home to a great number of animal and plant species[1] and, of course, an important oil- and gas-producing country. But for the majority of people in the West, Iran remains a tantalizing mystery, a challenge to established patterns of thought, a source of paradoxes. Just like Rumi's elephant, Iran is different things to different people, whereas in fact it is more than the sum of its parts.

A (PERSIAN) ROSE BY ANY OTHER NAME

The country we now know as Iran (which means "Land of the Aryans") has always been called that by its own people, but for centuries Europeans and others referred to it as *Persia*, mainly due to the writings of Greek

historians. The name *Persia* was derived from the southern province of Pars (or Fars), where the main centers of the ancient Persian civilization (Persepolis and Pasargadae) were located. In 1935 the first Pahlavi King Reza decreed that Persia should be known as *Iran*, a name that harks back to the glories of the Aryan race and pre-Islamic Iran.[2]

Persian (*Farsi* in Persian) is the official language of the Islamic Republic of Iran, which is Iran's formal name. Persians are the largest ethnic group in the country, outnumbering others such as Azeri Turks, Kurds, Arabs, and Lurs. The term *Iranian* includes members of all ethnic groups, much like the term *British* includes the Welsh, the Scots, the English, the Irish, and all immigrant minorities. In the same way, Iranian ethnic groups may speak different mother tongues but are conversant in Persian.

I avoid using the term *Farsi* to refer to the Persian language in deference to the Iranian Academy of Persian Language. The Academy is concerned that many English speakers don't know the term *Farsi* and that it may give the impression that Farsi is a dialect or a new language. *Persian*, on the other hand, correctly evokes the country's history and civilization, as this term has been used throughout the years in Western scholarship. In this book I use *Persian* for the language, carpets, and miniatures, and *Iranian* for society, people, culture, and the New Year holiday, although this distinction may sometimes seem arbitrary and its use inconsistent.

THE COUNTRY . . .

Iran, with its present borders resembling the outline of a sitting cat, occupies a vast area of 636,000 square miles (1,650,000 square kilometers), located between the 26th and 40th parallels north of the equator, and between the 44th and the 64th meridians east of Greenwich. Most of the country is mountainous, except a large desert in the center and areas of less than 650 feet (200 meters) altitude lying along the southeast border with Iraq and the south coast. As a result, most of the country has very hot, dry summers and cold winters. The only exceptions are the Caspian littoral in the north and the Persian Gulf coast in the south, both of which

are humid because of their proximity to water, and the northwest province of Iranian Azerbaijan which, according to the Bradt guide, boasts a climate similar to that of Switzerland.

Iranians take pride that the country has four seasons and view this as a balanced and complete universe. Each season begins at its appointed time, exhibiting its typical weather and bearing its own fruit. And maybe surprisingly to those from nations covering a smaller land mass, each of the seasons can be found somewhere in the country at any time of the year. The weather forecast usually mentions the coldest and warmest spots in the country, ranging from around freezing in winter to over 100° Fahrenheit (around 40° Celsius) in the summer.

. . . AND ITS NEIGHBORS

Iran shares its long western border with Iraq and a northwestern one with Turkey. After the break up of the Soviet Union, its former neighbor all along the northern border on both sides of the Caspian Sea, Iran now borders the republics of Armenia and Azerbaijan to the northwest and Turkmenistan to the northeast. Its eastern neighbors are Afghanistan and Pakistan, the Gulf of Oman to the southeast and, past the Hormuz Straits, the Persian Gulf across which lie (from east to west) Oman, the United Arab Emirates, Saudi Arabia, and Kuwait.

Be careful not to use any other name to denote the Persian Gulf, such as "The Arabian Gulf" or simply "The Gulf" as it sometimes appears in newspapers and on some maps. Iranians consider this almost blasphemous and point out that the Persian Gulf has always been called so since antiquity.[3]

CALENDARS IN USE

The first-time traveler to Iran will notice a different concept of time, which is as much a cultural construct as anything else. The organization of the day and the week differ from what a Westerner is used to. The day

begins at the moment of true dawn—about an hour and twenty minutes before sunrise—with the call to morning prayer. This timing variation through the seasons influences Iranians' everyday life. Iranians often feel that in winter, when the noon call to prayer is made at about 11:55 and the evening one can be as early as 5:00 P.M., that the days are short and that they can't get many tasks done. In the summer, when days are long, there are more hours in the day. The rest of the day is punctuated by another two calls to prayer, at about 12:00 noon in the autumn and winter, and about 1:00 P.M. in the spring and summer for the noon/afternoon prayer, after which lunch is usually eaten. The most marked difference happens with the variation of the evening prayer, which can be as early as 5:00 P.M. in the winter and as late as 8:45 P.M. in the summer. Traditionally, meals are served after the evening prayers, so in the summer dinnertime may be as late as 9:30. Office and school hours, however, don't vary with seasons.

DAY OF REST

As in other Islamic countries, the day of rest in Iran is Friday, with schools and some offices working a half day on Thursday. The first working day of the week is therefore Saturday, so many embassies have their weekend on Fridays and Saturdays. Traditionally, the day ends at sunset, so "Thursday night" can also be expressed as "the night of Friday." Consequently, Iranians often celebrate birthdays and anniversaries on the eve of the day itself.

The Iranian New Year (*Noruz*) begins with the spring in the northern hemisphere, at the exact moment that the Sun enters the northern hemisphere on the vernal equinox on March 20th or 21st. While at first this may seem unusual to Westerners, consider this: the first month of the horoscope is Aries (March 21–April 20), and the extra day for a leap year is always added to February and not, say, to December, which points toward some ancient link to the natural cycle of the seasons.

The exact calculations are much more complicated than this, but the general idea is that the new year is linked to the new life generated on earth by the advent of spring. The Iranian calendar consists of twelve months: the first six have thiry-one days each, the next five have thirty, and the last month twenty-nine, or thirty in leap years. The names for the Iranian months derive from old Persian names of Zoroastrian deities, the religion of Iranians before the advent of Islam in the seventh century A.D. It was at this point that Iranians adopted the Islamic lunar calendar, which was used until the late nineteenth century, at least for administrative purposes. But the Iranian solar calendar was not forgotten: it was recalibrated in the eleventh century by a group of scholars, including the famous poet, mathematician, and astronomer Omar Khayyam, and was eventually enshrined in Iranian law in 1925 (see appendix B for the months of the Iranian and the Islamic years).

For example, our year 2010 corresponds to the Islamic solar year *anno Persico* (A.P.) 1388–89 and to the Islamic lunar year *anno Hegirae* (A.H.) 1430–31. Both of these calendars are in use today in Iran: the former for governmental and administrative purposes and the latter for religious observances. These calendars begin the reckoning at A.D. 622, with the *Hijra* (*Hegira* in Latin), the Holy Prophet's migration from Mecca to Medina. So why are they out of synch?

The Islamic lunar calendar consists of twelve lunar months, making it about 354 days long, which means that every lunar year is eleven days shorter than the solar year. Starting the calculations at the same point in time, after fourteen centuries the two dating systems have ended up with forty-five years' difference.

The implications of this "discrepancy" reveal themselves in different ways. For example, Islamic observances, such as the mourning ceremonies for Imam Hossein, clashed with the New Year celebrations between 2002–2006, and the fasting month of Ramadan edges forward toward the summer. Ramadan began on September 13 in 2007, September 2 in 2008, August 22 in 2009, and so on by eleven days every year. And, of course, calculating your age in lunar years may makes you feel slightly older. (Multiply your age in years by 365 and divide the result by 354 for a rough calculation.)

USE OF THE DIFFERENT CALENDARS

The Iranian calendar (*sâl-e hejri-ye shamsi*, Hijra solar year) is used for administrative and fiscal purposes and for birthdays, wedding anniversaries, and other memorable dates.

The Islamic calendar (*sâl-e hejri-ye qamari*, Hijra lunar year) is used for religious festivals and occasions, for example Ramadan, the annual pilgrimage (*Hajj*), Imam Hossein's martyrdom, and the feasts of Eid Fitr and Eid Qorbân (see chapter 4).

The Western Christian calendar (*sâl-e Milâdi*, year of the birth [of Christ]) is used in transactions and correspondence with the rest of the world, international days, for example, World Labor Day, international fairs, and foreign travel bookings.

Date books and calendars published in Iran bear all three dates for every day of the year, so it is always easy to check correlations. Newspapers also include the three dates on the first page.

IRAN THROUGH THE MILLENNIA

The Iranian plateau contains evidence of people living in the Lower Paleolithic times (800,000 years ago), and the first Aryan nomadic tribes settled in the area at the end of the second millennium B.C.

Because of its geographical location, Iran has been at the crossroads of civilizations and movements of people from both Europe and Asia. Over the millennia, Iran was invaded by the Greeks, Arabs, Mongols, and Turks, with every invasion introducing new influences into the culture. Iranians have proved remarkably adaptable in the face of successive occupations, assimilating elements of every conqueror's culture and giving them an Iranian flavor, while the conquerors also adopted elements from Iranian culture. However, Iranian peoples have always reasserted their national identity and have developed as a distinct political and cultural entity. (For a brief overview of Iranian history, see appendix A).

WHAT IRAN HAS GIVEN THE WORLD

Iranian civilization has made numerous contributions to the world in agriculture and animal husbandry, cultural products, and architecture. It is responsible for peaches (*Prunus persica*), tulips, spinach, saffron, barberries, pistachios, and the domestication of goats and chickens. The lute (*târ*), the precursor of the guitar, and the game of polo also have Iranian ancestry.

Bricks, windmills, the architectural form of the ziggurat, underground water canals (*qanât*), and, of course, hand-knotted carpets are credited to Iranian creativity and artistic innovation. The first mail system (The Royal Road) and the first taxation system were introduced in the Achaemenid period. The Cyrus Cylinder, dated between 539–530 B.C., which declared the principles of respect for other humans, religious tolerance, and freedom of worship and is often considered the first charter of human rights, is now kept in the British Museum, and its replica is at the U.N. headquarters in New York. It was translated into all the U.N. official languages in 1971.

THE SYSTEM OF GOVERNMENT

Iran is an Islamic Republic, the only one of its kind in the world, established in 1979 by a popular movement (the Islamic Revolution) which overturned Mohammad Reza Pahlavi and abolished the institution of monarchy.

The establishment of an Islamic Republic is predicated on the principle of the regency of the jurisprudent (*velâyat-e faqih*) that was propounded by Ayatollah Khomeini. In simple words, this principle means that in the absence of the twelfth Imam (see Imam Mahdi, Appendix C, and chapter 4 "Other Religious Texts") the most learned theologian in the Shi'a world is entrusted with the governance of the Islamic community.

Based on this principle, Western media often refer to the Islamic Republic as a 'theocracy', but this designation is both inaccurate and misleading, as it does not acknowledge the 'Republic' part of the term.

In Iran there is universal suffrage over the age of 18, and 46.5 million electors were entitled to vote in the June 2009 presidential election, in which a record turnout of 85 percent was recorded.

The 1979 Constitution voted after the Islamic Revolution instituted the division of power among different bodies in order to ensure that no individual or body would ever be able to seize absolute power. The electorate vote directly for the president of the republic, the parliament, local government and the Assembly of Experts, who elect the Supreme Leader and act as his advisors in matters of state. The Guardian Council is the most powerful body and consists of twelve jurists, six appointed by the Supreme Leader and six proposed by the judiciary and subject to parliamentary approval. The Supreme Leader also appoints the head of the judiciary and must give his approval to the president-elect before he can take up office. The Expediency Council is another advisory body to the Supreme Leader and has the final say in cases of disagreement between the parliament and the Guardian Council.[4]

HOW TO GET THERE

Many major European and Middle Eastern airlines fly to Tehran, Shiraz, Isfahan, and Mashhad. At the time of this writing, the Iranian national carrier Iran Air has three scheduled flights per week from London to Tehran. The vast majority of Iran Air's clientele consists of Iranians, and it is worthwhile to fly Iran Air because it will help you get into the Iranian spirit. The in-flight meal always includes a specialty cooked by an Iranian chef, and you are bound to meet a few gregarious Iranians who will be interested in you and the reasons for your trip, and who will be forthcoming with advice and information. (Chances are you will be invited to visit them during your stay, too.)

Iran Air includes a complimentary domestic air ticket to any Iranian city, which is useful if you are visiting at a busy time. In addition, Iran Air's generous baggage allowance was only recently matched by other airlines serving this route: every passenger can check in 65 pounds (30 kilograms), plus have 11 pounds (5 kilograms) of carry-on baggage.

Iran Air's Thursday flight from London is the most popular because it lands in Tehran early on Friday, which is the weekly day of rest; consequently, families can go to the airport to welcome travelers. For those who are returning after a long time, this is especially important.

The new Imam Khomeini International Airport (IKIA) in Tehran opened to air traffic in the late summer of 2007, and has provided long-overdue relief from the cramped conditions of the old Mehrabad Airport, which now only handles domestic flights.

Standard customs limitations apply in Iran, so travelers with nothing to declare should go through the green channel, otherwise the red channel should be used. You should, however, bear in mind that bringing alcohol into Iran is strictly forbidden, so travelers cannot take advantage of their duty-free alcohol allowance when coming to Iran.

In addition, decks of playing cards and publications containing photos or images that may offend public mores are also not allowed into the country, but apart from obviously pornographic material, it is difficult to define what is considered 'offensive'. Indicatively, offensive pictures would depict men or women in close contact or wearing revealing clothes. However, the worst that can happen is having the offensive publication confiscated.

Once through customs, an airport taxi desk will arrange for a taxi to take you to your destination. These specially marked airport taxis charge a standard fare agreed upon at the desk in advance. It is always helpful to have your destination written down in Persian, although the taxi desk staff should speak English, even if the driver may not (for more on fare transactions, see chapter 3).

IDENTITY DOCUMENTS

All Iranian nationals have an identity document (*shenâss-nâmeh*). This is a booklet with a red plastic cover carrying all personal information, including names of spouse and children. By looking at a person's identity, one can find out whether a person is married, whether s/he has ever been divorced, and how many children s/he has. This identity document

is issued as soon as a baby's birth is registered, but does not carry a photograph until the holder is about 16 years old. It needs to be used throughout one's life, from school enrollment until one's death.

In recent years a national ID card scheme (*kârt-e melli*) has been introduced, bearing the holder's digital photograph and a unique bar-code. Increasingly, the national card is now used more widely, but it is not meant to replace the original identity document.

Travelers to Iran need a valid passport with a valid visa.

URBAN VIEWS

As you walk or drive through Tehran today, you will notice that there are very few traditional houses left, and those are mainly around the bazaar in central Tehran. The older houses have been replaced by two- or three-story houses dating from the 1940s onward, or by more recent multi-family homes and apartment complexes. You will most likely be struck by the enormous variety of designs and forms; every house and apartment building sports its own design of doors, windows, and finishing materials, which visitors interested in architecture will find particularly fascinating.

The yards of Iranian houses face south. Thus, the houses on the northern side of a road running east-west are accessed through the yard, while those on the south side are entered through the house itself and have the yard at the back of the house. A south-facing garden, making the most of sunshine, is a positive asset to properties in the northern hemisphere; in Iran, all properties boast sunny, south-facing gardens. In terms of town planning, this practice means that streets feel more spacious than they would if the buildings came up to the boundary on both sides. There is also more greenery in the form of trees and plants, at least on the northern side of the road.

Houses on streets running north-south afford their residents a wider choice. Since the yard always faces south, the street runs along one side of the house, giving owners the choice of either a yard or a building entrance, or often both.

INSIDE A TRADITIONAL IRANIAN HOUSE

The first time I visited Iran, in February 1989, I was working for an Iranian governmental company in London, and I was invited as an official guest for the celebrations of the tenth anniversary of the Islamic Revolution. Hossein and I were already married, and this was the first time I would meet his family, who lived in Tehran.

I already knew enough to take off my shoes in the yard just outside the front door of his parents' house. Being extra careful not to do anything wrong and following what others did, I noticed that as soon as his father came inside the house, he took off his socks, stuffed one inside the other in the shape of a ball, and tossed them behind the door. I did the same except for the tossing, and I sat down, thinking that, as in Greece, socks are probably classified with underwear and thus better kept out of sight. Nobody said anything about it until later in the afternoon when visitors were due. Then Hossein's mother whispered to her daughter, "How can I ask her to put her socks on?" obviously worried that I might take offense. Thankfully for both of us I understood and complied, without knowing why. I had yet to work out that many rules apply differently to men and women, and also vary in the presence of close family or guests.

FOOTWEAR ETIQUETTE

Always be prepared to remove shoes, if required. If you wear shoes without socks, it is a good idea to have a pair of socks with you, even thin deniers for women, so that you can wear them should you need to go indoors. Bare feet are an indication of intimacy and generally disapproved of in the presence of guests or non-intimate relatives (*nâmahrams*; see chapter 2). This rule, as many others, is not absolute, but my advice is always to be conservative rather than too forward and unwittingly causing offense. Once inside a household, you can always adjust accordingly.

An important reason behind the practice of removing shoes outside the house ensures that the carpets remain free of street dirt and other

impurities, and are therefore ritually clean to be prayed on, slept on, and having a meal spread set on them. This practice makes excellent house-keeping sense and reduces the need for more intensive cleaning. (Even the poorest of households are kept clean and tidy.)

If you visit a house without furniture, try to sit with your legs folded, as far as creaky joints allow. If after a few minutes your legs get stiff, as mine do, you can apologize for having to stretch your legs, which is considered too informal and impolite, especially in the presence of guests or those older than you. If you are female, cover your legs with a shawl or jacket.

In most households this problem does not exist anymore because a suite of furniture has become common. The standard "living room" set consists of two love seats and four armchairs, often in an imitation French style—the more elaborate and gilded, the more expensive and classy—although in recent years younger families choose contemporary design styles. Carpets in cream or other light-colored backgrounds are generally considered more elegant than the traditional dark red or navy blue.

For members of the more traditional classes, possessing furniture is a sign of status and wealth rather than a necessity: they may feel constrained by the formal air of the reception room with its heavy furniture, and if they feel intimate enough with their guests, they may well ask them if they mind sitting in the family room.

As in many other cultures, Iranian behaviors and practices take slightly different forms in privacy with close family than in the presence of acquaintances. One such instance is the two different styles of furniture. In flats where space is usually limited, the "front room" principle or separate guest area is distinguishable by furnishings in one fairly large reception area. If there is space for one furniture suite, it is mostly used by guests; if for two, one usually is more elaborate and expensive for guests and the other is fully upholstered and more comfortable to relax on.

When with close family and peers, it is permissible to slouch on a chair or sprawl on the floor (unless an elder is present), so the soft, more relaxed furniture is appropriate for everyday family use. Conversely, in the presence of non-intimates (see chapter 2) or on a formal occasion, such as a marriage proposal, the rules of politeness dictate that one must sit upright and in full control of one's posture. This duality, the "outside"

or formal/distant mode (*zâher*) and the "inside" or informal/intimate (*bâten*), permeates many other behaviors (see chapter 11).

ON HOME TURF

If an Englishman's home is his castle, you could say an Iranian woman's home is her stronghold. Once the threshold is crossed, she is the indisputable mistress of the household, although she may be assisted by other family members in the everyday running of the household.

The sons of the family often do the daily shopping, buying fresh bread, yogurt, and herbs. They also generally help with the housework, such as cleaning up after meals and taking their turn washing dishes. Occasionally they also carry out more demanding household tasks, such as washing the windows, carpets, and walls.

THE SMALLEST ROOM

In older houses the toilet is in the yard, at the farthest point from the house. Plastic slippers are kept by the front door, with the yard functioning as a buffer zone between the clean house and the "unclean" toilet. People put on the plastic shoes before going out to the toilet, and then take them off upon returning to the house. Usually there is only one pair of these plastic slippers for everyone's use, so visitors do not need to ask for permission to use them.

More recent houses and flats have "hole-in-the-ground" type toilets (called *Irâni*, i.e., Iranian). Because of the impurity of the toilet (see "Ritual Impurity"), after every use, the whole bowl and the surrounding area are rinsed with running water. In flats, which don't have a yard as a buffer zone, the slippers are placed just inside the toilet and not outside, which is meant to be ritually clean. Following the traditional placing of the toilet as far away as possible from the rooms, some modern flats have the Iranian toilet positioned very near the front door, even if the

bathroom that has a tub and shower and sink, as well as a flush toilet (called *farangi*, i.e., Frankish, European), is elsewhere in the flat.

RITUAL IMPURITY

A vital condition for Muslims' prayers to be valid is the ritual purity of clothes and the place of prayer (*pâki*). Ritual purity is linked to cleanliness: blood, urine, feces, and semen make people and objects ritually unclean (*nâjes*). Ritual impurity is transferred by moisture. This means that if you touch a ritually unclean (*nâjes*) but dry piece of clothing or the floor, your hand or foot does not become unclean. However, if the object becomes wet before it is ritually cleansed, your hand or foot also becomes ritually unclean. The easiest way to make something ritually clean is rinsing it under running water or three times with water from a container, which is what the water hose or plastic water jug in the toilet is for.

Under no circumstances should you wear the slippers used in the toilet anywhere in the rest of the house.

For Iranians the concept of "house" (*khâneh*) traditionally encompasses the building as well as the yard. In quoting the size of a property, the total area in square meters is given along with the area occupied by the building (*zir-banâ*). The yard is therefore understood as an integral part of the house and kept clean and tidy just like indoors.

Older houses often have an ornamental pool. In traditional houses rooms were arranged around the central courtyard, much like houses in classical Athens, and the pool was the focal point of the whole house. In the days before piped water, the pool was used to store water for washing. Nowadays, although the pool has lost its practical importance, it still retains a spiritual significance and resonates deeply with the Iranian psyche: it is seen as the expression of a household's purity of heart and the source of calm reflection. Elderly people, in particular, who have always lived in houses with a yard and pool cannot imagine living without them in an apartment.

LINKS WITH FENG SHUI

For centuries Iran was part of the Silk Road, along which cultural beliefs and practices were traded together with silk and spices. Some of the principles of Feng Shui ("wind and water" in Chinese) are used in traditional Iranian architecture, for example, in the layout of a house and the use of water. Moving water in the garden is good in Iran, just as in Feng Shui, because it refreshes the Chi (life force) and soothes the nerves. The pond water should always be clean and never be allowed to stagnate; a goldfish in the garden pond encourages prosperity.

In Feng Shui, the eight-sided shape *bagwa* has been used for centuries to deflect negative energies. In traditional Iranian houses, the entrance was through an octagonal vestibule in the shape of a bagwa called *hashti*, through which the other areas of the house were accessed.

In many traditional and rural households, rooms do not "belong" to anyone nor are they designated for a certain use (e.g., bedroom), as is the practice in the West. Obviously this practice is only possible in the absence of furniture, which determines the ownership and use of rooms, but it is now on the way out among urban households. A sign of family members' intimacy is that they do things together—sometimes moving from one room to another depending on the activity and sometimes the season—or are engaged in independent activities sitting in the same room. Iranians feel safe and warm when together and dislike being alone; even sleeping alone is generally considered deplorable. Hossein's grandmother, who passed away at the age of 95, had never slept even one night in her whole life on her own in the house.

The next chapter describes in more detail the importance of family and relationships in Iranian culture, but before that, let's look at some practical housing matters.

A PLACE OF ONE'S OWN

Being a tenant is not a desirable situation for a variety of reasons. In Iran the concept of the furnished flat does not exist, except for expensive prop-

erties usually intended for overseas tenants. When one moves, the house is stripped bare, including the curtains and sometimes the light bulbs. This means that the tenants will have to fit their belongings in a new property that may be smaller, in which case some things will have to go to storage, or bigger, in which case they may not have enough carpets to cover the floor in all the rooms. Carpets are used all year round and by everyone regardless of income level and for Iranians, the laying of carpets turns a new house into a home. Therefore, being short of carpets can be problematic in a new property. Furniture and big electrical appliances may be damaged while being moved, and often tenants need to buy new curtains, which in Iran are a substantial outlay.

Relations between landlord and tenant are considered (and sometimes are) hard to negotiate. Tenants are usually careful not to offend the landlord in any way and some landlords act like feudal lords. A popular proverb goes, "A bad landlord makes the tenant a homeowner," because tenants try to buy their own place, even if it is only a 538 square foot (50 square meter) flat, instead of dealing with a landlord. Therefore, as in many other countries, everybody dreams of buying their own house.

Ownership of a place to live is often vital. During the marriage negotiations of a male relative of ours, the father of the bride stipulated that the young couple should not live in a rented flat. Luckily, the groom's mother owned a small one-bedroom apartment, so the young couple lived there until they were able to buy their own place. Another relative owns a three-story house that is, in effect, three apartments. His family lives on the ground floor, one floor is rented out, and the third has been temporarily used by each of the family's four sons as they married one by one. The first son stayed for three years until he was able to buy his own property and move out. When the second one married, he lived in the apartment for a few years until the third one married, and so on. Now the fourth son lives there with his young bride until they are able to afford a place of their own.

Not everyone is so lucky, though. Many young couples, especially from less affluent backgrounds, rent a place until they are able to afford one after years of saving and borrowing from the bank, or until they are offered a social housing option, which is sold or rented at preferential rates by governmental agencies.

When many older houses in Tehran were demolished, either because they were beyond repair of because families needed more space, they were replaced by two- or three-story buildings with one flat on every floor. The original owner usually lived in the ground floor unit and rented out the other floors. In this arrangement, the building is still considered a house and not a block of flats, and the landlord acts as the building manager without charging a maintenance charge. Each tenant is responsible for cleaning the communal staircase that leads to their flat from the floor below, unless a cleaner is employed and paid by all.

If you have to rent a flat, there are three options. The first way is paying monthly rent, as in the rest of the world. Another system, which I have only come across in Iran, is called *rahn*. Rahn is usually translated as *mortgage*, but not as we know it. This is how rahn works: the tenant pays the landlord a lump sum of money, roughly one-fifth of the total value of the property, and moves in. At the end of the rental term, the landlord returns the same amount to the tenant, who only moves out upon receipt of the money. This is a useful system for landlords, who may run a business or may have borrowed from the bank in order to buy the property, or who can live off the interest of this (often considerable) sum. Until recently, when the interest rates were high, this option was attractive for many landlords. The third way, at present the most popular, is a combination of rahn and monthly rental.

OVERSEAS TENANTS

A small number of fully furnished luxury properties located in the northern suburbs of Tehran are available for overseas staff and embassy personnel. These are usually advertised in the English-language newspapers and their rent is payable each month in U.S. dollars.

TWO

Relationships and "Face"

Those ten days in Iran in February 1989 were a kind of crash course in Iranian culture. I understood very little of the language and much less of the culture, and the rules took a long time to work out. Iranian friends in Greece and England had given me some guidelines on behavior (don't laugh out loud; don't stretch your legs; only reply with a yes/no and a restrained smile to questions), but these didn't help me understand any better, only made me tread more carefully.

O bservation of one's own culture is notoriously difficult, mainly because we are so steeped in it that we take it for granted, and it can be difficult to see it from another perspective. A move to another culture may initially give rise to varying degrees of culture shock but usually later engenders fresh understanding, not only of the host culture, but of one's own culture too. Something like that happened to me, only with English culture thrown into the bargain as well. However, after twenty-three years I am now sufficiently acculturated to Iranian culture to be able to make sense of what I witness (well, most of the time anyway.)

ONE MAN'S BELCH IS ANOTHER MAN'S COMPLIMENT

Once in a very crowded shopping street in Athens, Hossein was walking ahead of me. Just behind me I heard a man telling his wife, "Look at how Arab men walk ahead of women; that shows how little they respect them." Although this happened many years ago and I tell myself that my compatriots are now less prejudiced than they used to be (or is it my wishful thinking?), this incident exemplifies how our judgments of "others" are often formed by applying the rules of our own culture to behaviors that stem from the rules of another culture.

In Greece at that time the accepted thing was for a man to open doors for a woman and to walk behind her. Therefore, the Greek man reasoned, the 'Arab' who doesn't do that is being disrespectful to his companion. In our case, Hossein was walking ahead to make way for me in the crowd, and there may be equally valid reasons in the Arab practice, if it indeed exists.

In Iran when a woman walks with an unrelated male (e.g., a colleague) or a nonintimate (*nâmahram*) relative, if there is no space for both to walk abreast, she usually prefers to follow rather than walk in front, because many women feel uncomfortable turning their posterior toward a nonintimate male. (see below "Relatives and Strangers") The male accompanying a female will always offer to give way to her, as she will too, but will probably not insist as much as he would with another male, out of consideration for her comfort.

GIVING WAY

Whether you are male or female and you are escorted by an Iranian man or woman, upon reaching a place that only one person can go through (e.g., a corridor, door, or elevator), your companion will invariably stop and give way to you as a show of respect. The usual Iranian practice goes thus: A stops and gives way; B does the same; A insists and so does B. If A is male and B female, A is likely to apologize and walk on. If both A and B are of the same gender, the more senior in years or status will usually be prevailed upon to walk through first, always after apologizing for

---

doing so. However, it is also possible for the senior person to insist even more or even physically guide the other person through the door, thereby showing his/her humility.

As a foreign visitor you are considered a guest, so Iranians, even those older than you, will give way to you. If you would like to exhibit some good old Iranian manners, you can give way to them too saying *shomâ befarmâ'id* (after you)—but don't expect your offer to be accepted.

This discussion is the cornerstone of understanding and engaging with a foreign culture: behaviors are best understood when examined in the context of that culture's values and worldview. The same behavior analyzed under a different set of values may result in divergent interpretations: polite and considerate, or intrusive and downright rude. However, even the word *intrusive* means different things to different people.

Take an inter-city train trip, for instance. In the United States and England passengers will scarcely exchange any conversation except, perhaps, for, "Excuse me, would you mind if I take this seat?" and then will take refuge behind a newspaper or book or by putting on headphones. They might as well stick a sign around their neck saying, "Please do not disturb."

To the gregarious Iranians, such behavior is exceedingly strange: that you would travel for hours next to a stranger and leave the train still not knowing your fellow traveler is almost inconceivable. Iranians, who are used to striking up conversations with strangers, often think that the Americans and English are too cold and aloof, and that you can't make friends with them. That, however, is because different values and social rules prevail in those societies. The Americans and English value privacy, freedom of action, and freedom from imposition, whereas for Iranians involvement, warmth, and friendliness are more important.

FAMILY CIRCLE

For Iranians, as in most societies, the nuclear family is the basic unit of social organization. However, unlike some Western societies, the extended

family has much greater psychological and practical significance. If we wanted to represent this idea schematically, we could draw a series of concentric circles, with their center being the individual. The innermost circle includes the individual's immediate family: parents and siblings if single, or spouse and children if married. In the latter case, in the next circle out are the parents, siblings, and their families and the person's own in-laws. The circle beyond that includes paternal and maternal uncles, aunts, and cousins, and their spouses and children. All these relations provide the basis of the social network that every individual in a given family belongs to.

Traditionally the family fulfilled many roles that in Western societies—and now increasingly in Iran, at least in urban settings—are played by financial institutions, day care centers, family counselors, and even doctors. Need a short-term loan to tide you over for a month? Cousin Majid will be able to help. Invited to a wedding without the children? Mom or auntie will look after the baby for the evening. Disagreement with your spouse? You ask an elder to be involved and help reconcile the difference. Ten-year-old son got a cold? An aunt makes chicken barley soup for him and buys herbal tea from the local herbalist on her way to your house.

As we will see throughout this book, family and social groups play a major role in Iranians' daily life and sense of self. The importance of belonging to a family is so critical to Iranians that one of the first things Iranians do after arriving in a foreign country is to find out the favorite haunts of other Iranians, Iranian shops or restaurants, where they can begin to make new acquaintances. In time, they create a surrogate social network to replace the one they left behind. According to the 2000 World Values Survey, in Iran over ninety-five percent of respondents said that family is very important in life, whereas only thirty percent rated friends as very important and fifty-two percent as rather important.

THE CIRCLE

Membership in a family or social/friendship group not only fulfills psychological needs, but practical ones, too. The circle of one's extended

family, friends, acquaintances, colleagues, and neighbors constitutes a reliable and permanent support network on which one can call at times of need. In this large group, one person is bound to know where you can get what you need, or at least knows someone who does. For example, when we were looking for a new school for our son, Hossein's maternal uncle's son's brother-in-law, who is an employee of the Education Department in our area, was able to advise us on suitable schools, confirmed that the school we had chosen was a good one, and gave a reference in support of our application to the school.

But a support network is not useful only for special favors. Very often Iranians will introduce tradespeople or professionals to their relatives and friends, for example, a tailor, doctor, or private tutor, who in most cases will pay special attention to the new customers and make sure they receive special attention.

Belonging to the Circle, of course, also entails reciprocal duties and responsibilities: the demands on time and effort one makes on a Circle member may have to be returned in the future, either by the original recipient or by a relative. This social debt is not considered a burden or an imposition, but is seen as a basic ingredient of interactions, the give-and-take of everyday life. The sense of belonging to the Circle gives an Iranian a feeling of safety: one is not alone in the world.[1]

IN-GROUP AND OUT-GROUP

The scene: a large, busy drug store in central Tehran. I put my prescription on the counter. The assistant behind the counter is deep in conversation with her colleague, and even though she has seen me, she seems determined to ignore me for as long as she can. When she finally turns to me, she does it without so much as an apology or a smile and picks up the prescription without saying anything. While she looks for the medicines, an acquaintance of hers comes into the shop. She interrupts her search and turns to him, exchanges extensive greetings (see chapter 3), smiling and nodding her head, and asks how she can help him. He reciprocates the greetings, thanks her, but goes to the end of the line. She returns to looking for my medicines and, reverting to her former reserved attitude, hands them over.

After an experience like this, you may begin to doubt what you have heard about Iranians being friendly, welcoming, and hospitable. However, once the mindset behind these two interactions is understood, things become clearer. In this situation, the male customer is an "insider" (*khodi*), that is, he belongs to the shop assistant's in-group, whereas I am an "outsider" (*qarib*), a member of the out-group.

From what we've discussed about relationships in the family, the Circle, and within professional groups, it follows that khodi/insider relationships are characterized by mutual help, self-sacrifice, and warmth, and, as described in the following section, strong "face" considerations and showing of respect. Because the exchange of goods and action is expected of members as a matter of course, Iranians in service positions try to maintain out-group status with customers to avoid excessive demands being made on them, hence the clerk's serious attitude toward me.

Outsider status is not, however, written in stone: a casual remark or a realization of common ground may relay an outsider into the in-group. And while the ideal of self-sacrifice may remain just that, it is nevertheless a principle to be strived for, even if never to be attained.[2]

RELATIVES AND STRANGERS

An important distinction to comprehend as we delve further into Iranian society is the classification of relationships into *mahram* (intimate, forbidden to marry) and *nâmahram* (not intimate). The mahram category includes close blood and in-law relatives of the opposite gender with whom marriage isn't permissible, such as parents, grandparents, siblings and their children, a spouse's parents, one's own children and their spouses, grandchildren, and blood uncles and aunts.[3] Everybody else is nâmahram, whether relatives or strangers, with whom marriage is technically permissible, even though it may be impractical or undesirable. This distinction influences behavior, predictably, more familiar/intimate conduct with mahrams. We will see how this distinction affects behavior and dress in later chapters.

COLLECTIVISM VS. INDIVIDUALISM

According to Geert Hofstede, one axis of classification of cultures lies along the poles of individualism and collectivism—the latter referring to the group, not to a political system. In individualist societies, members' ties with each other are loose, and the only close ties are among members of immediate families. In such societies, individuals are expected to look after themselves, defend their own rights, and choose the groups they want to belong to. The U.S., Great Britain, and Australia rank the highest on the individualism scale.[4]

At the other end of the spectrum, collectivist societies contain ingroups—stable and cohesive groups like extended families and/or lifelong professional organizations. In such settings, the individual pledges loyalty to the group and receives protection and support in exchange. Hofstede's studies found that Latin American cultures are the most collectivist, and Iran was rated at 41 on the Individuality vs. Collectivity scale.

Our research[5] also suggests that Iranian culture tends toward the collectivist end of the spectrum. The fact that Iranians thrive within the family framework is manifested in diverse ways in social practices and the mass media. Adult children live with their parents until they marry, and sometimes live close to their parents after marriage. The concept of an unmarried adult child moving out is unthinkable, as is the concept of divorced partners living on their own, even if they are responsible for any children. If divorced, both spouses return to their parental homes until they remarry, because Iranians feel they need the practical and emotional support that one's own blood family can provide.

A person's identity is defined through family roles: headstones often contain the appellation *Mother* or *Father* where applicable, and a quatrain referring to the loss of the deceased, often written by family members. A headstone I saw for a woman who died unmarried was inscribed *Amme jân*, "Dear paternal aunt."

Another indication of the importance of family ties is that the responsibility of caring for the elderly rests with the immediate family, not with a stranger who is paid to provide it. Apart from the social approbation it receives, caring for an elderly parent is considered a labor

of love that, in Islam, attracts ample divine reward. (This does not mean that elderly people are never looked after by strangers, but that this is considered the least desirable alternative.) Instead of seeing this duty as a burden, many families see the presence of the elderly parent as a blessing and as a focus for the extended family, who when visiting the elderly relative, at the same time visit other family members, too. Both of these are considered commendable activities in Islam.

The results of a small survey of character traits I conducted for this book highlighted the importance of group values. Positive concepts such as duty (*vazifeh*), dutifulness (*vazifeh shenâssi*), self-sacrifice/selfless devotion (*fadâkâri/khod-gozashtegi*), and blending in with the group (*hamkhâni/hamrang budan* or *tâbe'ye jam*) cropped up often in respondents' views, as did some negatively judged concepts: selfishness (*khod-khâhi*) and individualism (*fard-gerâ'i*), the latter often being mentioned in connection with Western culture.

Iranians view the nuclear family as the source of all of the good and bad tendencies and behaviors that manifest in society. If individuals receive appropriate socialization and a good upbringing from their parents, they will grow up as responsible, well-rounded people who will in turn raise their own children well. Similarly, children exhibiting poor behavior—impoliteness, irresponsibility, selfishness, lack of consideration for others and of social responsibility—are not considered to have been brought up appropriately.

The importance of the family is also clearly seen in the media, especially television, which has wide appeal. In addition to advertisements for products and services in which depicting families is expected, such as household appliances and funfairs, advertisers also capitalize on this theme in commercials ranging from bank promotions and facilities to dishwashing liquid. These ads often feature happy nuclear and extended families enriched by the presence of grandparents. Iranian television regularly produces animated short films as part of various campaigns (e.g., energy and water conservation) in which the stereotypically headstrong father is eventually shown the error of his ways by the mother or a younger member of the family who has internalized the campaign message.

This inclusiveness also appears in public settings, such as the mass media and public lectures. After beginning their talk with an invocation

to God (*Bismillâh ar-Rahman ar-Raheem*, In the Name of God, the Compassionate, the Merciful), presenters, news anchors, and public speakers offer formal greetings to the viewers and to their colleagues, using a variety of terms of address, such as "Dear and respected listeners/ guests" (*shenavandegân/mehmânân-e aziz-o arjmand*) and references to "our dear colleague Mr./Ms. X" (*hamkâr-e azizemun Âqâ -ye/ Khânum-e X*) and to "our beloved country" (*keshvar-e aziz-e-mun*). On special occasions like festivals or a mourning day, speakers also offer wishes or condolences. This interpersonal ritual gives audiences the feeling that they are in the presence of acquaintances and helps hold their attention.

QUANTITY VS. QUALITY OF LIFE

Another classification proposed by Hofstede, Masculinity vs. Femininity, was later changed by some users to Quantity vs. Quality of Life. One presupposition behind this axis is that women's values across cultures are more similar to each other, whereas men's values across cultures show a greater variation. This principle includes competitiveness, assertiveness, and the importance of wealth and material possessions at the masculine end of the scale, and modesty, a caring attitude, and the importance of relationships and quality of life at the feminine end of the scale. Predictably, "masculine" societies also feature gender-related roles along traditional lines and a greater variation between men's competitive/assertive modes and women's modest/caring modes, whereas in "feminine" societies gender roles are less rigidly applied and males and females display less marked behavioral differences. Hofstede rates Japan as the most masculine culture, Sweden the most feminine, and the Anglo cultures somewhere in the middle.

Interestingly, Iranian culture does not fit neatly into this classification axis. As we will see, diverse behaviors point toward the overarching importance of family and interpersonal relationships in Iranian culture, to the extent that such considerations often spill into an individual's professional life. Business appointments may be cancelled or

apologies offered for missing meetings because of illness in the family or an emergency and, importantly, these are met with understanding and compassion, not with annoyance because of their negative impact on business.

Many male partners often undertake household and child-rearing tasks that may traditionally be seen as feminine, such as preparing herbs for cooking, bathing babies, and putting them to bed.[6] On the other hand, despite the great inroads that Iranian women have made into education, employment, and social presence in the last thirty years, males and females generally perform traditional gender roles.

A simple lifestyle, considered more conducive to an individual's spiritual growth, is viewed as an ideal of the recent past to be upheld or returned to. Traditionally, wealth is seen as God's blessing and as a means to helping others who are less fortunate, beginning with the needy members of one's family. These elements may be interpreted as pointing toward the feminine end of Hofstede's axis. However, within the last generation the emphasis has shifted from simple living to ostentation, to the amassing of wealth and material possessions as signs of social status and, sometimes, to outright waste, especially among the urban *nouveaux riches*. In this sense Iranian culture seems to be shifting toward the masculine end of the axis.[7]

HIERARCHY VS. EQUALITY

Another of Hofstede's classification relevant to the Iranian distinction between hierarchy and equality is the axis of Small vs. Large Power Distance. This category refers to the perception of power difference, not to the actual differences, which are present in every society. Whereas in all societies power is distributed unequally, in some societies this inequality is encoded in behavior, for example, in the way subordinates and those above them address and interact with each other.

According to Hofstede, in Large Power Distance societies, such as Malaysia or Slovakia, less powerful members in families and institutions

accept the unequal power distribution in their societies and the autocratic and paternalistic relations with those in power that stem from this inequality. They expect that those in power wield more authority by virtue of their position and that subordinates won't question decisions coming from above. On the other hand, in Small Power Distance societies (e.g., Austria, Denmark, and New Zealand), subordinates relate on an equal footing with those in authority and feel able to contribute ideas and make comments on decision making, so relations tend to be more democratic.

Hofstede rated Iranian society at 58 on the scale, and at first glance, Iranian culture seems to tend toward the Large Power Distance pole. Iranians acknowledge that some people within families and social groupings naturally command more authority and power, stemming from their position, seniority, or knowledge, and this authority is encoded in language (see the discussions about deference and humility in chapter 3).

However, both respect for authority and consultation within groups are highly commended values in Islam, so collaborative, not authoritarian, decision-making is viewed positively in families and social groups. Achievement of *rezâei'at* (contentment, willing obedience) of the group members, or at the very least taking their views into account, is often a prerequisite of decision-making. Iranians are usually forthcoming in offering their views, suggestions, and criticism on the way things are done at home, school, university, or in the workplace, and decision makers often try to adopt a course of action that meets general consensus. Group members also try to be flexible in order to accommodate the wishes of the majority.

Asymmetrical relationships involve some exchange of actions and material goods. The senior person provides favors and rewards to subordinates, and in return orders the junior person to provide goods or action. Subordinates provide services and tributes to superiors and petition them to provide goods or action. Symmetrical relationships also involve an exchange, but differ in that in these relationships no status difference exists and the parties exchange help and support without need for order or petition. Both kinds of relationships can be rewarding in Iranian culture.[8]

A WARNING AGAINST "GIVING ROPE"
(*RU DÂDAN*)

Certain positions, such as teachers and university lecturers, are expected to maintain a status and power difference. People in such positions who behave in an egalitarian way toward students (e.g., foreigners operating according to the rules of their own culture) are likely to have difficulty establishing an appropriate relationship (see also "Familiar and Polite Pronouns" and "Naming Practices and Terms of Address" in chapter 3 and "Terms of Address" in chapter 5).

FACE

The concept of *face* relates to the image that people project of themselves to the world. According to Erving Goffman, it is their most intimate and valuable possession, the source of their security and pleasure, but it does not belong to them unconditionally. It is lent to them by society on condition that they behave in ways appropriate to the face they project. People maintain face by taking account of their social position, exhibiting behavior appropriate to that position, refraining from actions that are not in keeping with it, and even carrying out actions that may be costly or difficult from duty to themselves, which Erving Goffman defines as "pride."[9] Other behaviors include the way people handle their body, emotions, or material objects, which Goffman characterizes as "dignity." He concedes that such behavioral strictures function as a jail, but that does not necessarily mean that people dislike their cells.

Apart from upholding and protecting their own face, individuals are also concerned with others' feelings and strive to help them uphold their face because they empathize with them. Goffman emphasizes that both face orientations—the defensive one toward the speaker's own face and the protective one toward the face of others—are often simultaneous, even though one of them may be predominant at times.

Against the background of collectivity and group values, it would be easy to think that the identity of an Iranian is lost among the group. Personal identity is distinct, however, and is developed by cultivating one's talents, abilities, and social relationships; in this way one becomes a rounded, useful member of their group. Personal responsibility in behavior and action is of overarching importance, because individuals reflect on their group. Iranians are in charge of their destiny and bear the responsibility of maintaining and enhancing their own face and, by extension, the face of the family or the group they belong to. Consequently, if anything, the stakes of losing face are much higher, because an individual's loss of face reflects adversely on his family's or group's collective face. This is one of the main roots of the elaborate Iranian politeness.[10]

Face in Iranian Culture

Zâher-ra hefz kon *(Keep up appearances)*

—A Persian phrase often heard in conversation

Let's look at the two main aspects of face in Iranian culture.

- *Shakhsiat,* also referred to as *âberu* (personality, character, self-respect, social standing)
- *Ehterâm,* also referred to as *ezzat* (respect, esteem, dignity)

Shakhsiat, a person's identity, is the result of one's education and upbringing. *Ehterâm,* on the other hand, is shown through a speaker's adherence to the politeness/*ta'ârof* rules (see chapter 3), such as making offers or issuing invitations. Although the former is static and the latter dynamic, their manifestations are closely related. People demonstrate their *shakhsiat* through their behavior, by, for example, conforming to social manners and paying the appropriate amount of *ehterâm* to an interlocutor. (The next chapter looks at the principles of politeness and at specific behaviors in more detail.)

Face in Use

In the same way that the government and advertising agencies use Iranians' sense of belonging to a family and their community spirit, the

strong sense that Iranians have of upholding their *shakhsiat* is also coming in handy in persuading Iranians to observe safety regulations and their civic duties. For example, in the Tehran subway system, which becomes extremely crowded during rush hour, a sign above a door reads: "Dear Passenger [note the direct address], observance of order in boarding and alighting [from the train] shows your superior culture and personality." (*Mosâfere aziz, bâ ra'âyat kardane nazm dar savâr shodan va piâdeh shodan, farhang va shakhsiate valâye khod râ neshân midehid.*) A sign on the back of bus prompts: "The timely submission of your tax return is an indication of your social standing." (*Tasleem bemoq'e ezhâr-nâmeh mâliâti neshângar shakhsiat-e ejtemâ'i e shomâst.*)

A short, computer-animated film on driving safety features a skeptical middle-aged man and his marriageable-aged daughter going out for a drive in order to find out more about a prospective groom's *shakhsiat* by observing his driving behavior. The father argues that you can learn a lot about a person by the way he drives and follows the groom's car closely behind. However, the father himself does not observe the safety distance and crashes into the back of the groom's car at a traffic light. The groom calmly gets out to inspect the damage and, recognizing the man and the young woman, good-humoredly says that it's all right, these things happen when driving. By the humorous twist of showing the father's negligence of safety rules, the film promotes the message that responsible driving and calm reaction shows not only the character (*shakhsiat*) of the prospective groom, but also that of the older driver who sets out to see if the younger one breaks rules.

Face Compromise and Loss

Iranians feel that their face has been compromised mainly if one of the following happen:

- If any information they would rather keep secret about their private life becomes known
- If they behave in a way not in keeping with their *shakhsiat*
- If they are treated in a less respectful way (*biehterâmi*) than appropriate for their age and social position

It is also generally felt that dismissive parenting may lead to a child's development of a weak personality (*shakhsiatesh khurd mishe*, "his/her personality is crushed"). To guard against this, the child or young person has to be addressed respectfully, given responsibilities, and generally treated with respect (*ehterâm*). In this way young people develop a social identity that enables them to assume their positions effectively in society.

Linked to face loss is the strict religious proscription against backbiting (*gheibat*) which, according to a tradition of the Holy Prophet, is a grave sin worse than adultery. Imam Khomeini (known to Westerners as Ayatollah Khomeini), in his *Forty Hadith* collection of moral lessons, explains that backbiting about believers destroys their social standing and reputation, and what's worse, the unwitting victims can't defend themselves. Part of the perpetrators' punishment in the other world is to be shamed in the presence of the Prophets, the Imams, and the believers, thereby tasting the wrong they did in life many times over.[11]

An area that warrants more research is the different perceptions of face loss in men and women. Based solely on my observations, it seems that some Iranian men have more serious concerns about their country's image outside its borders, whereas some Iranian women are more interested in making their own viewpoints known and their voices heard, both inside Iran and abroad.

In June 2007 the Muslim Students' Association in Hammersmith, London, screened the documentary *Divorce Iranian Style* by Ziba Mir-Hosseini and Kim Longinotto (1998). This fly-on-the-wall documentary, filmed over several weeks in a family court in Iran, aims to "provide a unique window into the intimate circumstances of Iranian women seeking escape from unhappy marriages,"[12] and to show the means women employed (firmness, foxiness, and charm) to influence the judge's decision in their favor. In a couple of cases, although the judge might have been inclined to issue a judgment in favor of the woman, his hands were tied by the law. The directors' intention in making this documentary was to present a positive image of Iran by showing the complexity of the Iranian reality.[13]

After the screening, Ziba Mir-Hosseini took questions from the audience. I expected that questions would focus on the content of the

documentary, possibly on whether things have changed in the nine years since the documentary was made. Surprisingly, the first question was about the reasons behind the production of this documentary. Didn't Dr. Mir-Hosseini, asked the male viewer, consider the potentially negative impact that the screening of this documentary could have on Iran's image abroad?

I have had similar experiences with readers of earlier drafts of this book. Despite explaining that the reason for writing this book has been to make Iranian culture and everyday life better known to Western readers, male readers repeatedly have expressed concern that the book would provide "grist to the mill" for Iran's enemies by including facts or opinions that might show Iran in a negative light. Women, on the other hand, generally thought that my work was an accurate representation of Iranian culture and everyday life.

In summary, face loss may occur when facts that were meant to remain secret are revealed, or when adverse or negative facts about one's character or actions become known. Keeping up appearances (*zâher-râ hefz kardan*), keeping secret facts that should be kept secret, and not revealing information that may cast an unflattering light on someone are all part of maintaining people's face and that of their social group. This sentiment has a strong bearing on Iranians' behavior, deportment, and relationships.

THREE

Minding Your Ps and Qs

In the late eighties I worked for an Iranian company in London, where the Iranian colleagues had worked together for decades. I heard an Iranian female colleague being addressed by her Iranian male colleagues by her first name, and, since she used my first name too, I thought I could do the same. But when I did, she drew herself up to her full height and said haughtily, "I am not Zari; I am Mrs Rahmati!" My mistake was that she was much older than me and we had only known each other for a short time.

As members of families and other social networks, Iranians maintain a large number of relationships, all of which must conform to expected rules of behavior. Starting at a very young age, Iranians are socialized to follow the unwritten rules of the culture and polite behavior that then become second nature to them. They grow up understanding the main reason why they should do so: as a religious duty to behave with respect and cordiality toward others in order to nurture positive and rewarding relationships. Without these, families and other social networks could not function effectively or promote

their members' interests. In naming desirable character traits in children, 90 percent of Iranian respondents included "having good manners."[1]

In social situations, Iranians generally shun behaviors construed as impolite, such as raising one's voice, arguing, swearing (very rare), or not acknowledging an acquaintance's presence by exchanging warm greetings, as we saw in the drugstore situation in the previous chapter. All of these ingrained behaviors often affect Iranians' interactions with foreigners.

PERSIAN POLITENESS

Persian politeness broadly follows three principles, the application of which gives rise to a wide variety of behaviors. These principles are deference, humility, and cordiality, with the first two often occurring together in practice. According to the Deference principle, speakers address a person as superior or better, and in keeping with the Humility principle, they present themselves as junior or less favored in terms of accomplishments, abilities, knowledge, or possessions. The Cordiality principle requires that a speaker show interest in others' affairs and concern for their needs and comfort, and to claim common ground with others.

The principles are rooted in qualities and behaviors that are highly commended in Iranian culture: *adab* (good manners), which includes respect, especially to seniors, teachers, and one's superiors; cordial manners; and modesty. Although I present these principles separately here for the purposes of analysis, they often coexist in interaction and are expressed in a wide variety of behaviors, as discussed in this chapter.

INTRODUCTIONS

When Westerners first meet an Iranian, they may find themselves being asked many more questions than they may be used to, including some they may perceive as being quite personal. For example, Iranians will ask how old someone is and how much they earn; whether they are married or have children, and if not, why not; or how much someone has paid

for something. In turn, Iranians will also probably volunteer similar personal information. Iranians ask these questions to classify new acquaintances by placing them in appropriate social categories of marital status or occupation, and they expect to be grouped in a similar way themselves. Seen in this light, such an exchange of information helps an Iranian choose appropriate modes of behavior, and is an indication of cordiality, as it shows that the speaker wants to include that person in their circle of acquaintances.

Foreigners married to Iranians will almost certainly be asked how they met, whether they had to embrace Islam in order to marry, and whether their in-laws are nice.

FAMILIAR AND POLITE PRONOUNS

In common with some European languages (e.g., French, German, and Spanish) but not English, Persian has two pronouns of address, a singular, familiar (*to*) and a polite plural (*shomâ*).[2]

The use of the singular familiar pronoun is generally considered impolite, even rude, outside very intimate or familial settings. In addition, intimates or close relatives, who would use the familiar pronoun when alone, will use the plural to each other if people outside the immediate family are present.[3] Because the use of the familiar pronoun (*to*) is so limited, the plural pronoun (*shomâ*) is much more widespread than in other languages and functions as the default pronoun.

It is also acceptable to use the familiar singular to address young children and household help, where there is a marked status difference, as well as to address God, who, according to the Holy Quran,[4] is more intimate than one's jugular vein. So, the default pronoun in addressing a stranger is the polite one, unless a driver cuts in front of you and you shout, "Get out of the way, you [singular] idiot!" But apart from situations of status difference, such as intimacy or deliberate impoliteness, there is another case where the singular pronoun is used.

I find that as soon as a stranger, for example, a shopkeeper, bank clerk, taxi driver, or even doctor, realizes that I am not Iranian, they switch to the singular pronoun. Initially, I thought I was being treated as

a grown-up child. However, a conversation with a friend helped me understand this practice and underscored the duality between the external and the internal aspects of existence, *zâher* and *bâten*, which are often at variance in everyday life (see the discussion in chapter 11). Iranians follow the politeness rules to show respect to the person they are talking to (I knew that from spending four years studying politeness in Persian), but they feel that form and appearances are not too important to foreigners, so they can speak to them in a more intimate, relaxed way. "After all," my friend added, "Iranians are invariably friendly and welcoming toward foreigners, so they would never intend to offend you!"

I've come to realize that Iranians feel that in the presence of foreigners formalities are superfluous, and they are prepared to drop the conventions that govern their relationships with their compatriots. This unwonted openness might jeopardize their face in conversation with an Iranian, but is thought to be innocuous in conversation with a foreigner, who probably does not perceive this behavior as loss of face.

THE ROYAL *WE*

Unlike in English, where the first person plural pronoun *we* is used primarily by royalty (as in "We are not amused") and denotes authority and elevated status, in Persian the use of the corresponding pronoun "we" (*mâ*) shows the exact opposite: humility and (nominally) low status, through the diffusion of the self.

NAMING PRACTICES AND TERMS OF ADDRESS

During a lecture on effective relationships with teenage children, the speaker, a well-known psychologist and family counselor, urged parents to address their youngsters with *Ali Âqâ* (Mr. Ali) and *Fâtemeh Khânum* (Miss Fatemeh) rather than only "Ali" or "Fâtemeh." This is the same form of address normally used with adult relatives, so, he argued, youngsters who are addressed in this way feel respected and valued, and are more likely to behave maturely.

This recommendation acknowledges the importance of names among Iranians. If you are on first-name terms with someone, there are two options: as just described, use their first name and *Âqâ/Khânum* (Mr./Lady), or their first name and *jân*, which means "soul, life" and therefore "dear as one's life." It is sometimes pronounced *jun*, the latter option being more common. In relationships within the family circle, this is something of a paradox. By definition, family relationships are defined by intimacy or, at least, familiarity. On the other hand, two other considerations are also important: age, and whether a person is *mahram*, because an age difference and being a *nâmahram* can create a notional distance between speakers. In other words, a fine balance must be struck between deference and cordiality, with some speakers tending more toward the one or the other principle, often depending on the speaker's temperament, mood, or character. Hossein's mother was addressed as '*Mâmân-jun*' ('dear Mum') by her children, grandchildren, sons-in-law and daughters-in-law, but not by her husband Hâj Nâsser, who addressed her respectfully as Hâj Khânum ('pilgrim lady').

WOMEN'S SURNAMES

Iranian women do not legally adopt the husband's surname upon marriage. In professional settings, therefore, they are known by what in English is called their *maiden name*, although in social settings their husband's name may be used. The title *Khânum* does not specify whether a woman is married or not; it simply means "Lady."

In professional settings, Iranians use *Âqâ/Khânum* and the person's family name. Female colleagues who become friends may address each other by their first names and *jân* when they are alone, but will use *Khânum* and the person's family name to refer to and address each other when others are present. Similarly, in girls' high schools, students use first names among themselves, but in an announcement over the PA system, students are addressed with *Khânum* and their family name. If male colleagues are friends, they usually address each other with only their family

names without *Âqâ*, as do male high school students among themselves. Surnames are often prefixed with any educational titles, for example, *Âqâ-ye Mohandes* [engineer] and family name, or *Khânum Doktor* [doctor] and family name. The title of *doctor* is used not only for medical doctors but for academics too, even outside academia. For more detail on address conventions in professional settings, see Terms of Address, chapter 5.

On the whole, terms of address are used very often in Persian to convey deference or cordiality, but the use itself of a term, rather than its absence, has the function of establishing common ground and warmth.

Using only someone's first name, or even *Âqâ/Khânum* and their first name, is reserved for only when people know each other well or when addressing household help or children. Because the use of a first name in English can convey informality but not necessarily familiarity or intimacy (as among colleagues, between boss and employee, or students and university staff), English language speakers need to be aware that in Iranian society informality is linked to intimacy, and they had best avoid first name usage in public settings.

Foreign names follow slightly different conventions. Because foreign surnames may be difficult for Iranians to pronounce, foreigners tend to be called by their first names in more situations than Iranians are. However, if you are called by your first name, don't think you can reciprocate: you need to gauge whether deference or cordiality would predominate in each situation.

So what should a foreigner do?

If unsure, err on the side of deference: use *Âqâ/Khânum* and the person's family name instead of their first name, even if you are addressed by your first name. (If your companion would like you to address them otherwise, they will probably tell you.)

But then, how can you balance deference with cordiality? Use other means, such as compliments, body language, and smiling. Some caveats here, though: touch between *nâmahrams* is generally forbidden in Islam, so don't make a move to touch a person of the opposite gender, even to shake hands, unless they make the first move. However, you may be hugged and kissed by persons of the same gender much more often than you may be used to. A similar convention applies to smiling and laugh-

ing. Try not to smile too much toward the opposite gender or laugh out loud, especially if you are female, although, in my experience, this is almost always recognized and excused as the mark of a foreigner.

Public displays of affection between spouses are also frowned upon, at least among the most conservative social strata. During a discussion in my class, a student mentioned a scene she had witnessed at the airport when pilgrims were leaving for the major pilgrimage to Mecca. A large group of relatives accompanied a male passenger up to the gate, where they had to part. The man kissed the well-wishers one by one, including some women who must have been his *mahrams* (his mother and sisters), but not his wife. My student thought this practice was too prudish, which indicates that this avoidance is not absolute, but, again, erring on the side of caution might be the best course.

OPENINGS AND HEALTH INQUIRIES

Conversations typically open with the Islamic greeting *salâm aleikom* (peace be upon you) or *salâm* (peace) for short, and answered by the same phrases, not by *wa aleikom us-salâm*, as in Arabic, which is more commonly used by clerics. Junior people are expected to "offer a *salâm*" first as a sign of respect to someone senior irrespective of gender, but offering a *salâm* first without regard to age or status is greatly commended in Islam as a sign of humility in the face of God. It is important to greet people you are acquainted with one by one, including children, instead of a collective greeting like "Hello, everyone."

In fact, offering a *salâm* to somebody you know and responding to another's *salâm* is obligatory, even if it means interrupting proceedings, such as a meeting. During a gathering in the assembly hall at my daughter's high school, the headmistress addressed about a hundred parents who were there to elect new members of the Parent-Teacher Association. From the podium she also faced the door through which latecomers were trickling in. Her speech went something like this: "This year we have implemented a shakeup of the school counseling system—*salâm*

aleikom—employing younger counselors much nearer the girls' age—*salâm aleikom*—and we hope that we shall soon see the positive effects of our decision on the girls' performance—*salâm aleikom.*" The repeated *salâms* had no effect on the audience, who continued to listen.

An opening is immediately followed by formulaic health inquiries and responses that do not require factual answers, as in English. These responses may overlap as they are issued simultaneously by both parties, and they encompass members of the immediate family, like spouse and children, even if the speaker has never met them. Formulaic phrases are often used in response, for example:

"How is your husband?"
"May God be praised, he is well. He sends his *salâms.*"
"Convey my regards to him."
"I will convey your greatness to him. And your children, how are they?"
"They kiss your hands."

I am often asked about my parents (who live in Greece) by friends and relatives who have never met them and probably never will. Conversations run like this:

Relative/friend: "And how are your parents?"
Sofia: "May God be praised, they send their *salâms.*"
Relative/friend: "Give them my *salâms* too."

All these health inquiries are not empty talk, though. The anthropologist Bronislaw Malinowski and, after him, John Laver, named this kind of talk *phatic communion,* a kind of social lubricant that serves to get the interaction off to a good start and cultivates relationships.[5] The fact that a speaker goes through the motions of asking about my spouse, children, and parents, thus for a moment sharing my concerns, shows the speaker's cordiality toward me and establishes common ground.

Health inquiries have another function: that of marking a new stage in the conversation.[6] If conversation stops and one of the partners wants the interaction to continue, that person initiates a new round of health

inquiries, which function as a springboard for a new topic of conversation. When they serve as a restart or a filler of a conversation they can, but by no means must, be treated as genuine questions, and they provide the impetus for the start of a new topic.

KEEPING IN TOUCH

Eating together and sharing food are socially significant activities and cement group ties. Most Iranians tend to socialize as families and eat dinner together in each other's houses. This *commensality,* as anthropologists call it, is extremely important among Iranians, who generally believe visits do not reach "consummation" unless accompanied by a shared meal. This attitude underscores the central position of food in Iranian culture, which all of chapter 9 is devoted to.

If they live close enough, married couples usually visit both sets of parents at least once a week, and almost always have a meal with them too. On feast days, like New Year's Day (*Noruz*) and *Eid Fitr* (the feast at the end of Ramadan), apart from visiting parents, Iranians have to pay their respects to other family elders, or, failing that, telephone them. Younger people now exchange text message greetings on mobile phones. Greetings cards have never been popular, probably because they lack the all-important, oral contact that a visit or a telephone call provides.

In Iran, the telephone is firmly established as a tool for socializing. A visit in person is obviously the best way of maintaining family and friendly relationships, but a telephone call is the next best thing. My two sisters-in-law speak on the phone at a certain time every day, and they used to do the same with my mother-in-law, much as my sister does with my parents back in Athens.[7] A telephone conversation follows similar conventions as face-to-face interactions—openings and health inquiries—and plays a phatic role in exchanging everyday news. One difference from American and English conventions is that callers don't usually identify themselves until asked to do so, unless, being a foreigner, the caller volunteers this information.[8]

CALLING FRIENDS

If you make new friends during your stay in Iran, you should expect them to call you from time to time to ask how you are, and they will probably expect you to do the same. Such telephone calls do not need to be very long: they serve as a reaffirmation of friendship ties. The following phrases introduce the closing-off sequence that you need to recognize and can use:

"Well, I just called to ask how you are."
"Sorry I've taken up your time." (Means: "Gotta go now.")
"Do come to our house." (A *ta'ârof* invitation that means: "Let's meet some time.)

TA'ÂROF, OR RITUAL POLITENESS

Years ago in England, when Hossein was studying, we rented an upstairs bedroom of a family's house. This one room served as our bedroom, study room, and dining room. I had just got home from work and was resting. Suddenly Hossein burst into the room, evidently perturbed, woke me up, and said that a fellow student, who had given him a ride home, was coming upstairs for coffee.
"Why on earth did you invite him in?" I asked him.
"I was only doing ta'ârof; *I didn't know he would come!" he said.*

Ritual politeness can mean different things in different cultures: among Iranians, an off-hand invitation like Hossein's is an indication that the speaker would like to bring the interaction to a close. At the same time, it serves as a "sincere expression of thanks or regard,"[9] even though it is not meant as an invitation proper, as the expression of good intention counts for more than the outcome. Hossein issued an invitation for coffee to his fellow student as an expression of thanks for the ride he was given.

Ta'ârof is a style of polite communication, or "ritual courtesy,"[10] that permeates much of Iranian communication, and its practice is related to religious teachings of hospitality and generosity. The word *ta'ârof* is

44

Arabic and means "mutual knowledge," which emphasizes the important function of *ta'ârof* as a tool for negotiating relationships.

THE STATUS OF THE GUEST

Iranians feel that visitors attract God's blessings into one's home, and therefore visitors are always treated with respect and warmth. A popular phrase is *mehmân habibe khodâst* (a guest is loved by God). Guests are always given the most comfortable seat and the best food. They are pressed to eat, are offered tea without being asked whether they want any, and are generally fussed over. At the end of the visit, they are thanked for visiting and asked to come back soon.

Guests also express their thanks repeatedly during the visit, ask their hosts not to go to so much trouble, assure them that they are comfortable, and at the end of the visit thank them profusely for their hospitality and ask them to repay the visit.

Social visits have no definite beginning or end as far as the hosts are concerned. Guests are free to arrive and leave at their convenience, but it is good manners to keep in mind the hosts' comfort.

Ta'ârof is generally used to express the speaker's deference, humility, and cordiality toward a speaker. Here's a conversation I heard between two brothers-in-law:

> A: Where have you been? We haven't seen much of you lately.
> B: We are [i.e., I am] under your feet.

Ta'ârof may sometimes be seen as an empty formality when the outward expression of these positive qualities (e.g., hospitality, warmth, and respect) is not accompanied by sincerity of feeling, but going through the *ta'ârof* motions conveys respect and enhances the face of both speakers.

OFFERS AND REFUSALS

A beggar, Mohammad Âqâ, used to come to Hossein's parents' house for charity every Thursday evening. One evening Hossein went out by the front gate and struck up a conversation with him. Mohammad Âqâ

carried a heavy sack and two long pieces of wood, the proceeds of his evening's begging. Hossein asked what the pieces of wood were for. Mohammad Âqâ answered, "You can have them if you want," to which Hossein answered with a refusal and thanks.

The beggar, who barely had anything to call his own and depended on others for survival, had this innate sense of offer and sacrifice: in this case, even though he didn't expect Hossein to accept his offer, he issued it as an expression of his gratitude at receiving charity.

This exchange exemplifies *ta'ârof* behavior. In fact, one of the main meanings of *ta'ârof kardan* (to do ta'ârof) is "to offer something," as in "he offered us tea and fruit," as well as the rather cumbersome "to make an offer without expecting it to be taken up," as in the earlier example with Hossein and the friend who gave him a ride. Another meaning attached to *ta'ârof* is that of "refusing something because it is the expected form." According to *ta'ârof* conventions, an offer must be made and refused at least once.

MAKING AND RESPONDING TO OFFERS

If you want your offer to be accepted, you need to insist for much longer than you are used to, at least twice or three times, reassuring the person that you can spare it, it's no inconvenience, and you want them to have it.

If you want to accept an offer of help or service, decline it at least once with "*barâye shomâ zahmat mishe*" (it'll cause you trouble), which conveys your desire to accept. The person will insist it is no trouble at all and then you can accept it using the formulas "*râzi be zahmat nabudim*" (I didn't want to give you this trouble) and "*kheili mamnun*" or "*mersi*" (thank you).

Declining the offer as a way of saying you really don't want it usually does not work: it is part of Iranian hospitality to be pressed to eat and drink, even beyond your capacity. If you do, however, want to decline an offer, be prepared for insistence: use the thanking formulas again, adding "*injuri râhatar-am*" (I am more comfortable like this), which should do the trick.

APOLOGIES

If the English use *please* and *thank you* more than any other nation, Iranians must be the uncontested champions of the ostensible apology. But in the same way that the English "thank you" is not always an expression of thanks, as in "That'll be all for now, thank you," an Iranian apology can be anything from an expression of humility, gratitude, thanks, or indebtedness when offering a present, or even a move to a closing sequence, as in "Sorry I've taken your time."

The most common form of apology is *bebakhshid* (the plural imperative form of the verb *bakhshidan* (to forgive), which is used in ostensible or *ta'ârof* apologies, such as at the end of a visit. This kind of closing sequence often takes this form:

Guests have indicated their intention to leave.
Host: Sorry you've had a bad time [with us].
Guest: Sorry for the trouble we've given you.

The host or hostess nominally apologizes for bad food, lack of comfort, and waste of the visitors' time: in short, they present their hospitality as being worse than the visitors deserve in a show of deference toward the guests and humility toward themselves.

Ta'ârof offers and apologies can occur in unusual situations. Once I boarded a taxi with my father-in-law, Hâj Nâsser. During the ride the taxi driver recognized my father-in-law from a time when he had visited Hâj Nâsser's blacksmith workshop. When we reached our destination, the taxi driver said that the fare was not worthy of us, that is, he showed deference by nominally refusing to accept the fare. Hâj Nâsser insisted, and after some more refusals and insistence, the taxi driver apologized profusely for accepting the money because he considered himself Hâj Nâsser's distant acquaintance and therefore, in an ideal world, he should not have charged him for the ride—in this way abiding by his "obligations" as a member of Hâj Nâsser's circle of acquaintances. On the other hand, Hâj Nâsser insisted on paying the fare out of consideration for the taxi driver, thus following the cordiality principle.

COMPLIMENTS

Depending on the content, compliments are often expressions of both deference and cordiality. The initiator of the compliment pays face (*ehterâm*) to the recipient by acknowledging the recipient as superior and himself as inferior, and in so doing, enhancing his own *shakhsiat*. If the compliment is about an object or an item of clothing, a *ta'ârof* offer of the object in response to the compliment is often made, as in this sequence:

> A: This is a nice pen.
> B: It's not worthy of you (*Qâbeli nâdare*, meaning: You can have it.).
> A: Thank you very much. (Always meaning, "No, thank you.").

Even though a speaker humbles himself and elevates the interlocutor, he hardly expects the latter to agree with the force of the compliment because of the humility principle.

The expected response would be a "mirroring" of the speaker's behavior: the interlocutor will humble himself and elevate the speaker. A possible response to a compliment is *Ekhtiar dârid, mâro sharmande mikonid* (You are free to say anything you like, but what you say embarrasses me). Some Iranians will characterize a speaker as immodest or arrogant if he responds with an expression of thanks as acceptance of a compliment.[11] Here's an example of how to respond appropriately:

> A: That is a nice pen.
> B: It looks nice in your eyes. (i.e., "You are so good, you see everything as being nice." (Meaning: "Nice of you to say so.")
> A: You are very kind.

GIVING AND RECEIVING COMPLIMENTS

Keeping the politeness principles in mind, the offer itself of a compliment expresses cordiality, although it may be phrased in terms of deference. The socially acceptable response is a thanking expression—which, however, does not mean acceptance as in English—or an expression that deflects the compliment back to the originator (deference).

> If you compliment someone on their abilities, achievements, or their children, always use *mâshâ'âllâh* (literally, "what God wants") as a talisman against the evil eye.

REQUESTS AND REFUSALS

Reza receives a telephone call from his former colleague and family friend Abbas, asking if he knows of a bank where he can borrow five million tumans (approximately $5,260 [£3,450] at June 2009 rates) for a month. Reza says he can spare a million tuman ($912/£600) for a month, if this would help. Abbas politely thanks him anyway and hangs up.

While in many countries this might seem like Abbas was looking for information, in Iran Abbas's question could also be understood as an indirect request for a loan. Why did Abbas make the request indirectly? Because if he asked directly, and Reza either didn't have that amount of money or was unwilling to lend it, both of them would lose face, which might reflect adversely on their ongoing relationship. On the other hand, if Reza were in a position to help Abbas out, he would make an offer of a loan, thereby showing his cordiality and strengthening their ties of friendship.

The moral of this interaction is: Don't ask for something directly if you can do so indirectly.

> ### MAKING AND REFUSING REQUESTS
>
> If you have to make a request, explain your need without focusing on how the other person can help you. For example, if you are looking to rent a flat, explain how you've talked to several rental agents and looked at a number of properties without success. If the other person can help, he will make the offer.
>
> If a friend confides her problems to you, you can offer to help or make a general comment as a default refusal: "I hope it gets sorted out eventually." In the unlikely possibility that you are asked for something directly,

find a reason beyond your control for refusing, against which nobody can argue (e.g., you car's not running right or the baby is sick), unless, of course, you are in a position to help.

CLOSINGS

Just as elaborate openings of interactions and health inquiries are important in showing mutual respect (deference) and establishing goodwill (cordiality), the ending of conversations have similar functions. In many interactions, even business meetings, Iranians often adopt the roles of the host and guest.

Near the end of a visit, guests will indicate their intention to leave, but the hosts will usually insist that they stay longer. When they finally rise to leave, the hosts will escort them to the front door, often downstairs to the front gate and even to the street. This custom shows the hosts' unwillingness to part from the guests and expresses their deference and cordiality toward them.

PARTING EXPRESSIONS

The usual parting expression is *Khodâ hâfez* (May God preserve you), much in the way that *good-bye* in English comes from the old expression "God be with you."

IRANIANS AND FOREIGNERS

In Saeed Assadi's 2007 film *Mehmân* (The Guest), Caroline (American actress Caroline Peach), an American engaged to Hamed, an Iranian student in the United States, is unwilling to tie the knot until she visits Iran to see for herself the reality behind the media's negative images of the country. She stays in Hâmed's affluent family home, where, still distrustful of Iranians, she goes to sleep with her passport under her pillow. Mis-

understanding an overheard conversation in Persian between Hâmed and his parents, she runs away early the following morning to take refuge in the Tehran hotel where her friend Julia is staying. The problem is that she doesn't know the address and can't remember the name correctly.

Enter poor but honest Majid, the taxi driver whose taxi Caroline boards. Initially he loses his temper when she urges him to drive on but is unable to tell him where. When he realizes that she is a foreign guest, his attitude completely changes: he buys her fruit juice but doesn't let her pay for it, takes her to a traditional restaurant even though he can hardly afford it, and eventually, late at night, he sneaks her into his house secretly from his mother, while he settles to sleep in the taxi.

When Majid's mother comes into his room and sees a *nâmahram* woman asleep in her son's bed, she flies into a rage and chases Caroline out into the yard with her slipper. Majid, hearing his mother's screams, rushes into the yard. Majid explains and the mother's attitude changes instantly: she shakes Caroline's hands and welcomes her in broken English.

Although the changes in attitude toward the foreign guest are some-what exaggerated for comic effect, they nevertheless reflect reality. I have often experienced such changes of attitude in taxi drivers or shop assis-tants, who, although usually stern and unsmiling (default behavior toward out-group members), change completely when they realize they are talking with a foreigner. I believe this is a combination of two factors: Iranians' innate sense of hospitality, which accords a guest privileged status, and a desire to show their nation's best image, or "face," to an outsider.

THE KINDNESS OF STRANGERS

Iranians feel that foreigners, even those living permanently among them, occupy the position of a guest, and they try to help and give advice in any way they can. Taking advantage of any offers is likely to save you time, embarrassment, and frustration while you get acquainted with the new culture. However, if their help sometimes becomes too much, you can thank them for their kindness and assure them that whenever you need anything, you will definitely ask them. This usually works.

Iranians see foreigners (i.e., Westerners) in paradoxical ways. Despite the fact that Iranians may disapprove of the policies of a foreign government, they are invariably helpful and friendly toward nationals of that country because of their hospitable nature and their sense of duty to show respect to guests.

Iranians feel that foreigners lack the refinement of manners and ritual politeness that plays such an important role in cementing relationships, but they are prepared to make allowances for this lacking. On the positive side of this deficiency, they feel that foreigners always say what they think directly, so one knows where one stands with them. And Iranians often admire foreigners' punctuality, accurate planning, and obedience of the law, though they attribute those characteristics to the fact that interpersonal relationships are not as strong as in Iranian culture.

FOUR

In His Name: Religion and Calendrical Feasts

This scene was recounted by a friend of mine who went to visit Imam Rezâ's holy shrine complex in Mashhad, in eastern Iran. As my friend sat inside the mosque to read the pilgrimage supplication (ziyârat-nâmeh), a woman behind her said, "That is all for now, sir . . . with your permission I shall take my leave." The woman was talking to the Imam as she would to an acquaintance: this is how close Shi'a Muslims feel to the holy Imams.

Iran is in many ways a distinctive Muslim country. It is the only non-Arab majority state among the Middle East Muslim countries, and the only one where a language other than Arabic is the official language (Arabic is used, of course, for devotional purposes). Shi'a Islam, (also sometimes spelled Shia, Shi'i or Shi'a), itself a minority denomination of about 20 percent of the world's total Muslim population, is Iran's official religion and forms the basis for its system of government (see chapter 1). The majority of the world's Muslims are

Sunnis (from *sunnah*, meaning "tradition of the Holy Prophet"), and most of the basic guides on Islam available in English mostly discuss Sunni Islam, although some basic information on Shi'ism is usually included.

All Muslims share the same main beliefs in the Oneness of God, the prophetic status of the Holy Prophet Muhammad (peace be upon him),[1] and the Day of Judgment, but just like with Christian denominations, there are doctrinal and devotional differences between Sunnis and Shi'as. Since the official religion of Iran is Shi'a Islam, the focus throughout this chapter is on this denomination.

Iranian culture is closely tied to Islam and Shi'ism in diverse ways. To appreciate this connection, we will look at the five fundamental principles (*Usul-e Din*) of Shi'a Islam and its ten secondary articles (*Furu-e Din*)[2].

ISLAM AND SHI'ISM

Introductory books to Islam list the five pillars of Islam as creed (*shahâdah*), prayer (*salât*), alms-giving (*zakât*), fast (*sawm*), and pilgrimage (*hajj*). In Shi'a Islam the creed is included in the five fundamental principles and the other four pillars in the secondary articles.

Shi'a Islam has five fundamental principles, or roots: the Oneness of God; God's justice; Prophethood; Imamate, the vicegerency of the prophet; and the Day of Judgment.

Oneness or Unity of God (Tawheed)

The concept of *Tawheed* means that there is only one God, one who has no partners and who created many worlds, including the physical world. On a deeper level, the unity of God is manifested in the harmony of nature and through the actions of believers whose motives should always be to follow God's will. On an even deeper, more mystical level, *Tawheed* refers to the oft-repeated idea in the Quran that humans will eventually be reunited with God whence they came. Of course, this is a huge oversimplification of the most important belief of Islam, on which numerous volumes have been written.[3]

God's Justice ('Adl)

Throughout life, believers do good deeds and try to avoid committing sins. An account of checks and balances is kept, and when the physical world is destroyed and God raises the dead, everyone will be called to account on the Day of Judgment. Although all Muslims hope for God's mercy, they believe that He will reward or punish everyone according to their deeds.

Prophethood (Nobovvat)

Throughout the history of humankind, God has sent prophets who communicated God's will and tried to guide humanity on the straight path. These include Abraham, Moses, Elias, Jonah, Solomon, Jacob, Joseph, all the prophets of the Old Testament including those not mentioned by name, John, and Jesus. There are 124,000 prophets, and all are revered in Islam.

MUSLIM-CHRISTIAN COMMONALITIES

- Jesus and his mother, the Virgin Mary, are deeply respected by Muslims.
- Jesus' miraculous birth is mentioned in the Quran.
- Jesus is referred to 154 times in nineteen *suras* (chapters) of the Quran, many more times than Muhammad.
- *Sura* 19 of the Quran bears the name of the Holy Virgin, Mariam (Mary).

In Islam, Jesus, although fully human, is one of the five main prophets in Islam (Adam, Abraham, Moses, and Muhammad). His mission was to complement the Mosaic law and to pave the way for the complete message that would be delivered by the last of the divine prophets, Muhammad.

Muhammad received the call to prophethood during a meditation in the Cave of Hira on a mountainside outside Mecca in the year A.D.

610. On this occasion, the whole of the Quran descended into the Prophet's heart, although it was many years before it was revealed in its totality. That very first revelation ordered Muhammad to proclaim God's message to his fellow humans (*sura* 96, *Iqra'*—Recite!), and for the next twenty years Muhammad preached first in secret, then more openly, until the hostility of his tribe in Mecca forced him and his followers to flee to Medina, where he established the first Islamic community in 622.

Imamate, or the Vicegerency of the Prophet (Imâmat)

The principle of the Imamate relates to the Shi'a belief that the Holy Prophet appointed Imam Ali as his successor to the leadership of the Muslim community. During his prophethood, the Holy Prophet Muhammad fulfilled several functions. Upon receiving the first revelation, he became the receptacle of the Quran, God's last revelation to humankind. When he established the first Islamic community in 622, he also became a temporal ruler, managing the political, practical, and spiritual affairs of the community. Just before his death in 632, during the last pilgrimage he undertook, he assembled the Muslims and told them that his end was near, but that he was leaving them two things that would continue to guide them until the end of time: the Holy Quran and his household (*Ahl-e Bait*). The means to their salvation lay in holding on to them both. Then he lifted the hand of Imam Ali, his cousin, who was the husband of Muhammad's only daughter, Fatemeh (also spelled Fatima), and announced that whoever recognizes him as his leader should recognize Ali too, and whoever loves him should love Ali—in effect, appointing Ali as his successor. Then he prayed to God that may those who love and follow Ali enjoy God's blessings and love, and that those who do not taste God's wrath.

This event, the feast of *Ghadir Khom*, celebrated every year on the 18th of the lunar month Zil Hajjeh, marks the beginning of the divergence between the main Muslim denominations of Sunnis and Shi'as. Although both groups accept the authenticity of the traditions relating to this event, their interpretations differ. Sunni Muslims see the event only as a confirmation of Ali's moral worth, whereas Shi'a Muslims view

Ali and the chain of his eleven direct descendants, the Imams, as the Prophet's vicegerents, who were not chosen by a consensus of believers but were divinely appointed and entrusted by God with the spiritual guidance of the Muslims.[4] All the imams except the last one were killed by their political enemies, who disputed their legitimacy, resented their popularity, and schemed to destroy their spiritual succession (see appendix C).

The Day of Judgment (Qiyâmat)

In common with their brothers and sisters who follow the other two Abrahamic religions, Judaism and Christianity, Muslims believe that at a time only known to God, the world will come to an end, the dead will rise from their graves and will stand before God, who will judge their worldly deeds and send them to paradise or hell. On that day inanimate objects will bear testimony about human behaviors, so that no actions remain unaccounted for.

THE TEN BRANCHES, OR SECONDARY ARTICLES, OF SHI'A ISLAM

Shi'a Islam has ten branches, or secondary articles: prayer, fasting during Ramadan, pilgrimage to Mecca, alms, surplus income levy, struggle in the way of good, enjoining the good, forbidding the evil, loving and respecting the Holy Prophet's household, and disassociating from the enemies of the Holy Prophet's household.

Prayer (Namâz or Salât)

Iranians, like all Muslims, pray five times a day, but the call to prayer (*azân*) is only made three times a day in Iran: at the moment of true dawn, at noon, and at sunset (see chapter 1). These calls punctuate the lives of believers with constant reminders of God's presence. After the noon call to prayer, the noon and afternoon prayers are offered, and after the evening call to prayer the sunset and the night prayers become due. The

timings vary every day as the position of the earth to the sun changes slightly, another reminder of God's omnipotence and omnipresence, and of the celestial harmony that subsists in the universe as His manifestation.

Men and women pray in exactly the same way. The three main physical positions in prayer—standing, bowing, and prostrating—have spiritual counterparts. The believer stands in the presence of God's greatness and mercy, then bows in awe in the face of God's majesty, and prostrates with the forehead touching the ground in a symbolic image of obliteration of the believer's physical self and the awakening of inner awareness.[5]

SURAS USED IN PRAYERS

These are two *suras* (chapters) of the Holy Quran used in prayers. The first is always used, while the second one can be replaced with any other, usually a short *sura*.

Sura 1, *Fatiha* (The Opening)

In the name of Allah, Most Gracious, Most Merciful.
Praise be to Allah, the Cherisher and Sustainer of the Worlds;
Gracious, Most Merciful;
Master of the Day of Judgment.
Thee do we worship and Thine aid we seek.
Show us the straight way,
The way of those on whom Thou hast bestowed Thy Grace,
Those whose portion is not wrath, and who go not astray.

Sura 112, *Ikhlâs* (The Purity of Faith)

In the name of Allah, Most Gracious, Most Merciful.
Say: He is Allah, the One and Only;
Allah, the Eternal, Absolute;
He begetteth not, nor is He begotten;
And there is none like unto Him.

—Translation by Abdullah Yusuf Ali

FASTING DURING RAMADAN (*RUZEH* OR *SAWM*)

During the holy month of Ramadan, during which the Quran was revealed, Muslims abstain from food, drink, smoking, and physical relations from the break of dawn until sunset. This abstinence, which becomes more demanding when Ramadan edges forward toward the summer (the first day of Ramadan in 1430 A.H. fell on August 22, 2009, and will fall eleven days earlier every subsequent year), has multiple goals. Believers develop self-control, but not only over their physical needs: they abstain from lying, backbiting, and other behaviors that God disapproves of; empathize with the poor and the needy; and learn to appreciate God's blessings in their lives. Sharing food with the poor, inviting people for the meal that breaks the fast (*iftâr*), giving to charity, and completing a reading of the whole Quran during this month attract numerous divine rewards.

MANNERS FOR VISITORS DURING RAMADAN

If you visit Iran during Ramadan, it is good manners to abstain from eating and drinking in public out of consideration for those observing the fast. Fast food outlets and restaurants are closed during daylight hours, but grocery shops are not, and you should be able to have meals in hotels (all travelers are exempt from fasting).

After the evening call to prayer (*azân-e maghreb*), the fast is broken with dates, sweet tea, bread, cheese, fresh herbs, thick herb soup with noodles (*âsh-e reshteh*) or porridge, halva, rice, and saffron pudding. If you're walking through the city at the time when the fast is broken, you will be offered dates, tea, or soup by believers who may have made a pledge for a sick person to become healed, or for the fulfillment of any other wish. The response to such offers is *Inshâ-allâh qabul bâsheh'* (May God accept your pledge [and assign a reward for it]).

The end of Ramadan is celebrated on Eid Fitr with congregational prayers.

PILGRIMAGE (*HAJJ*) TO MECCA

Every year during the twelfth month of the lunar calendar, thousands of Muslims from all over the Islamic world make a pilgrimage to the holy city of Mecca. It is believed that every adult Muslim who is physically able and can afford it should make the pilgrimage at least once in a lifetime. The rituals that have to be observed for the pilgrimage to be valid have a deep, spiritual meaning. The donning of all-white, simple garments for men and women signifies the shedding of class and status divisions and underscores the equality of all believers before God. The brisk walk or run between the hills of Safa and Marwa harks back to Hagar's, the handmaid of Abraham, desperate search for water in the desert when she was exiled there with her son Ishmael. Eventually God answered her prayers and brought forth a spring, the spring of Zam Zam, which is still there. The deeper symbolism of this hastening between the two hills reminds believers of the futility of chasing worldly gains.[6]

Going on a major pilgrimage is an important rite of passage for Muslims, and is usually taken when one is middle age or older. Relatives and friends see pilgrims off at the airport and then welcome them back with flowers. Their return is also marked by a celebratory banner hung outside their house, which formally welcomes them back home. A few days after returning, the pilgrim hosts a large dinner for relatives, friends, and neighbors either at home or in a reception hall, after which others address the pilgrim as *Hâj Âqâ* (pilgrim sir) or *Hâj Khânum* (pilgrim lady).

ABRAHAM'S SACRIFICE

In the biblical story, God, in order to test Abraham's faith, asks him to sacrifice his son (in the Hebrew-Christian tradition this is Isaac, Sarah's son; in the Islamic tradition this is Ishmael, Hagar's son). Abraham prepares the boy for sacrifice. As he is about to plunge the knife into the boy's throat, God stops him and sends down an animal to be sacrificed instead.

In remembrance of Abraham's deep faith and unquestioning obedience, pilgrims cast stones at three stone pillars that stand for Satan. This ritual signifies the rejection of Satan's wiles from the heart of every believer. On the Feast of Sacrifice (*Eid Qorbân* in Persian; *Id-ul-Adha* in Arabic), which concludes the pilgrimage every year and is celebrated all over the Islamic world, every pilgrim sacrifices a sheep, again in Abraham's remembrance.

In Iran, the custom of sacrificing a sheep also marks rites of passage (the birth of a baby, the entry of a bride into her new husband's house) and other auspicious occasions, such as the purchase of a house or shop. Before the sacrifice the animal must have its fill of water, in remembrance of the martyrdom of Imam Hossein and his faithful followers (see Appendix C). Iranians feel that this sacrifice diverts any potential harm from people and property to the animal, just as in the biblical story, and ensures good luck and protection from the evil eye. The meat of the animal is then distributed to the poor in exchange for their prayers, or it is cooked and shared with neighbors.

CHARITY OR ALMS (*ZAKÂT*)

Zakât is an amount payable by farmers on some agricultural produce, cattle, silver and gold at the rate of 2.5%, to the Imam's representatives, who during the absence of Imam Mahdi in our era, are the learned theologians (*marja' taqlid*, pl. *maraji' taqlid*; see Appendix C and below, under 'Other Religious Texts') The proceeds of zakat are managed by the theologians' offices and are put to various uses, among which are helping the needy, funding educational institutions and student bursaries, and paying off debts of those who face imprisonment because they cannot discharge them (subject to conditions.) Apart from *zakât*, Iranians believe that regular, voluntary donations to charity increase wealth and bring blessings to their daily income—along the lines of what goes round comes round.

If you visit Iran, you may notice some metallic hexagonal boxes painted blue and yellow erected on poles at street corners. These are *sadâqeh* boxes. *Sadâqeh* is a small amount of money given or set aside

voluntarily every day, A central charity organization administers these funds either in the form of emergency payments, or to fund long term projects, such as teaching a trade to needy people, so that they can earn a livelihood. The practice of setting a small amount of money aside every day is believed to keep danger away from all family members as they go about their daily business.

ANNUAL LEVY OF ONE-FIFTH (*KHOMS*)

All adult Muslims need to set a day every year on which to carry out an audit of their yearly income, yearly expenses, and outstanding loans. If after settling all loans and bills there is a surplus, one-fifth of this amount is given to the poor and the needy. This account must be settled before a believer sets off on a pilgrimage to Mecca.

STRUGGLE IN THE WAY OF GOOD (*JIHAD*)

Probably the most controversial and misunderstood aspect of Islam over the centuries and especially in recent years, *jihad* is now being construed differently by some groups to further their own aims and to justify their actions. The triliteral root of the word *jihad* is j-h-d, which means "struggle." For some people the struggle can only be violent, and they justify this stance by using certain Quranic verses out of context. The Holy Quran makes it very clear that the killing of innocents is absolutely and categorically forbidden: ". . . anyone who kills any person [. . .] acts as if he had killed all mankind."[7] Not only does this belief *not* glorify suicide bombers, but it also consigns them to the category of grave sinners and excludes them from paradise.

Armed struggle is obligatory in defense (*Jihad-e Asghar*, Lesser *Jihad*), but the spiritual dimension of *jihad* (*Jihad-e Akbar*, Greater *Jihad*) lies in the believers' daily struggle to overcome their negative impulses and to reach spiritual perfection.[8]

As for the other four branches, or secondary articles of Shi'a faith, enjoining the good (*amr be ma'ruf*) and forbidding the evil (*nahi az*

munkar) refer to the believers' duty to encourage others to behave in ways that are pleasing to God and to abstain from actions that are forbidden or reprehensible. Loving and respecting the Holy Prophet's household (*tavallâ*), and disassociating from the enemies of the Holy Prophet's household (*tabarrâ*) are self-explanatory.

THE HOLY QURAN

When Iranians move to a new house, the first object they take into it is their Quran. This book occupies a special place in even the humblest Muslim household. All prophets before Muhammad demonstrated God's majesty through miracles: Moses parted the Red Sea, Joseph had the gift of interpreting dreams, Jesus healed the sick and raised the dead. Muhammad's miracle is the Quran itself, a collection of exquisite writings, in a style that is both poetry and prose, dealing with practical topics and metaphysical concepts. Jews and Christians will recognize the prophets and their stories from their scriptures. The Quran, which was recorded as it was revealed to Muhammad in classical Arabic, has remained unchanged throughout the centuries and provides daily spiritual inspiration to anyone who turns to it with a pure heart.[9]

OTHER RELIGIOUS TEXTS

Many religious rules and everyday practices and sayings of the Holy Prophet are preserved in collections of stories (singular: *hadith*; plural: *ahâdith*) transmitted through an unbroken chain of people and collected in writing. Many ahâdith are accepted as authentic by both Sunni and Shi'a Muslims, and some only by one group.

Along with the Quran and the hadith collections, Shi'a Muslims also use a number of other texts for devotional and educational purposes. *Revâyât* are the life stories and sayings of the Holy Imams and contain gems of wisdom and guidance for the believers. The *Nahj ul-Balâgheh* (The Peak of Eloquence) is a collection of Imam Ali's sermons, sayings, and political advice, giving an insight into the greatness of a man who is

respected and loved by all Muslims. The *Mafâtih al-Jinân* (The Key to Paradise) is a collection of recommended (i.e., nonobligatory) prayers and supplications for special days and for every day in the year.

Another important book found in pious homes is a collection of religious rules (*Resâleh al-'Amaliyeh*). In the present time when the last Imam (Mahdi) is absent (see appendix C), learned theologians (*âyatollâh*, which literally means "sign of God") act as his deputies and are entrusted with the guidance of the Muslims. Some learned *âyatollâhs* reach such high levels of scholarship and understanding and can interpret the holy texts in light of their knowledge of sources, application of deduction methods, and current conditions. Upon publication of a *Resâleh al-'Amaliyeh* they become "a source of emulation" (*marja' taqlid*). Every Shi'a Muslim is required to make an informed choice of a *marja'* and to follow that *marja'*s rulings relating to religious practices. Every *marja'* has an office in Qom, the centre of theological learning, in Tehran and in other cities, and can be consulted by telephone, email or in person on issues relating to religious conduct and everyday practice.

POPULAR BELIEFS AND PRACTICES

For Shi'as, life is a series of checks and balances: some acts attract divine reward while others, such as arrogance, anger, backbiting, or envy, divine punishment. This is why it is important that believers improve their record during their lifetime. Helping others, giving to charity, feeding the poor, rendering service to the community, teaching and learning, reading the Quran, offering prayers regularly, and taking part in religious ceremonies are all activities that attract divine reward.

In Shi'ism, visiting the graves of the deceased, the Holy Imams, and their descendants is felt to be spiritually beneficial for both the dead and the living. On Thursday evenings or Friday mornings, families visit the graves of their loved ones. Whenever we visit the grave of my parents-in-law, we buy a bouquet of flowers, a box of pastries or a bag of candies, and a bottle of rose water. Hossein washes the gravestone with the rose water, scatters the flower petals on it, and sits cross-legged on the nearby grave to read *sura* 55, *Ar-Rahman* (The Compassionate), of the Quran,

a chapter enumerating God's blessings. The children walk around offering pastries or candies to other mourners, who ask God's forgiveness for our dead and offer a Fatiha prayer (see earlier in this chapter) for them.

Thursday evening is also a busy time for a visit, or *ziârat*, to an Imam's or a saint's mausoleum. Pilgrims remove their shoes by the entrance and can leave them with an attendant who gives them a pigeon-hole number. Once inside, they borrow a booklet containing the special supplication (*ziârat-nâmeh*) of the shrine and stand or sit to read it. They usually offer a short prayer, and if the time is right, their obligatory prayers too. Pilgrims add their own personal supplications here: prayers for other people, a cure for an illness, an offspring's successful marriage, a solution to financial difficulties, or admission to a university, as in the story that began this chapter. If a pilgrim attains a connection (*tavassol*) through the Imam or saint, a channel opens for the supplication to be heard by God.

Some people make a point of touching the elaborate grille that surrounds the saint's tomb, push money through it (the money is used for the upkeep of the shrine), or tie strips of green fabric on it, a visual metaphor of the knotty problems of their lives. It is believed that when the problem represented by the green knot is solved through the saint's intercession to God, the knot unties itself. At the end of the visit, pilgrims walk out into the large courtyard and through the huge wooden portal, bid farewell to the saint, and step out refreshed into the hustle and bustle of the bazaar and of ordinary life.

Similar rituals take place all over the Shi'a world where Imams and saints are buried: in Iran, in the city of Mashhad, where Imam Reza is buried, and in Qom, where Imam Reza's sister, Fatemeh Ma'sumeh, rests. Appendix C lists where all the Imams are buried.

THE NEW SOLAR YEAR (*NORUZ*)

So far in this chapter we have discussed Islamic beliefs and customs that are inextricably linked with mainstream Iranian culture. But the one yearly festival that is celebrated by all Iranians irrespective of religion is the beginning of the new solar year, *Noruz*. The ancient Iranian calendar

contained a number of celebrations, two of which have survived in modern Iran: Noruz and the eve of the winter solstice (*Shab-e Yaldâ*). Some people also celebrate the ancient harvest festival of Mehregân in late September.

The feast of Noruz has its roots in the ancient worship of Mithra, who was the Sun God in Iranian pre-islamic religions, and was also worshipped in Ancient Rome. It was believed that during the first days of the new year the spirits of the ancestors descended from heaven and visited the homes of their descendants, so it was imperative that the houses be clean and tidy, and well stocked with food and candies. On the eve of the last Wednesday of the year, fires were lit on the rooftops to guide the ancestor spirits, a custom that now survives in the guise of street bonfires, over which young (and sometimes not so young) people jump.

HAPPY NEW YEAR

Today, Afghanistan and other Central Asian nations celebrate Noruz on March 21 and use the Iranian calendar, albeit with different month names. The Romans also began their new year around March—the names of the months September, October, and November are derived from the Latin words for seven, eight, and nine. In England New Year's Day was the Day of the Annunciation, March 25, from the thirteenth century until 1752, and the present fiscal year starting on April 6 uses a calculation based on the same day.

The spring equinox (March 21), along with the occurrence of the full moon, also carries special significance for the Christian churches in determining the exact day of Easter. (Greek Orthodox and Western churches often celebrate Easter at different times because they use slightly different formulas for the calculations.)

At least a month before New Year, families start the thorough spring cleaning that must be completed before the beginning of the new year. All furniture must be moved, floors cleaned and polished, wardrobes cleaned out and tidied up, and curtains washed; in short, everything in the house must be cleaned, and whatever is no longer useful or service-

able given away or thrown out. The physical cleaning out of the house corresponds to a psychological and spiritual reality, as in the saying, "out with the old and in with the new."

Everybody in the family, but especially children, will have new clothes and shoes. This is a time of new beginnings, not only in the physical world by buying or having new clothes made, but spiritually too: Iranians make a point of wiping the slate clean, sorting out differences and making reconciliations, so that the new year will find everybody in the best frame of mind.

About ten days before Noruz the women of the family soak lentils or wheat until they sprout. Then they spread them on a plate and cover them with a piece of gauze which is kept moist. By New Year's Day the sprouts have grown to a height of about four inches (ten centimeters). They are then tied with a red ribbon and become one of the main items, the *sabzeh*, for the New Year decorative spread (*sofreh haft sin*).

When Hossein's parents were still alive, all their children and grandchildren arrived at their house just before the change of the New Year. Mâmân-jun (my mother-in-law) would put an embroidered piece of fabric on the floor in the middle of the room and lay the New Year decorative spread on it—every object from the natural world symbolizing an abstract ideal. She put out her wedding mirror and candlesticks for purity, light, and joy, took out one of her goldfish from the pool and brought it in a bowl to represent freshness, and had her grandchildren decorate eggs to represent new life. In keeping with tradition, she had to have seven items whose names begin with the letter *s* in Persian: *sabzeh* (green herbs), *serkeh* (vinegar), *sir* (garlic), *sib* (apple), *samanu* (a paste similar to halva but made of germinated wheat), *somaq* (sumac, a sour spice used in kebab dishes), and *senjed* (dried lotus fruit) or *sombol* (hyacinth flower). (For the traditional New Year meal, see chapter 9.)

Although Noruz is not an Islamic feast and is celebrated by Iranians of every religion, its celebration has been fused in the Iranian psyche with the worship of the one God and Islam, so most Iranian Muslims also place the Holy Quran on the New Year spread too and read a special supplication (*Du'â Sâl-e No*) in Arabic.

On the first day of the new year younger people visit the elders of the family, starting with the parents and grandparents and then the aunts

and uncles. It is customary for the elders to give children and newly married brides an *eidi*, a present of money in the form of newly minted banknotes that have been kept between the Quran leaves. This need not be a large sum, its significance being the blessing bestowed by the old upon the young. Hossein's grandmother, who was a descendant of the Holy Prophet (*sâdât*), always had a pad of new banknotes stamped with her name. She gave one to everyone who visited her on New Year and on Eid Ghadir, the feast of the Prophet's descendants, and told them that if they kept their banknote in their wallet, it would bring them luck and prosperity, and their wallet would never be empty. Over the years I've collected a fair number of such notes, some of which I have sent to my parents and sister in Greece, friends in England and Greece, and my editor in Boston, thereby expanding the circle of blessings.

Throughout the next twelve days short visits are exchanged among family and friends, in keeping with the idea that relatives should see each other at least once a year, even if everyday life doesn't let this happen more often. The younger visit the older people first, and toward the end of the twelve days, the older people reciprocate those visits.

During the Noruz visits, apart from the staples of tea and fruit, other traditional items are offered: several kinds of pastries, sometimes homemade, but nowadays mostly shop-bought; candies or chocolates; and a mixture of seeds and nuts containing pistachios, almonds, dried chickpeas, pumpkin, watermelon seeds, and other nuts. All of these, and sometimes more, will be pressed upon you during a Noruz visit, so you will need a lot of stamina (to keep refusing) or a strong stomach, or both.

The New Year feast ends on the thirteenth day, when Iranians go on a picnic. Margaret Shaida in *The Legendary Cuisine of Persia* writes that many Iranians believe that the *sabzeh* (lentil or wheat sprouts), which has begun to wither by this time, attracts the devil's attention, so it is cast away in running water on this day, thus exorcising the evil. On the following day, everyday life resumes its normal rhythm again.

The other notable day in the Iranian calendar is Shab-e Yaldâ, the night of the winter solstice and the longest night of the year, usually falling on December 20 or 21. Friends and family gather in one house and while away the long night telling stories and jokes, reading Hafez's

auguries to each other, and munching nuts, dried fruit, candies, and fresh melon or watermelon as a reminder of the long summer days.[10]

PERSONAL CELEBRATIONS

Mâmân-jun and Hâj Nâsser didn't know exactly when they were born; the dates on their identity documents were chosen arbitrarily when compulsory registration was introduced by the first Pahlavi monarch Reza in the 1930s. They didn't celebrate their birthdays or their children's birthdays either. This practice emphasizes the lack of importance that personal occasions such as birthdays or wedding anniversaries were traditionally accorded.

One generation later, those now in their 40s, 50s, and younger may exchange presents quietly on their wedding anniversary or on birthdays, but they will celebrate their young children's birthdays. Since the custom of the birthday party is imported from the West, parties are similar, but have acquired an Iranian flavor. Immediate family and friends are invited, the house is decorated, and the birthday child blows out candles on a cake and opens presents. The main difference is that the child's birthday is another occasion for a family get-together, and after the cake-cutting and the presents, a dinner party like any other follows.

FIVE

The World of Work and Business

In 2000, when an English friend of mine visited Iran she exchanged £120 (then about $160) for six wads of banknotes—so many that she had to carry them in a plastic bag.

"I feel rich!" she exclaimed. "I've never had so much money in my life."
After shopping for an overcoat and scarves, however, about one-third of her money was gone.

IRANIAN CURRENCY AND EXCHANGE

The official Iranian currency is the Iranian rial, exchanging at approximately 9,500 rials to the U.S. dollar and 15,000 rials to the British pound in October 2009. Apart from the many zeros involved in any transaction, foreign visitors need to be aware that prices are always quoted in *rials* when written, but are quoted in *tumans* in speech. One *tuman* is equal to ten *rials*. The tuman unit has no official standing, but has the obvious practical use of getting rid of one zero. (In early 2009 an Iranian MP proposed an overhaul of the monetary system that would do away with the numerous zeros, but nothing came of it.)

Banknotes are used a lot, both because the use of credit cards is still limited and because coins are only minted for very small values (250, 500, and 1,000 rials). Paper money comes in denominations of 10,000, 20,000, and recently 50,000 rials, which are too small for substantial purchases, but I am told that not minting higher denomination bills helps keep a check on inflation. In recent years a useful innovation has been adopted which does away with the need to carry bags of money when going shopping. It is called *chek-pul* (check money) and works like a traveler's check but doesn't have a name written on it, so it functions as a large denomination bill. The most common denominations of chek-puls are 500,000 and 1,000,000 rials, but even higher ones are used in large transactions. They can be bought from any bank and, after the streamlining of the financial system in 2008, they are accepted everywhere.

At present, Iranian currency can only be bought in some Middle East countries, so if you are coming from anywhere else, you will need to buy rials after you arrive. There is a currency exchange office at the new Imam Khomeini International Airport in Tehran as well as several more in the center of Tehran and other big cities. A network of currency exchange offices operate in Tehran and in major cities under the licence of Iranian National Bank. Many banks also offer foreign exchange facilities, but not in all branches. Your host and hotel staff should be able to advise you further.

SHOPS AND SMALL BUSINESSES

A corner shop near our flat has a small sign over the entrance reading *Huwa ar-Razâq* (He [God] is the Provider). In a country where, apart from the central Tehran bazaar and a few chain stores, retail trade is in the hands of small shops dotted around cities and towns, one's own enterprising skills together with God's blessing—rather than a corporate body of technocrats—ensures business success.

SHOPPING IN SMALL SHOPS OR BUSINESSES

Once inside a shop, don't wait for the clerk, who could well be the owner, to ask what you would like. The usual practice is to ask for what

you want yourself, or in a small grocery shop where there are no shopping baskets, to pick your items and then put them on the counter while you look around for some more items. Customers who walk into the shop after you may be served before you, possibly because they are faster to ask for what they want (this happens to me all the time). Complaining that you were there before them will probably work, but Iranians will consider this strange, because in shops the understanding is "ask and you will be given." Lines are formed in banks, government offices, and traditional bakeries because it is clear that a customer wants something. This is not the case in shops, where customers may not find what they are looking for, or may be trying to decide what to buy, so customers don't line up.

Iranians are seasoned negotiators, having developed their skills since childhood, and, apart from the financial gain, often enjoy the bargaining experience for the sake of it. In Iran, almost everything apart from retail groceries and restaurant and hotel bills is negotiable.

Bargaining for an item or a service is a task that takes some getting used to. In the West, large shopping chains carry out their own kind of bargaining: chain stores undercut competitors with offers like "buy one and get one free," or promising to refund the difference if you find the same item cheaper elsewhere. Because this bargaining takes place at a corporate level, Western visitors are generally not used to bartering in the context of everyday shopping in the same way that Iranians are.

Shopkeepers believe that the first sale of the day (*dasht-e avval*) carries a special blessing. If it is an expensive purchase such as clothes, shoes, or electrical goods, shoppers will have an advantage when it comes to bargaining, as we will see later in this chapter.

HOW TO BARGAIN SUCCESSFULLY

First, you need to convince the seller that you are a serious buyer and aren't just browsing. Ask the price and express surprise or disappointment in words or by facial expression. The seller will respond with something like, "This is the market price," or "You won't find it cheaper elsewhere." You can say that the shop in the next street sells it cheaper,

and quote a much lower price than the one you are prepared to pay. He will lower his asking price a bit. If you aren't prepared to pay it, or you enjoy the game for its own sake, raise your own price but don't match his yet. Depending on the seller's and your resilience, this back-and-forth may go on for some time. When he reaches his absolute lowest price, he will often signify it by saying, "XXX thousand tumans, last offer." You can then agree or still not make a purchase.

Once you have agreed on a price, your Iranian interlocutor will say *qâbeli nâdare*—"It is not worthy of you" (i.e., "You can have it for free"). Shopkeepers and taxi drivers also say the same when you ask how much you should pay them. This offer is, of course, not to be taken at face value even if repeated, as it only indicates the speaker's goodwill and pure intention. The idea expressed by this offer is that in an ideal world you would be his guest, but this is not an ideal world, and everyone has to get paid. The response to this offer is *khâhesh mikonam* (please), which acknowledges the intention, followed by your payment.[1]

THE BÂZÂRI CLASS

Every provincial capital has its own central bazaar that provides shops in their province with locally produced goods and food. Imported or manufactured goods are usually sold wholesale from the Tehran Grand Bazaar (*Bâzâr-e Bororg-e Tehrân*), which is the commercial heart of Tehran and of the whole of Iran. Some provincial bazaars are centuries old, but the Tehran Grand Bazaar developed from clusters of specialty small craft markets about 150 years ago near the then seat of Qajar royalty, the Golestân Palace (which is just up the road and well worth a visit).

The bazaar is a maze of narrow alleys in which small shops and stalls sell goods and commodities. Some alleys take their name from the goods sold there, for example, *Bâzâr e Mesgar-hâ* (coppersmiths' market) or from a famous person. The visual effects of the bazaar range from the dazzling, as in the goldsmiths' market, to the uniformly muted, as in Kilo-ee-ha Alley, where shops stock only black chador fabric, and everything in between: shoes, clothes, household goods, stationery, and anything else you can imagine.

Some stalls sell on a retail basis, but many others are only shop windows—they showcase the merchandise available in the large storerooms that wholesalers maintain elsewhere and only sell to these potential wholesale buyers.

In addition to the wholesale and retail shops, the bazaar contains banking and credit facilities, where prices for gold, commodities, staple goods, and foreign exchange rates are determined and influence nationwide prices. Thus, the Tehran Grand Bazaar is the financial heart of the whole country, much like Wall Street or the City of London. The *bâzâri* class includes those employed in wholesale trade and financial institutions, workshop owners, distributors, and middlemen, and they represent the solid, conservative social strata. Traditionally, the *bâzâri* families have enjoyed familial ties with the clerical class (*ulemâ*) and, exercising their financial muscle in conjunction with the *ulema's* spiritual influence, have often brought pressure to bear on the Iranian monarchy's autocratic tendencies.[2]

SHOPPING HOURS

Grocers and greengrocers are open every day and keep very long hours, opening early in the morning and not closing until late at night. Other shops open about 9:30 A.M. and their shopping hours vary according to location. Neighborhood shops that are likely to be owned and run by a local resident usually close after the noon call to prayer for lunch and a siesta, and then reopen from about 4:30–8:00 in the winter and about 5:00–9:30 in the summer. Centrally located shops or larger stores are more likely to remain open throughout the day until late at night, although in the height of summer they are unlikely to have any customers after lunch, so they may pull down the shutters halfway to indicate that they are resting. If you plan to go to a specific shop, call ahead before setting off.

The bazaar keeps different hours from retail shops. It is open Saturday to Thursday from about 9:30–5:30 (but closes at about 3:00 on Thursdays) and is closed on Fridays and public holidays.

STATE EMPLOYMENT AND RETIREMENT AGE

A large percentage of the workforce is employed by the state in government offices, local authorities, and educational establishments, or by state-related organizations and institutions. Jobs range from cleaners and tea attendants to blue-collar workers, and from technical, administrative, teaching, and management personnel to the highest positions of managing directors.

State employment is highly sought after for a variety of reasons. Although basic salaries have increased to acceptable levels over recent years, they are not exceptional. The attraction of a state job lies mainly in other benefits available to workers, such as subsidized travel, opportunities to buy land or new homes at low prices, interest-free loans, family cash allowances, medical insurance, and a pension plan. Another important consideration is the fact that a government job is for life: once you have it, you have a guaranteed salary for the rest of your working life and a pension to the end of your days.

According to current legislation, male state employees retire after thirty years of service and females after twenty-five. Women also have the option of early retirement after twenty years on a reduced pension. In response to the increased numbers of young people entering the workforce every year, there is talk of lowering the retirement age for men to create more job opportunities.

FOREIGN INVESTMENT

Iranian state-run and private companies now welcome and actively invite foreign investment, especially in trade, manufacturing, infrastructure, and leisure and tourism industries. To facilitate such investment, the government has introduced incentives that facilitate funds transfer, reliable insurance cover, and tax exemptions.[3] The Persian Gulf island of Kish constitutes a free trading zone (Kish Free Zone Organization—KFZO) and vies with neighboring Dubai as a trading, tourism, and leisure

destination. It offers offshore banking and trading facilities and, as a further incentive, non-Iranians can travel there without a visa.

DOWN TO BUSINESS

To conduct business successfully, visitors need to bear in mind that the principles of communication outlined in chapter 3 (deference, humility, and cordiality) apply not only to social relationships, but to business relationships too. All visitors, whether on business or for leisure, are considered guests, and as such can expect to be treated with respect, generosity, and warmth and to be looked after and entertained.

On the other hand, visitors should realize that Iranians will exhibit politeness and warmth, behave with deference toward guests, and display humility because they follow their own cultural rules about acceptable behavior. Don't, however, misinterpret a business partner's humility as an underestimation of the latter's abilities, or someone's show of deference and respect as an indication that the Iranian partner sees the foreign visitor as superior. Iranians are proud of their nation, its ancient civilization, and its culture and expect to be seen and treated as equal partners in projects and partnerships, able to offer as much as they are likely to receive.

INTRODUCTIONS

In keeping with the importance of collectivity, group values, and the in-group/out-group distinction in Iranian culture, Iranians prefer to conduct business with those they know and trust, or at least with those introduced by such people. As a result, it is almost essential that you find a "way in" for every company you would like to do business with. Your first contact could be the staff in the commercial section of the Iranian Embassy in your home country; they should be able to give you information on local representatives and events that you can use for networking.

Any Iranian friends or acquaintances you have are bound to know people you can contact for help and introductions.

ARRANGING AN APPOINTMENT

Make an appointment at least four to six weeks in advance of your trip. It is advisable both to telephone and e-mail to confirm the time and place about a week beforehand, as well as after you have arrived in Iran. On the day before a meeting, it is often worth calling to verify the meeting and the time.

TIMES TO AVOID FOR BUSINESS TRAVEL

Certain times of the year are best avoided for business purposes:

- Noruz officially lasts four working days, but in practice nothing much happens in terms of business between mid-March until the first week of April.
- During Ramadan, the month of fasting, Iranians work shorter hours and cannot entertain guests. In 2010 Ramadan begins on August 11 and eleven days earlier every year thereafter.
- The Iranian calendar is dotted with occasional one-day holidays, so if your time is limited you might want to check these dates before you plan your trip (see appendix B for official holidays).

FIRST APPOINTMENT:
THE INTERPERSONAL DIMENSION

So far in this book a basic principle of Iranian life has become clear: personal relationships are very important. This section explores how this principle applies to business relationships.

As a general rule, the first appointment is an opportunity for the business parties to get to know each other. The success of your business venture depends on the impression you make during the initial meeting. Even once you have been introduced, don't forget that you are still considered a stranger. Iranians may appear formal and stiff, especially with a foreign business partner, and may take some time to become friendly (remember the in-group/out-group distinction discussed in chapter 2). Be prepared to spend time establishing your relationship by making small talk, and don't think of this time as wasted. Imagine yourself as a farmer preparing the soil for sowing, turning the sod, watering, and, most importantly, waiting patiently for the seed to germinate and bear fruit. Effort and time are the main ingredients of every personal relationship; in Iran, the same is no less true for a business one.

During "small talk" you may be asked personal questions about your trip, your family, where you studied and what educational qualifications you hold, as well as questions about your home country, ways of doing things, and what your city looks like. As mentioned in chapter 3, such questions help cultivate a personal relationship that can then establish the basis for a successful business one. Iranians are generally interested in other people's ways of life and they also enjoy explaining aspects of their own lives, habits, and beliefs to others. Showing photos of your hometown, university, and family also helps establish a personal relationship, as does the offer of small gifts or mementoes from abroad, such as keyrings, pens, or postcards.

Don't be in a hurry to move on to the business at hand: this may give the impression that you are uninterested in the personal relationship and you may come across as one-dimensional and untrustworthy. The safe course is to wait until your counterpart initiates a change in conversation to business matters.

When your Iranian counterparts state their own positions, they will most likely begin with a lengthy introduction about their company and the projects it has successfully undertaken in the past. Try not to show your impatience at what you may think is superfluous information. The rationale behind this "setting the scene" is to establish an acquaintanceship and to set the basis for negotiation.

FIRST APPOINTMENT:
PRACTICAL MATTERS

If you are met at the front door or in the lobby, you will most likely be asked to walk ahead of your escort. (For more details on the manners of giving way, refer to chapter 2.) Shaking hands with people of the same gender is acceptable. The best approach regarding handshakes is not to initiate one, especially with someone of the opposite sex, but to respond to a proffered hand. A bow of the head and a smile will do instead of a handshake.

When a new person enters the room, follow others' lead in standing up to greet them. Similarly, others already in the room will stand up to greet you when you enter, as a sign of politeness and respect. Good manners require that you ask them to remain seated out of consideration for their comfort. (Keep in mind the three politeness principles from chapter 3.)

In all likelihood you will first meet and hold initial discussions with junior members of a firm or government organization before you meet senior members or officials. One of these junior members is most likely to be a person with a good knowledge of English and, if you haven't brought your own interpreter along, s/he will probably do the interpreting. Your meeting with this person is a useful opportunity for you to establish a good working relationship and to find more about the company and its workings.

ENTERTAINMENT

While you wait and throughout the meeting at least two rounds of tea will be served with pastry and possibly fresh fruit. The normal practice is for the tea attendant (every office has one) to place tea and refreshments in front of guests and for guests to wait until the host invites them to eat and drink. Smoking, which used to be quite common, is now rapidly on the way out, at least in closed spaces.

DRESS

The next chapter gives detailed guidelines on appropriate business dress, but the general principle is to be conservative and follow the lead of the

Iranian hosts. Avoid anything excessive, such as chunky jewelry (both men and women), and do not remove any item of clothing, even a coat, if others are keeping theirs on.

TERMS OF ADDRESS

Refer to chapter 3 for a discussion of terms of address. Remember, though, that Iranians are fond of educational titles and like to be addressed with their full title, especially in business and educational contexts. Formal terms of address take this form:

- *Âqâ-ye* [Mohandes/Doctor] + family name (e.g., *Âqâ-ye* Mohandes Mohammadi, Mr Engineer/Dr. Mohammadi)
- *Khânum-e* [Mohandes/Doctor] + family name (e.g., *Khânum-e* Doctor Mohammadi, Ms. Engineer/Dr. Mohammadi)

Making a point of knowing your partner's qualification and using the appropriate title (Doctor, Mohandes) often will help establish a positive working relationship.

DOCUMENTS AND BUSINESS CARDS

To facilitate the work, all documents should be available in both English and Persian. If you want to prepare these before you arrive in Iran, the Iranian consulate in your home country should be able to help you find qualified translators. Translation services are also listed in Persian magazines and newspapers that are usually on sale in Iranian shops abroad.

Similarly, a dual-language business card that includes your position and educational qualifications ensures that your partners will remember your name correctly and understand your rank. The polite way of offering your business card or anything else is with both palms open.

CONCEPTS OF TIME

Generally speaking, Iranians are relaxed about time, interpreting it in a rather loose way. An old client of a *bâzâri* may telephone the latter's

shop to arrange a business meeting and say, "Come for lunch and we can talk then." Lunch is any time after the noon call to prayer, which, as described earlier, can be as early as 12:00 noon in the autumn and winter (September 21–March 20) or as late as after 1:00 during the spring and summer (March 21–September 22), so a precise time may not be mentioned for such a meeting.

The timing given for meetings and lectures is usually an approximation of when participants are normally expected to arrive, with the meeting beginning as much as fifteen to thirty minutes later than the scheduled time. If the organizers really intend to start the meeting at the time announced, they will mention the arrival time too. However, Iranians are aware that foreign guests tend to arrive promptly, so don't make the mistake of arriving late. Meetings with foreign partners are likely to start closer to the time that has been planned.

Timing may be even more elastic if you are dealing with government organizations, because officials often need to deal with issues that come up unexpectedly. Similarly, last-minute schedule changes and new arrangements may take place. Once again, showing understanding, patience, and flexibility will work in your favor.

If you need to hold more than one meeting on the same day, leave ample time between each one, because, as discussed, the first meeting is likely to last longer than you anticipate. Looking at your watch or appearing impatient to bring the meeting to a close will leave a bad impression—that time is more important to you than the progression of the meeting—and you will be seen as untrustworthy.

Be forewarned that in Iran meetings can be frequently interrupted by staff entering for short consultations as well as mobile phone and landline telephone calls—both business and personal ones. Again, be patient and try to see things from the Iranian point of view: life is like that.

DEADLINES

As with the sense of time, deadlines are also generously interpreted. If you have been given a deadline by which a job should be accomplished, don't expect it to be adhered to as strictly as you may be accustomed to,

because events beyond one's control may happen. For example, one might have unexpected visitors, become ill, or have a family emergency. Iranians understand that such eventualities could happen to anyone and see them as inevitable in the course of human life. This is the reason why Muslims usually say *inshâ-âllâh* (God willing) in every conversation about the future: humans make plans and arrangements, but since all affairs lie in God's hands, delays and missed appointments have to be accepted as an undeniable fact of life.

On the other hand, any insistence by your Iranian business partner on a deadline that you feel is too tight may stem from a similar expectation that it will not be punctually met and may in fact be an attempt to factor in a delay. You can always explain your position by pointing out that your deadline will be met promptly (*inshâ-âllâh*, your partner may add).

USING AN INTERPRETER

Negotiations will probably take place through an interpreter, which is an advisable practice even if you think your Persian is adequate or your business partner speaks English well. It may be useful to spend some time establishing a relationship with your interpreter before the meeting, which, as with other Iranians, will help the progress of your work in the long term. To facilitate the interpreter's work, speak slowly, especially at the beginning, and pace your speech. To avoid misunderstandings, avoid new and colloquial expressions, which an interpreter may be unfamiliar with, and use textbook/formal vocabulary, not informal, chatty words.

If you or one of your associates speaks Persian, communication will be easier generally and, since Iranians are well-disposed toward a foreigner who has made the effort to learn their language, the presence of a Persian speaker, even one who is not fluent, is likely to contribute toward the overall good feeling.

NEGOTIATIONS

As in all business interactions aimed at reaching agreement over future actions or on terms for a contract, the negotiation process follows

similar lines. Each party has in mind the absolute maximum amount of terms they are prepared to grant, but start off with the minimum to allow themselves the leeway to show flexibility and goodwill.

When it comes to the negotiation itself, again you need to be patient. As must have become clear by now, interpersonal relationships are very important among Iranians and are developed gradually through interactions. If a speaker feels that a point could be construed as criticism or is likely to cause confrontation or disagreement, it will probably be made in a long-winded or indirect manner in order to minimize its potentially offensive impact. Try to read between the lines of a seemingly irrelevant point; ask your interpreter for help if necessary.

As discussed in chapter 2, such indirectness is linked to face issues. Any criticism or comments that may be construed as such should always be done indirectly and gently, and certainly not in the presence of other people, as the danger of loss of face is too great. Even then, the addressee may offer an explanation or justification rather than a proper apology (quite different from the ostensible apologies described in chapter 3), which often seems to result in loss of face.

Iranians frequently use the inductive method to make a point. They build up an argument gradually, sometimes using anecdotes and analogies (*qiyâs*) until they reach their main point. This discourse style takes some getting used to by those accustomed to making the main point first and then supporting it with evidence. Learn to listen for the main point near the end of the talk rather than at the beginning.

As mentioned earlier in this chapter, Iranians are seasoned negotiators. This ability comes into its own in business dealings; they enjoy bargaining in their attempt to get advantageous concessions and, most importantly, they know that time is on their side. Try not to show that you are under time constraints, as this can be used as a negotiating tactic against you. In Iran patience, not time, is of the essence.

NEGOTIATING: AN EXAMPLE

As negotiations progress, Iranians will offer stronger arguments in support of their case. Once I witnessed a business negotiation between the

director of a cultural institute (X) and a member of the board of directors of the same institute (Y), both female. Agreement had been reached on the format and the starting date of a course the institute was going to offer, and then the topic of fees came up. X felt that the institute should charge the same amount it charged in the previous series (50,000 tumans per person for ten three-hour long sessions).

Y argued that the fees should be higher now because this was a specially designed course that couldn't be found elsewhere. She added that language institutes charge roughly the same fee for teaching ready-made courses for a term (two 1½ hour classes per week for ten weeks), and that they can afford to do that because they have many students and thus can keep the unit cost down. If Kânun, an extensive network of language schools, got wind of the idea of this course, they would set it up and offer the course at a very high fee. Therefore, she argued, the institute should charge 80,000 tumans.

X said that not many people would be prepared to pay this amount, so they may not get enough students. Y countered that every service has gone up and cited her hairdresser, who charges 10,000 tumans for a facial hair removal and eyebrow shaping. Once when she was at the hairdresser's a woman was having her hair highlighted. Every foil cost 5,000 tumans, with a total of twenty for the full head coming to 100,000, plus the face make-up at 80,000 tumans. Then she joked that the woman was prepared to pay this amount for going to a wedding reception and would have everyone tell her, "You look so awful!"

X still didn't look convinced and asked Y to agree on 60,000. Y stood her ground. She used the example of her own counseling center, where she has built up a good reputation but charges low fees. She now finds that the expenses of the center are too high, and has to top them up from her own pocket. She asked Y to agree on 70,000, which she did.

This interaction demonstrates the principle of not conceding too much too soon, as well as the use of a favorite strategy in argument, that of analogy (*qiyâs*). If a woman is prepared to spend that much on her appearance for one night, she would also pay for something intellectually useful.

DECISION MAKING

From everything discussed so far, readers may have already guessed that decisions are also reached and implemented slowly, although this has more to do with company organization and layered bureaucracy rather than time management. Companies and organizations are structured hierarchically, and decisions have to be deliberated by the top person or by a small board of directors. To speed things up, you can apply gentle pressure through follow-up calls or e-mails, although the most effective way is to ask the person who introduced you to check in or to find an influential contact who can do so more effectively.

SOCIAL ASPECTS OF A BUSINESS RELATIONSHIP

During your stay in Iran you are likely to be invited for a meal. On such occasions the boundaries between business and personal relationships are blurred even further and, again, you should make use of this opportunity to cultivate the relationship.

If the invitation is to an associate's house for dinner, good manners require that you bring a small present, such as flowers, candies, or baked goods, but no alcoholic drinks. If you bring chocolates from abroad, which are always appreciated, make sure they do not contain alcohol. Small souvenirs from your home country are also welcomed. Despite the religious and legal prohibition of alcohol, non-Muslim Iranians (e.g. Armenian Christians) are allowed to brew and consume alcohol in private. Some Iranian Muslims also drink in the privacy of their own homes, so if you are offered an alcoholic drink, you can accept it, since your host also drinks.

If the invitation is to a restaurant, convention requires that the host pays. You may try offering to pay (only *ta'ârof*), but do not expect the offer to be accepted. Meal etiquette and related issues are covered in chapter 9.

AFTER THE MEETING

Even if you are pleased with the progress of your business project, in today's hectic life your meeting may easily be forgotten. If you want to maintain a long-term business relationship with an Iranian firm, ideally you should return to Iran as often as possible, but also keep up the relationship via e-mail and the occasional telephone call, as well as Noruz wishes.

THE ETHICAL DIMENSION

A business needs to make a profit to remain viable, of course, but profit isn't the only measure of success. Iranians consider the moral and ethical dimensions equally important, as well as maintaining a work-life balance. This doesn't mean that there aren't any businesses purely driven by profit or businesspeople whose lives haven't been taken over by their work, but be aware that a one-sided emphasis on profits at the expense of human considerations is an attitude generally frowned upon.

SUCCESSFUL BUSINESS IN IRAN (IN A NUTSHELL)

- Take the time to acquaint yourself with Iranian culture and manners.
- Keep interpersonal factors in mind.
- Remember and apply the three politeness principles that guide behavior: deference, humility, and cordiality).
- Be patient.
- Be flexible.

SIX

Dress and Make-Up

In October 1997 we were invited to what would be my first Iranian wedding. The bride was the daughter of Hossein's maternal uncle. I had a new outfit made, a two-piece suit made of complementary fabric in turquoise, and this was as far as my preparation went. On the day, I washed and blow-dried my hair, put on an overcoat, scarf, and shoes, and off we went.

It was Thursday evening, a favorite time for wedding receptions and all kinds of social activities, so traffic was heavy and we arrived at the reception hall late. Past the front door Hossein and I parted ways: our son Yusef went with Hossein over to the men's hall, and our daughter Athena followed me to the women's part upstairs. We stopped by the vestibule to remove our scarves and overcoats. A woman with her hair in an elaborate hairdo stood in front of the mirror applying lipstick. I gave my hair a quick brush, took Athena's hand, and walked into the main hall.

I thought I had walked into the wrong reception: the hall was full of women with their faces made up in bright colors of eye shadow, rouge, and lipstick, and their hands dazzled with gold jewelry and nail varnish. I didn't recognize anyone.

"Mummy, Mâmân-jun's there," Athena said, tugging my hand toward the table where Hossein's mother was seated. We were at the right place after all.

It took some time to adjust to matching the women in their new—for me—guise with the mental images I had in my mind of their everyday appearance in black chadors or loose overcoats, heads under dark scarves, and unadorned faces.

ISLAMIC DRESS (*HIJAB*)

When the prospect of a trip to Iran is raised, the very first thing prospective visitors, especially women, worry about is how to dress appropriately. All travel guides to Iran contain a section on this topic and my advice follows later in this chapter, but before we get down to the specifics, the *hows* and the *whats*, it is useful to look at the *whys*—the principles behind the dress rules of *hijab* (modest dress). Understanding the rationale behind this practice is essential to truly comprehending the culture and its standards.

The distinction between intimates and nonintimates, discussed in chapter 3, also influences dress codes. The Holy Quran lists the intimate (*mahram*) males before whom women can display their beauty: parents, grandparents, siblings and their children, a spouse's parents, one's own children and their spouses, grandchildren, and blood uncles and aunts. By extension, this rule implies that all other males are nonintimate (*nâmahram*) and that, consequently, women should be modestly dressed in the presence of these men.[1]

A prophetic tradition (*hadith*) mentions that a woman's whole body should be covered, except the face and hands, and it is generally agreed that the outfit should be loose enough so as not to outline bodily curves. The term *hijab* literally means "curtain," in other words, something screening off what should not be seen. So, if every item of clothing covers a woman's frame and hair, she may be described in current usage as being "in full *hijab*," that is, observing all the rules. A woman would be considered in "bad *hijab*" if wearing a too-tight blouse or overcoat, her hair wasn't fully covered, or by wearing flashy make-up. However, among English-speaking Muslims, *hijab* sometimes refers to the head covering only.

This principle allows considerable freedom in the choice of dress: we all know of wide variations across the Islamic world, developed out of preexisting cultures, climatic conditions, and practical considerations. Thus, some women cover the whole face, some half, others tie the headscarf behind the head leaving the neck uncovered, and still others wear knee-length skirts without tights.

"But why?" non-Muslims often ask. "What's the point?"

This is a controversial topic on which innumerable books have been written arguing divergent viewpoints. Western-style feminists argue that *hijab* is imposed on women in an obvious expression of patriarchal values, whereas pious Muslims point out that for many women the *hijab* is a personal choice they make in obeying God's orders. Opinions and views cover the whole spectrum, from the most liberal to the most conservative, depending on backgrounds and persuasions. But the fact remains that for many Iranian women from conservative backgrounds, the compulsory *hijab* has been a means of liberation and of extensive participation in society: a woman in *hijab* is meant to be seen and appreciated for her qualities as a person and not for her attractive appearance.

In response to the question "How important is it for a woman to wear a veil?" Seventy percent of Iranian male respondents said "very important" and 17.6 percent "rather important," while sixty-eight percent of female respondents said "very important" and sixteen percent "rather important," so both males and females have very similar opinions.[2] The theological arguments themselves fill volumes, but for the purposes of this book, here's a brief summary of the main social and practical reasons for observing *hijab*.

- To preserve women's dignity, respect, and freedom to participate fully in social life.
- To ensure equality among women and give them self-confidence, minimizing the difference between the attractive and the less attractive women. This promotes a relative equality among them. Every woman regardless of appearance is seen as attractive and desirable.
- To safeguard family stability and protect family life, because men can only see their own *mahram* women and are less likely to be attracted to a stranger and grow distant from their wives.

Of course, reality is far removed from this ideal, but this is the philosophy behind the *hijab*. Generally, when girls reach puberty they start covering their hair, but they may still be wearing slacks and T-shirts. As they get older, they start wearing a manteau, which is probably the most common item of clothing for Iranian women, and a headscarf or shawl.

The women who also wear a *chador*, may either wear it over a manteau or over a top and skirt or slacks.

THE CHADOR AND OTHER ISLAMIC DRESS

Thanks to photojournalists, the most well-known Iranian clothing item that most Westerners are familiar with is a black *chador* (*châdor meshki*). Shaped as a half circle with a radius of the woman's height plus four inches (ten centimeters), it covers the whole figure from head to toe and is usually clutched from underneath the chin with one hand. This simple outer garment, indigenous to the country and worn for centuries, has become a symbolic image of contemporary Iran, especially after the Islamic Revolution. Just walk into any bookshop that stocks books on Iran and count the covers showing women in black *chadors*.

Because it is so different from anything Western societies are used to, the *chador* is often the subject of misunderstanding and prejudice (I know this first hand, from my Greek relatives' not very flattering comments). Such prejudice takes different forms: some think that all women are forced to wear it and feel repressed, others think that only the militant, revolutionary, ultra-conservative, very religious women wear it. Very few outsiders realize that the *chador* is very common all over Iran and in Tehran, and also that another type, the patterned *chador* (*châdor rangi*) is also widespread throughout Iran, in both rural and urban settings. Women can choose from a wide variety of patterns and colors that reflect seasonal fashions and personal tastes. White fabrics with small, pastel-colored flowers are favored by young or newly married women, while beiges, greens, and darker colors such as browns and navy blues, all patterned with flowers or abstract shapes, are suitable for middle-aged and older women.

Sewn of a lighter, cooler fabric, the patterned *chador* stays in place more easily than the black one. In cities the patterned *chador* is only worn indoors by some women when *nâmahrams* are present. Rural women wear the patterned *chador* outdoors over blouses and slacks or a skirt, or over a traditional outfit.

Near Hosseiniyeh Ershad, toward the north of Tehran, a new business enterprise has recently opened: Laleh Chador Gallery. Housed in a flat, only women are allowed in during the working week, while men accompanied by a female relative can visit on Friday mornings. All sorts of different *chador* fabrics are stocked here: formal black of various thicknesses and weights, for outdoor wear; semitransparent lacy black, often with flower patterns, for prayer meetings (now also worn outside); opaque or semitransparent colorful, silky *chadors* for weddings and formal gatherings; white opaque or semitransparent for the bride's journey from the hairdresser's to the reception hall; colorful thin cotton or voile for everyday use; pastel-colored or white thick cotton for prayer use and (the latter) to wear while on the pilgrimage. Before I become familiar with Iranians, I could never imagine there would be so many different kinds of *chadors*; I thought it was just a plain black covering.

Chador fabric is normally bought by the meter: 5½ meters (6 yards) × 1¼ meters (a little less than 1½ feet) wide of fabric is enough for a woman of average height and is sewn at home or given to a tailor to make up. This is where Laleh Chador Gallery differs. A made-up sample of each fabric is available to try on for grip, drape, movement, and pattern before one decides on a purchase. Then a resident tailor can take the customer's order.

Apart from the standard, semicircular Iranian *chador*, which is still the most commonly used throughout Iran, there are other designs for black *chadors*, some older, others newly developed. Over a decade ago the Arabic style *abbaya* had gained currency especially among younger women and students. Because it has holes for the hands, it is more convenient than the Iranian *chador*, although not, in my view, as elegant. The *abbaya* enjoyed a period of popularity until new Iranian designs for black *chadors* emerged about five years ago: the national and the student *chadors* are two popular varieties that look similar to the standard one but they have sleeves and button up the front. These have now become popular choices among students and young women. A Qajar-period waistband chador, dating back to the nineteenth century, is uncommon but can be specially ordered and is making a timid comeback.

All these designs for outdoor use are always made in black. Some courageous shops have started to produce national *chadors* in other colors like brown or dark blue, but these are at present considered eccentric. Only time will tell whether this innovation will catch on.

A PIECE OF HISTORY

The chador has developed over the centuries into a national item of outdoor clothing.

Reza Pahlavi's campaign in the 1930s to modernize Iran deemed the *chador* as a symbol of women's repression and backwardness, banning it in public, forcing government employees to make their wives appear in public without a *chador*, and ordering the police to remove *chadors* by force. Predictably, this radical move resulted in more repression for the vast majority of women, many of whom immured themselves in their homes for fear of assault and humiliation. A governor's wife, who had to appear at public functions preferred to commit suicide rather than cast away her *chador*.[3]

This policy brought about change. Women in some urban families adopted modest European style clothing, some covering their hair with scarves or hats. But during the latter part of the reign of the second Pahlavi monarch (1941–79), under the influence of Mohammad Reza's "modernizing" policies, including television and banning women in *hijab* from workplaces, young women closely copied their European counterparts and wore whatever they wanted.

The Islamic Revolution gave the black *chador* a new meaning, that of returning to the nation's national identity and Islamic roots. At the time, some women who did not belong to particularly religious families adopted the *chador* in a show of allegiance with the ideals of the Islamic Revolution, hence the revolutionary image often associated with the *chador*. However, most Iranian women wore a *chador* before the revolution and many still continue to do so.

The *chador*, apart from its use as *hijab*, also has formal connotations. I have observed that some women who normally wear an overcoat will wear a *chador* to a funeral or a mourning ceremony in a mosque.

CURRENT DRESS CODES

Although the *hijab* is understood to be compulsory for all women when they reach puberty, not all women choose to observe the *hijab* rules, at least indoors and in their private lives. At the time of the Revolution, many women did not observe *hijab*, so when the *hijab* dress code became compulsory a couple of years after the victory of the Islamic Revolution, a new type of *hijab* was introduced and took its place along the *chador*. This took the shape and the name of *manteau*, a loose overcoat worn over top and slacks, or mid-calf skirt with thick hosiery and a headscarf. Women who didn't want to wear a *chador* could wear a manteau and a headscarf.

At first some thought that women who did not observe *hijab* wore a manteau and that the really pious ones wore a *chador*, but this belief has changed over the years, with many pious women wearing manteaus rather than *chadors*, or others wearing a *chador* because of work requirements (e.g. in some governmental agencies and in some universities) rather than by personal conviction. A wide variety of manteau styles have developed: casual (for leisure occasions), official (for university or work), and formal (made of heavy, black fabric, often embroidered, for weddings or for mourning).

As with all fashions, styles vary with age. Students, teachers, and working women wear manteaus with black trousers and a headcover in the shape of a wimple (*maghna'eh*) in black or a dark color, and if they are *châdoris* (i.e. they always wear a *chador* outdoors), with a *chador* on top. School uniforms for girls consist of loose overalls with pants made of the same fabric and a dark blue, gray, or black wimple.

Wearing a headcover has assumed an air of formality. In my daughter's girls-only high school, where all staff are female and no males are allowed on the grounds during the school day, teachers wear black chadors, manteaus and wimples to school and then change to colorful scarves or shawls once inside, unlike the girls who remove their wimples upon entering the school and replace them before leaving the school. In this case, when no males are present, wearing a headscarf underscores the difference in status between teachers and students.

When out of uniform, many teenage girls sport tight, short overalls that look more like longish shirts, usually black, over tight denim jeans, although jeans and fashionable sneakers are common among all young women, whether they wear a *chador* or not. In fact, tourists can see young women dressing like this in the street, with the only difference that some will wear a *chador* over their top and jeans.

READY-TO-WEAR OR TAILOR-MADE?

Clothing is sold in small shops, ranging from those expensive boutiques importing single items from abroad, to those stocking products made in Iran. However, there is nothing like the Western department store chains that sell the same lines of products throughout the country and where one can find specific items. As of recent, a wider variety of clothing can be found in Iranian shops than was the case earlier, but finding the item in the size you need is either a challenge or an opportunity to shop until you drop, depending on your outlook.

This potential difficulty is compensated for by the fact that it is relatively easy to find a skilled tailor. Many Iranian women shop for dress fabrics themselves, choose a design from a fashion magazine at the tailor's shop, and have an outfit made by her. I say *her* because tailors for women's formal clothing, which requires precise measuring, are usually female, although I do know a male tailor whose female assistant takes measurements before he makes the outfits.

Most tailors are highly skilled and experienced, and they can make up a pattern in the correct size just by looking at a photograph and measuring the customer. Some can sew a new garment using an old one as a guide without taking any measurements. Some tailors specialize in engagement and wedding gowns, and they can sew anything featured in a wedding fashion magazine without having a pattern. And the best thing of all is that, by Western standards, tailor-made clothes are quite affordable. Tailors' fees may vary according to location and difficulty of the work, but as a guide, the tailor's fee for a simple blouse with buttons along the front may be about $20 (£13), while for a man's suit it can be $100 (£63) or more, at October 2009 exchange prices.

TAILORS

If you would like to have an outfit made by a tailor, get a friend's or a host's recommendation for a good tailor. You should expect to pay a deposit when you place your order and to wait for a few days until your garment is ready. At several points in the process, for example, when the fabric is cut, at the first fitting, and when the garment is ready, you may hear the wish *mobârak bâshe* (may it be blessed). The answer to this wish is *salâmat bâshid* (may you be healthy), or simply *mersi'* or *kheili mamnun* (thank you very much). The same phrases are used when you buy something new.

INFORMAL WEAR FOR MEN AND WOMEN

Generally, younger people's styles show a stronger Western influence than those of older people. Much like in the West, younger men tend to wear leisure items indoors, such as polo shirts, T-shirts, and sweatshirts, which are often used as sleepwear too. Older men and those from traditional backgrounds often wear loose, baggy trousers made of cool cotton fabric called *shalvâr kordi* (Kurdish trousers), especially in the summer, or striped pajama bottoms tucked inside their socks under their outdoor trousers in the winter for more warmth. These pajama bottoms then double as indoor trousers.

Women's indoor clothing follows fashions similar to those in the West when no *nâmahrams* are present: T-shirts, slacks, denim jeans, with younger women generally favoring pants rather than skirts. In the presence of *nâmahrams*, women who wear *chadors* outdoors will most likely wear a patterned *chador* over whatever they are wearing. Women who observe the *hijab* rules but do not wear a *chador* will most likely change into a loose, long-sleeved top and long skirt, or loose slacks and scarf.

PERMISSION GRANTED

When a *nâmahram* man is about to enter a room or any other space where women may have removed their *hijab*, he will announce his arrival with *yâllâh, yâllâh* (an invocation of God's name) so that the women can replace their scarves or *chadors* before he comes in, and he will wait for permission to enter. This permission is often expressed as *befarmâ'id* (at your orders).

FORMAL WEAR (MEN AND WOMEN)

In Iran the two-piece suit, often with a vest, is worn more than in the West. Office workers, technocrats, civil servants, doctors, teachers, and bank clerks wear suits not only to work, but also when visiting friends and family, going shopping, or traveling, especially if they are middle-aged or older. Artistic and engineering types, and those who have lived abroad, tend to dress less formally, with trousers and coat of different fabrics. As mentioned earlier in the chapter, ties are rarely worn, especially among the more conservative and pious strata, and are seen as a Western irrelevance.

FORMAL WEAR: WEDDINGS

Ties, however, are quite likely to be worn at weddings, and a groom may also wear a light colored suit like off-white or olive green rather than the more common gray or navy blue. Male guests usually wear darker colored suits.

On formal occasions like weddings, women dress like movie stars on premiere night. Because the genders are segregated on such occasions, women spare no effort to present an impressive image: low-cut dresses in

heavily embroidered fabrics revealing a lot of cleavage and bare legs are quite usual, even for women who generally observe the *hijab* rules in mixed company.

MAKE-UP

On the wedding morning, the bride and her close female relatives visit the beautician/hairdresser. Traditionally, single women had their eyebrows shaped and facial hair removed with a twisted thread for the very first time a couple of days before their wedding, a visual indication of entering marital status. On the big day the bride would be made up in bold colors, while any unmarried sisters and cousins would wear muted, low-key make-up. Her mother and middle-aged matrons would also wear make-up, but nothing excessive. However, these practices are now changing, at least among some urban families. Young women often have their eyebrows shaped irrespective of their marital status, while both married and unmarried young women may wear make-up as flashy as they dare, and sport quite extravagant hairdos. Even middle-aged women, if they are close relatives of the bride or the groom, now will dress more like the younger women.

Bridal make-up and hairdressing salons are booming businesses in Iran. A bridal party made up of the bride, her mother and sisters, and possibly one or two aunts will spend the whole day of the wedding until the evening at the hairdresser's salon getting prepared for the reception. The cost of a bridal make-up and hairdo ranges from about $400 (or £250) for the bride only (equivalent to a teacher's monthly salary), depending on the hairdresser's location. The total bill for the bridal party make-up is paid for by the groom.

Make-up fashion shows the influence of neighboring Arab countries, such as *Khâliji* (Gulf-style) and *Loobnâni* (Lebanese). Other current make-up fashion items are temporary tattoos on bare arms, the neck, and cheeks, make-up that looks like a tan, hair extensions, and color contact lenses.

FASHION VICTIMS

In recent years semipermanent lip liner and eyebrow "tattoos" have become popular, together with more drastic and permanent interventions, with nose jobs (rhinoplasty) being the most common. (Iran is reputed to be the nose job capital of the world.) With Iranians boasting more than a fair share of Julius Caesar noses and with the rules of *hijab* making a sizeable nose even more prominent, a significant number of mostly young women go under the knife in pursuit of happiness in the shape of a French nose.

Nose jobs are not limited to women. Quite a few young men sport layers of plaster across the nose and sometimes "tidied up" eyebrows. Such practices in young men, by the way, although frowned upon by older and more conservative people, do not detract from their virility and do not indicate homosexuality.

When the bride is dressed and made up in the beauty salon, she wears a specially made white *chador* or long cape and hood to cover her gown and make-up for the ride to the reception hall. The groom picks up the bride from the beauty salon in a flower-decorated car in which, if she is not particularly bothered about the *hijab* rules, she may take the white *chador* off. Brides that observe the *hijab* rules closely may also cover their faces because of the heavy make-up, probably the only instance of face-covering in mainstream Iranian culture. Covering the face is extremely unusual in Iran and is likely to attract curious stares.

FORMAL WEAR: MOURNING

For mourning, men who attend the funeral and burial often wear black shirts, while close male relatives of the deceased may wear black shirts for forty days after the death. Among the most religious or traditional groups, men also do not shave for forty days.

Close female relatives of the deceased usually wear black clothes for at least forty days, and traditionally refrain from using make-up or eyebrow shaping (see chapter 8 for more on mourning practices).

MALE TOURISTS

Anything middle-of-the-road is acceptable, with only two no-nos: avoid shorts at all times, as well as loud, bright shirts and tops (e.g., Hawaiian shirts). Some Iranian youngsters have recently taken to wearing tight-fitting, sleeveless tops, but this fashion is generally disapproved of and is limited to the very young and trendy. All other leisure wear is acceptable, although be aware that tracksuit bottoms are only used indoors or in gyms, so wearing those pants in the street is likely to attract puzzled glances and smiles. (Wouldn't you do the same if you saw a man walking in the street in his pajamas?)

Short sleeves are acceptable when sightseeing and shopping but not for formal or business occasions.

MALE BUSINESS VISITORS

As in the West, a suit is the generally acceptable dress code for men on business and formal occasions. The main obvious difference is the almost general absence of a tie, at least in government organizations and government-affiliated companies. This doesn't mean that you can't a wear a tie, because Iranians are aware of the different dress styles and may even expect you to follow your own—foreign leaders and diplomats always do. Iranian private businessmen are more likely to wear a tie.

WOMEN: GENERAL GUIDELINES

Iranian law requires that all women wear Islamic *hijab* upon reaching puberty, but it doesn't specify the form. Despite the common misunderstanding, the *chador* is not compulsory except when visiting some mosques and holy shrines, where you can borrow one at the gate or even, if fancy takes you, buy a ready-made one from a nearby bazaar.

Women visitors have to observe the *hijab* law, which at the time of writing applies not only to Iranian nationals but to all women. If you find others around you being more relaxed about *hijab*, you can do the

same. However, as mentioned in chapter 3, don't forget that Iranians are well disposed toward foreigners and generally appreciate an effort to fit in and show respect for their conventions, so a small inconvenience may be worth the goodwill it generates.

Technically, all hair should be covered, but you will soon notice that this isn't the case in practice. If you want to be comfortable and not have to worry about your scarf slipping back, tie long hair back and choose a light cotton or nonslippery scarf or shawl (Indian silk or cotton scarves are good, too) tied under the chin or draped back over the shoulders.

Colors

Generally there is no limitation on color, although it's best to avoid bright reds and pinks, especially during the month of Moharram, when Iranians observe mourning for Imam Hossein, and during the fast of the month of Ramadan. Apart from these, the anniversaries of the Holy Imams' martyrdoms are also scattered throughout the year, so you would feel rather awkward walking about in bright colors among people dressed in somber ones. I find that any shades of blue and green, from pastels to deeper hues, and browns and creams are generally acceptable. Turquoise is a favorite of mine, and matches the lovely multicolor tiles in the Isfahan mosques.

Female Tourists

Generally, women have to wear clothing that adequately conceals feminine curves and does not show bare flesh, except for the face and hands, and often a bit of forearm, lower calf, and feet.

Foreign visitors can wear a pair of not-too-tight slacks under a loosely fitting, long-sleeved top or tunic that covers at least half the thighs, though ideally longer. If you would prefer to wear a skirt, it should be at least mid-calf or longer, with nontransparent, darkish hosiery underneath. Ankle length skirts are unusual but acceptable. During late autumn, winter, and early spring (October to March), these requirements are easier to follow, as women visitors can wear a raincoat over pants. In the warm and hot months (April until late September), my advice would be to choose a linen jacket or even an oversized but-

ton-down blouse to get to Iran and then have your first shopping experience hunting for a cool overcoat once you get here. Your tour operator or host should be happy to advise.

Female Business Visitors

Apart from the general guidelines already described, if you are a business traveler, aim to have at least one dark color outfit (black, navy blue, brown, or dark green) and a similarly muted or dark color scarf to wear over your head. Beige raincoats are also appropriate.

SEVEN

From the Cradle to the Grave: Education and Health

Seek learning from the cradle to the grave.

—Imam Ali

Pursue knowledge even if it is as far as China.

—Holy Prophet Muhammad

*The first time I heard Persian being spoken was in May 1987, when I intro-
duced Hossein and his old friend Ja'far to my classmate Ghafour, who I
thought would have a useful tip or two to share with his newly arrived compatriots. The four of us sat at a table at the Academie Française in Athens.
Since I had studied English language and literature in Athens, at the same
time cultivating my hobby of learning languages, I settled down to a treat.
What would I make of it?*

*Like everyone who hears an unfamiliar language, my first impression
was of no word boundaries, a steady stream of sounds, much like birds twit-
tering, absorbing but incomprehensible. All that and a healthy measure of
hand gestures and other body language made me sit there transfixed, telling
myself that here was a language I would never, ever learn.*

With German as our common language, over the following weeks Hossein and I stumbled over German irregular verbs, case agreement, and misunderstood appointments (halb sechs in German really means half past five) before giving German up in favor of English, which all his friends understood. English became our default language, and Hossein tried his best to help me keep up with the Persian conversations with his friends. Gradually, the stream became less daunting, the shapes of some words emerged, and links with its cousins of the Indo-European language family became clear to me.

THE PERSIAN LANGUAGE

Because the Persian language is written in Arabic script, it is often mistakenly thought to be related to Arabic. In fact, Persian belongs to the Iranian branch of the Indo-European group of languages, together with English and German (Germanic branch), French, Italian, and Spanish (Italic or Latin branch), Scots, Irish Gaelic, and Welsh (Celtic branch), and Greek (on its own), whereas Arabic is classified under the Afro-Asiatic or Hamito-Semitic language family.

The Arabic alphabet was adapted for writing Persian after the Arab conquest of Iran in the seventh century A.D. by adding four characters to the twenty-eight characters of the Arabic alphabet in order to represent four Persian sounds that do not exist in Arabic: **p**, **g** (as in *get*), **ch** (as in *chair*), and **zh** (as in *leisure*).

Persian pronunciation is quite easy to master, except perhaps for three consonant sounds that may sound unfamiliar to English speakers:

- /x/, as in the Scottish *loch* or German *doch* and usually transliterated as /kh/, as in *Khomeini*
- /gh/, similar to /x/, but with voice, approximating the French /r/
- /q/, similar to the English *k* but articulated toward the back of the mouth, on the soft palate

Persian has only six vowels, which are similar to English. These have been represented in English characters as /a/ (*hat*), /â/ (*bath*), /e/ and /i/ (*bee* or *bin*), and /o/ and /u/ (*zoo*).

Spelling proves a bit trickier. After the Islamic conquest, numerous Arabic words entered Persian and are in current use, their pronunciation being adapted to the simpler consonantal system of Persian while retaining their original spelling. As a result, words like *zaferân* (saffron), *nazr* (pledge), *zarbeh* (a blow), and *zarf* (container), which all contain the sound /z/, are each spelled with a different letter with the sound /z/, reflecting their pronunciation in the original Arabic, where each of these letters is pronounced differently. A similar situation occurs with the sound /s/, which is represented in writing in three different ways, for example, *sang* (stone), *sabr* (patience) and *mesâl* (example), and with /t/ with two, as in *tâbe* (follower) and *tâher* (pure). Schoolchildren and teachers have a tough job!

However, once past the initial hurdle of the alphabet, the similarities of Persian with its sister languages become apparent. Cognate words such as *mâdar* (mother), *pedar* (father), and *barâdar* (brother) are easily recognized across the Indo-European languages, but numerous others are less obvious. For example, *dokhtar* (girl, daughter) must have borne a closer phonetic resemblance to the English *daughter* a few centuries ago when *gh* was still sounded in the English word. *Biveh* is a cognate of the English *widow*, the French *veuve*, and the Italian *vedova*. We could go on looking at other examples for a long time, but the point is clear: the Persian language is much closer to English than one may tend to think at first glance.

Many Arabic words are used alongside their Persian equivalents, resulting in prose rich in connotation and with fine nuances of meaning. A similar situation exists in English with Latinate (or Greek) and Anglo-Saxon words. Words deriving from Latin and Greek have undertones of high status and education, formality, refinement, and, in some situations, possibly of arrogance and a desire to flaunt or, worse, to pretend that one possesses any of these qualities. On the other hand, Anglo-Saxon words are short, informal, and neutral in everyday speech and writing, for example, walk vs. perambulate.

Other words absorbed more recently from European languages into Persian reflect influences on and imports to the culture. The educational system was based on the French model, so many *farangi* (i.e., Frankish, European) cultural practices were introduced by Iranians

who had studied in Francophone countries. As a result, many French words are used in these contexts: *lisâns* (Fr. *licence*, Bachelor's degree), *kelâs* (Fr. *classe*), *rufuzeh* (Fr. *refusé(e)*, not promoted to the next year), *diplom* (high school diploma), *concour* (Fr. *concours*, university entrance examination), *teâtr* (*theatre*), *consert* (*concert*), and *radiolozhi* (Fr. radiology), all of which have the stress on the last syllable as in French. With the advent of new technology, management training, the Internet, and the return of many Iranians from the West, many English words are now established in common use: telephone, computer, mobile, sandwich, hamburger, support, range, and pilot (as in "pilot study"). The Iranian Academy of Persian Language is trying to preserve the purity of Persian against the adoption of mainly English words by providing Persian alternatives that must be used in official documents and on the state media, for example, *târ-nâmeh* (website), *râyâneh* (computer), and *ravâdid* (visa). However, these alternatives also have undertones similar to the ones that Latinate words in English have, and are not in colloquial use.

In common with many of its cousin languages, Persian is an inflectional language, like Latin, Greek, Italian, and German. It retains inflectional suffixes for both singular and plural verbs, unlike English, which only marks the third person singular with –*s*. This means that every verbal form contains a different suffix that distinguishes the person and whether singular or plural. For example:

mi-rav-am (I go)
mi-rav-i (you [singular] go)
mi-rav-ad (he/she/it goes)
mi-rav-im (we go)
mi-rav-id (you [plural] go)
mi-rav-and (they go)

The noun and adjective system is very simple: unlike French or Italian, Persian has no grammatical gender, and nouns have only one form for the singular and one for the plural. Just like in English, adjectives are not pluralized. The plural of nouns is formed through plural suffixes,

although Arabic nouns are sometimes pluralized according to Arabic rules, for example, broken plurals, as in *ketâb* (book)/*kotob* (books).

A remarkable, in my view, aspect of Persian syntax is that the main verb of a sentence comes at the very end, just as in classical Latin. In formal writing, where sentences can be several lines long, this positioning of the verb has the effect of retaining the readers' attention. In addition, if I may venture that far, this pattern subliminally inculcates the virtue of patience: only after working through the parts of the sentence does one reach the most important component, the verb, without which the sentence has no meaning.

THE VALUE OF LEARNING

Until the founding of the University of Tehran in 1934, doctors, engineers, and university graduates got their degrees in the West, mostly France. Only the (male) offspring of the privileged classes and the aristocracy had access to higher education abroad. Consequently, a higher degree and the titles of Doctor and Mohandes (engineer) were indicative of privilege of birth and financial status at a time when the vast majority of the population was either illiterate or barely literate.

This class/educational divide continued until the establishment of the Islamic Republic in 1979, when an extensive program of adult literacy was launched and higher education aspirations were encouraged in young people who would never have dreamed of it even a few years previously. Thirty years on, the pattern is reversed: illiteracy is almost eradicated,[1] but many university graduates cannot find jobs commensurate with their qualifications. Some proceed to postgraduate study while others find jobs unrelated to their degrees.

Despite the number of college graduates, a degree is still seen as a passport to better job and marriage prospects, and a higher quality of life. Many young people take the *concour* (college entrance exams) each year, with slightly more women being admitted than men in the recent past. A degree from Europe or the U.S. is still seen as prestigious and desirable, and you may find that many Iranians will be interested in

where and what you studied, and what the educational system is like in your country.

TRADITIONAL TRAINING: APPRENTICESHIPS

As in most parts of the world, the traditional way of learning a practical job is through an apprenticeship. Nowadays special vocational schools (*kârdânesh*) cater to nonacademic youngsters and teach skills needed for jobs. However, not everyone can afford to continue formal schooling, so some young people are apprenticed with a master and learn on the job, at the same time getting paid for helping around the workshop. As in the past, goldsmiths, blacksmiths, coppersmiths, carpenters, tailors, barbers/hairdressers, musicians, and all traditional handicraft artists transfer their skills to the young in this way.

THE COMPULSORY EDUCATIONAL SYSTEM
AND ORGANIZATION

Schooling is organized into primary (years 1–5), lower secondary or guidance school (years 6–8), upper secondary (years 9–11), and one preuniversity year. School attendance is compulsory from ages six through fourteen (eight school years), and at the end of year eleven students are awarded a high school diploma.

The emphasis is mainly on rote learning; every question has only one right answer (see the discussion of uncertainty avoidance in chapter 11). In the minds of many Iranians, learning is the same as memorizing, except for mathematics, which is taught to a very advanced level. The marking of examinations and class assessments is out of a high of twenty, although recently "descriptive" assessments (excellent, very good, good, moderate, and poor) have been introduced in primary schools. Generally, a student needs to score at least ten out of twenty marks in every subject to progress to the next class. If students don't achieve that score by the end of the school year, they can retake the examination at the

beginning of the next school year and sometimes midyear in January/
February after having already progressed to the next class.

The school year is concentrated into nine months, September 23 to
May 21, with the final examinations between May 22 and June 21. The
only extended holiday during the school year is Noruz (March 20 to
April 2), with the occasional day off here and there. This means that the
summer holiday is twelve weeks long, during which time children and
youngsters often attend "leisure" classes they don't have time for in the
school year, such as swimming, drawing, dance, music, or foreign language classes.

POST-15 EDUCATIONAL SYSTEM

At age fifteen, students leave compulsory education and enter a three-
year upper-secondary education (*dabirestân*). After the first year students
choose their study direction: academic or art/vocational. Four academic
options are available (mathematics/physics, life sciences, humanities, and
Islamic studies) and numerous art/vocational ones, named *honarestân*,
including accounting, computers, architectural drawing, graphic arts,
and traditional handicrafts. Both academic and art/vocational courses
can lead to university studies, although the idea behind the latter is edu-
cating trained and experienced technicians who can fill the gaps at this
level of the job market.

An extensive system of coaching schools and experienced private
tutors prepare the thousands of candidates who take the university
entrance examination (*concour*). The university entrance examinations
are different for state and private universities and are held twice a year.

UNIVERSITY

Along with the immense population growth, demand for and attendance at higher education has increased manifold in the last thirty years.
Higher education is provided in state universities, where students do not

pay tuition fees. A number of state universities are based in Tehran, while at least one state university is located in every province. Among private universities that charge tuition fees, the largest is the Open Islamic University (*Dâneshgâh Âzâd Islâmi*), with branches all over the country.

The curriculum and the textbooks of every course are set centrally by the Ministry of Higher Education, so a degree in, say, English literature has the same content whether one has studied in Tehran or in a provincial university, although the quality of teaching may differ considerably.

FOREIGN LANGUAGE LEARNING AND OTHER ADULT CLASSES

English as a foreign language is taught as a compulsory subject from the age of eleven until the end of secondary education and throughout university. English is taught formally, with emphasis on mastering and actively recalling grammar rules, reading, and learning lists of words rather than listening to native speakers and conversing in English. Thus, most university graduates can usually cope with complex written texts using specialist vocabulary, but have considerable difficulty understanding native English speakers and speaking fluent, correct English themselves.

The focus on formal aspects of English is further complicated by the English university entrance examination, which all the teaching of English in schools is geared to: how to obtain the ideal of 100 percent in all multiple choice questions.

Other compulsory courses at all education levels include Persian Literature, Arabic from guidance school (age twelve), Religious Studies and, at undergraduate level, Family Planning.

Nowadays many Iranians, especially students and professionals, recognize the necessity of knowing English in their academic and professional lives and work hard to master it. English language teaching is a burgeoning business in Iran at present, both in organized language institutes as well as in private schools, and both offer classes focused on En-

glish for special purposes, such as business, embassy interviews, higher study (TOEFL, IELTS), or travel. General English courses are usually designated as "grammar" or "conversation," to distinguish these classes from the formal teaching of English in compulsory and tertiary education. Instructors with clear, educated, and authentic British or American accents are very popular, especially in conversation classes.

Adult education has expanded greatly in recent years and caters to every taste: from the artistic and creative to the religious and the literary. Many areas have their own "culture house," an adult education center that offers courses in understanding and appreciating poetry (e.g., Hafez and Rumi); Quran recitation, translation, and commentary; foreign languages; musical instruments and classical singing; and all kinds of artistic and creative courses such as calligraphy, drawing and painting, printing, making artificial flowers, cooking, and many more. Local mosques also offer lessons in the Quran and sometimes Arabic lessons.

TRADITIONAL MEDICINE

Zoroastrianism, the ancient Iranian system of religious beliefs, established a dualism that exerted a strong influence on all aspects of Iranian life. The ongoing battle between the God of Good/Light (*Ahura Mazda*) and the God of Evil/Darkness (*Ahriman*) was seen as an ever-present threat to the overall balance of the world. As a result of this struggle in the physical world, night followed day and winter followed summer as one or the other god attained temporary victory. A similar struggle between good and evil was considered to manifest itself in every human as illnesses, which were believed to be nothing more than a sign of imbalance within the body.[2] The ancient Greek physician Hippocrates (born A.D. 490) described this physical balance in more detail. Envisioning every human as a miniature of the cosmos, he linked the four natural elements (air, fire, earth, and water) to the four humors in the human body (blood, yellow bile, black bile, and phlegm) and classified each with the qualities hot/cold and dry/moist.

The following table summarizes Hippocrates' classification of the natural and physical elements.

Element in Nature	Element in the Human Body	Qualities
Air	Blood	Hot/moist
Fire	Yellow bile	Hot/dry
Earth	Black bile	Cold/dry
Water	Phlegm	Cold/moist

These elements, named *humors*, coexist in a delicate balance in a healthy constitution.[3] However, this classification pertains not only to humans but to all food, which can help sick individuals bring the system back into balance/health.

Traditional medicine has always been and still remains a reliable resource for maintaining family health, because it treats the patient as a whole and doesn't only address the symptoms. Every Iranian woman knows the basics of this system and combines them in the dishes she prepares for her family to ensure their health and well-being. Common ailments can be treated by applying these practices. For example, a stomachache, especially in children, usually indicates a "cold" predominance in the body and is usually treated with some crystallized sugar (*nabât*) in tea, both of which are "hot." A sore throat may indicate a surplus of "heat," so that person should eat "cold" foods (e.g. cucumbers) and avoid eating "hot" foods like pistachios and walnuts, which would exacerbate the condition. I understand that this system, known as Greek Medicine, is practiced in India too, whereas, surprisingly, modern Greeks know little about it.

When it comes to more serious or persistent conditions, Iranians seek advice from a professional herbalist (*attàri*), who can prescribe the appropriate remedy in the form of herbal brew, ointment, or potion, and who advises which foods to be consumed and avoided while the treatment lasts.

Until quite recently, traditional medicine was the first, and often the only, treatment for every illness. This practice is now being replaced by

Western or modern medicine, at least in cities, where there is access to a Western-style doctor. Hamid Dabashi, a professor of Iranian studies and comparative literature at Columbia University, writes that his mother, although illiterate, had a solid grounding in the principles of traditional medicine. During his childhood in the 1960s in Ahvaz, in southern Iran, he and his siblings were raised on herbal remedies prescribed by their local herbalist and they very rarely needed to see a modern doctor.[4]

A TRADITIONAL HERBALIST'S ADVERTISEMENT

A variety of herbal medicines for kidney stones, high blood pressure, diabetes, weight loss, and weight gain; natural herbal waters and essences.

WESTERN MEDICINE

Tehran and other big cities have many doctors in all specialties. A lot of these have been educated abroad and are also university professors and members of a university's academic board. Because many doctors work in hospitals in the mornings, they usually see patients three afternoons a week on either even days—*ruz-hâ-ye zowj* (Saturday, Monday, Wednesday)—or odd ones—*ruz-hâ-ye fard* (Sunday, Tuesday, Thursday)—although some see patients every day. Some use an appointment system, and you can make one by calling their secretary during office hours. Very popular doctors may not have appointments available for a few months, although a "friend of a friend" may be able to help you get one sooner. But even if you aren't able to see the doctor you want as soon as you'd like, you can always get an appointment on the same day with a specialist who isn't as busy. (Waiting rooms often look crowded because some patients are escorted by relatives.)

Doctors' offices can be identified by white rectangular signs on the outside of buildings, and these often have offices for several doctors as

well as related services like X-rays and microbiology laboratories. Most doctors speak at least some English and are, of course, familiar with the Latin names of conditions and illnesses, so you shouldn't have any major problems in making yourself understood.

IF YOU GET SICK

If you are staying in a big hotel, medical assistance should be readily available around the clock. If not, some private health centers operate 24/7 not only for emergencies but for everything else, even a sore throat or allergy.

IRANIANS' ATTITUDES TOWARD ILLNESS

Patricia Baker writes that Iranians could be the world's worst hypochondriacs, competing for this doubtful honor with the Lebanese.[5] Although I don't claim expertise in this area, there does seem to be some truth in this statement. As a general rule, Iranians are wary of catching colds and always wrap up well. In winter, many turn up the heat before taking a shower and in the summer turn off the cooling system so as not to catch cold, and many women cover their hair with a special scarf until it dries. If you complain of backache, neck ache, or leg pains, your problem is often attributed to cold, and you'll probably be advised to keep warm. People are concerned about sore throats and chest pains becoming infected, fearing serious heart problems. A doctor is usually consulted at once and, if the doctor's office is closed, a 24/7 health center will provide a prescription, and a 24/7 chemist will dispense it.

As a rule, Iranian doctors prescribe lots of medicines because (as some privately confess) if they don't, patients are likely to think they aren't competent. A pharmacist is therefore a lucrative occupation all year round. Penicillin injections are often used instead of a course of antibiotics and as prevention against infection. (Unfortunately, the practice of prescribing antibiotics for every minor ailment from child-

hood onward can actually have adverse effects on the immune system, which becomes increasingly unable to cope with even a minor infection and needs to be boosted with more antibiotics.)

When Iranians are hospitalized, they are accompanied by at least their spouse and possibly other family members. A common and expected practice is to have a relative of the same gender with them at all times, including overnight, to help look after them, liaise with nurses and doctors, and, very importantly, to help them feel less anxious and somehow at home. Children are usually accompanied by their mothers if they need to stay overnight. When I was hospitalized on the day before an operation recently, I happily spent the time alone except for the two visiting hours when my family came to see me that afternoon. The nurses, the food service woman, and the cleaner who came and went in the course of their duties repeatedly asked, "Don't you have a companion tonight?"

Visiting the sick is considered a highly commended religious duty that attracts divine reward. If a patient is likely to stay in the hospital for some time, close relatives visit often and distant relatives and friends visit at least once. When patients return home soon, they will be visited at home. Generally Iranians like to be visited when ill; the show of interest and goodwill gives them and their relatives courage and hope even in the face of serious illness.

Patients suffering from a serious, possibly life-threatening, condition aren't usually told the truth about their situation. Both doctors and close relatives usually agree that it is in patients' best interests not to be fully informed, for fear they may lose the will to fight. In such cases, the family assumes a more prominently supportive role in looking after the patient, not only in practical ways but psychologically too, making decisions on the patient's behalf.

ALTERNATIVE TREATMENTS

In recent years other traditional or alternative, mainly Eastern, treatments such as cupping, leeching, energy healing, and acupuncture have attained some popularity in Iran, although the vast majority of the population

view them as Western-imported fads and prefer to stick to orthodox, modern medicine often supplemented by traditional Iranian remedies.

FAITH HEALING

Sometimes none of these methods work: doctors have given up, other approaches have yielded no results, and the patient and the family are losing hope. At such times Iranians, like believers everywhere, turn to God. At this point they pledge charity in the form of money or other help for the needy, prepare and distribute food to neighbors in exchange for prayers, offer special prayers and supplications, and pray for the Holy Imams' intercession so that God will heal the patient.

Muslims believe that if a believer can achieve the blessing of connection (*tavassol*) through an Imam or with the Lady Fatemeh Zahra, who can intercede on his/her behalf and ask for God's grace, anything is possible. A student in my English class in Tehran shared this story about a patient who was healed miraculously.

> A 35-year-old woman suffered from multiple sclerosis (MS), and her condition had progressed to the point that she couldn't walk unaided. Many Iranians like to visit the shrine of Imam Rezâ, the eighth Imam, in Mashhad as a vacation, and this woman and her husband decided to travel there. When they went to bid farewell to the woman's mother, the mother asked her daughter to pass on this message to the Imam: "I have given two martyrs to the holy defense [i.e., they were killed in the Iran-Iraq war] and I cannot bear to lose another child through illness. If you don't ask God to help my daughter, I will complain to the Holy Fatemeh, your grandmother."
>
> When the couple arrived at the shrine, the man settled the woman in her wheelchair under the Steel Window and went inside the shrine to pray. The Steel Window (*panjareh fulâd*) is a large window with a steel grille, under which pilgrims express their fervent wishes and ask the Imam to intercede to God for their fulfilment. In the history of the Holy Shrine of Imam Rezâ, numerous miracles have been witnessed in this location. She prayed too and passed on her mother's message to the Imam. Then she heard a voice behind her, "Get up and come inside the shrine!" She answered, "If I were able to walk, I would have gone inside with my husband." The voice repeated, "Get up and come inside!"

She felt a surge of energy through her body and stood up. The people near her realized that a miracle had happened and the crowd made a commotion around her. The Imam's servants ran to her rescue, escorted her to their office, and one of them went to find her husband, who was awestruck, just as she was. This happened seven years ago and the woman has been well ever since.

MEDICAL RESEARCH AND ACHIEVEMENTS

If knowledge can be found in the Pleiades,
The people of the land of Pars will find it.

—The Holy Prophet

But all is not herbal remedies and prayers. In the thirty years since the Islamic Revolution a lot has changed in medicine, health standards, and technology, and Iran has become a pioneer in the fields of pharmaceuticals, nanotechnology, biotechnology, genetics, and stem cell research.[6]

Whereas just after the Revolution a large number of foreign doctors and surgeons met the needs of the Iranian population, now Iranian-educated physicians not only attend to the vastly increased population, but they are also able to offer their services to patients who come from all over the Middle East for treatment.

Medical research and innovation have also made numerous great strides, and the following discussion highlights just a few of the recent successes. The number of articles published in medical peer-reviewed journals has increased considerably in the last thirty years, and many innovative medical procedures now take place in Iran. For example, Iran was the second country in the world to perform a pancreas transplant successfully, and the fourth to do kidney transplants, and now performs more than 2,000 kidney transplants every year. The first liver transplant in Iran was performed in 1993, and well over forty transplants have taken place since the cerebral death law was passed in 2002.

Iranian laboratories have developed artificial compounds to repair cartilage, bone, and skin, and have used nanocrystals to mend damaged livers, esophagi, cartilage, and bones. An artificial liver, an Iranian

innovation, simulates normal liver function in blood detoxification and has improved the quality of life of those suffering from renal failure.

In pharmacology, Iranian laboratories have developed effective medications for the treatment of numerous conditions, such as diabetic foot ulcers (*Angipars*), HIV/AIDS (Immuno-Modulator Drug or IMOD), and MS (*CinnoVex*) among many others. They also mass-produce popular medicines, such as the antihistamine diphenhydramine chloride, which were previously imported.

Iran is currently one of ten countries that carry out pioneering work in the production of human embryonic stem cells and is considered the leading stem cell researcher in the Middle East. Iranian stem cell researchers have worked on human kidney stem cells, produced differentiated spleen and liver tissues in laboratory mice, and generated smooth muscle cells from human bone marrow. They have also done stem cell transplants for the treatment of a number of conditions including spinal cord injuries, liver cirrhosis, cardiac arrest, and vitiligo.

According to Anne Barnard of *The Boston Globe*, two important factors contributed to the progress of stem cell research in Iran: government funding and broad government approval to conduct research on cells from early-stage embryos left over from fertility treatments.[7] This freedom in conducting such vital research, which is often restricted in Western countries on moral and religious grounds, was made possible by a religious ruling of Shi'a jurists. (They pronounced that a soul is infused into an embryo after 120 days from the beginning of the pregnancy, and not earlier.)

Iran is also the first Middle Eastern country to clone a lamb that survived the usual postnatal complications of cloned animals. The lamb, Royana, named after the Royan laboratory that undertook the project, was born in Isfahan on September 30, 2006. The first cloned goat, Hana, was born on April 17, 2009.

Other areas where remarkable progress has taken place are birth control and infertility. From 1976 to 1996 Iran's population almost doubled, possibly as a result of increased fertility among the growing female population.[8] This put the country's limited resources under considerable strain when the economy was fighting, and then recovering, from the Iran-Iraq war (1980–1988). According to one projection, if the Iran-

ian population had continued to grow at the same rate, it would have reached 110 million by 2010. After the war the government launched a country-wide birth control program to stabilize the population growth, and this has proven to be very successful. This program, which the United Nations praised as the best in the world, reduced the fertility rate from an average of seven children per woman in 1986 to three in 2002. The annual population growth between 1989 and 2003 registered a sharp fall from 3.2 percent to 1.2 percent. (A well-known campaign slogan still printed on food packaging is "Fewer children—better life.") Many young couples and those in their mid-thirties now only have one child. The current U.N. projection is that by 2012 the average number of children per woman will fall to two, which is zero population growth.[9]

At the same time, improvements in primary health care even in remote villages have resulted in a significant reduction in infant mortality, from 79 deaths of babies under the age of one in every 100,000 in 1979 to 26 in 2000, with further reductions projected, and maternal mortality reduced from 237 in 100,000 in 1975 to 25 in 2009.[10]

Iran is currently the most progressive among the Muslim nations in assisted reproductive technologies (ART). According to Elizabeth O'Donnell of *Le Monde Diplomatique*, Iran has about fifty in vitro fertilization clinics, among the most of Middle East countries.[11] A *fatwa* (religious edict) by Ayatollah Khamene'i, the Supreme Leader of the Islamic Revolution, allows the use of donor sperm and eggs, both sometimes controversial practices elsewhere and one generally banned in the Islamic world. The article writer concludes that this *fatwa* shows the leadership's pragmatic and sensitive response to modern life issues.

EIGHT

Partners in Joy and Sorrow

*A close relative reported on how everything went at his wife's memorial serv-
ice as "âberumandâneh bargozâr shod" ("it took place with* âberu, *or
appropriate face maintenance"), a comment on the quality of fruit that was
bought, the appeal of the cleric's sermon, and the number of guests who
attended. He felt that all the components of the ceremony were in keeping
with the* shakhsiat *of the deceased and her family, a sentiment that seemed to
give him comfort in his bereavement.*

Humans everywhere celebrate life's milestones, such as welcoming a young person to the community's faith (cir-
cumcision, christening), initiation ceremonies (first communion, bar
mitzvah), weddings, and funerals. On these occasions, in Iran just like
elsewhere around the world, family and friends gather to reaffirm the
ties among themselves.

SOCIETAL VALUES AND CELEBRATIONS

Depending on their values, some societies celebrate life stages that in other places may go unnoticed. In Britain, for example, the 16th, 18th, and 21st birthdays, and sometimes passing one's driving test, call for a special celebration, because these occasions mark a young person's development and increasing independence. By contrast, Iranians don't celebrate these occasions because independence as understood in Western cultures isn't generally considered a high-value concepts and young people, irrespective of their age, are expected to show deference toward their parents' views.

Celebrations connected with children and young people are mainly birthdays, as we saw in chapter 4, a custom imported in recent decades from the West. Young people may also celebrate a university graduation with a dinner party for their extended family.

"MAY THEY GROW OLD TOGETHER": MARRIAGE

Matchmaking and weddings occupy a special position in Iranian social life, capturing the imagination of young and old alike. Marriage is seen as the successful culmination of parents bringing up their children and acknowledges their efforts and self-sacrifices. Marriage is considered so significant that the word *zendegi*, which means "life," is often used to mean "married life" and "household of a married couple." Iranians refer to a good marriage partner as "a man/woman to build a life with" (*mard/zan-e zendegi*), while partners in an unsuccessful marriage are said not to have had a good life and their divorce is described as "their life having fallen apart" (*zendegishun az ham pâshide*).

Such expressions indicate the very close connection between family values and the inner core of an Iranian's existence. Young and not so young unmarried offspring always live with their parents. Moving out on their own before marriage, so commonplace in the West, is unthinkable for singles, because Iranians view life as inconceivable without a family. Failure in married life is such a social stigma for both men and women that it can't be compensated for by other factors of one's life, for

example, even by their professional status. For women especially, whose identity within their own family (good wife, good mother) is the apex of social achievement, a divorce is almost a catastrophe. Similarly, never-married men and women past marrying age are very rare. Iranians disapprove of people not marrying, aligning it with shirking social duties and responsibilities that God enjoins upon everyone. Islam recommends that young people marry early, but in recent years the marrying age has gone up, possibly because young people tend to study for longer and also because of their high expectations of prospective spouses. Divorce is also much more common now than it was a generation ago.

So how do Iranians ensure their children make a good marriage match? An established process helps the prospective couple—and equally importantly, their families—get to know each other. Beeman writes that marriage negotiations take the form of a corporate merger, and that the skills, professions, and social connections of the two families factor into the success of a match.[1] Although a lot has changed since Beeman's 1986 work, a kernel of truth in this view still persists, especially in the conservative social strata, where matchmaking mostly follows traditional patterns.

The mothers of the prospective spouses are the primary movers and shakers, at least in the beginning. Until the recent past, and still among the conservative social strata, the groom's mother approaches families with daughters of marriageable age or she asks friends, neighbors, relatives, and colleagues about eligible women. She will then telephone the young woman's mother and ask for permission to "come to their service for a good cause" (the formulaic expression for a matchmaking visit).

Some years ago the prospective groom's mother, together with her married daughters or other experienced female relatives, would make the preliminary visits during the day, when the men were at work. In effect, the women of the household would vet the family and the young woman before the young man had a chance to see her and possibly be unduly influenced. But in recent years this convention has changed: both sets of parents and both young people are at the first meeting, assess each other in terms of appearance, and talk of general matters, such as the educational background of the prospective couple and their lifestyle.

If the groom and his family would like to pursue the relationship, a few days later his mother will call the bride's mother. If the bride and her family are also positively disposed, her mother will normally indicate their willingness to enter into detailed negotiations by saying something along the lines of their family being at the service of the groom's family whenever they will give them the honor of visiting again. However, if the prospective bride's family isn't interested, the mother will use an indirect strategy and say that the young woman does not intend to marry just now or that she has decided to pursue further study. This indirectness cushions the rejection and preserves the groom's and his family's face.

For those interested, a second visit is then arranged at the young woman's house, during which the young people will have the opportunity to talk with each other in private to evaluate their compatibility of character, temperament, and outlook on life. The prospective spouses may also discuss conditions for their future life, which may or may not be included in the marriage contract. Such conditions may include an understanding that the groom will not ask the bride to leave her home town, or the groom's agreement if the bride decides to continue her studies or take up paid employment. Some couples need more than two or three meetings until they feel well acquainted with each other; marriage counselors always advise prospective spouses to spend as long as they need at this stage, which can take from a couple of weeks to a couple of months. A definite marriage proposal is not made until after this stage has been successfully passed to the young people's and their families' satisfaction.

At some point during this or a subsequent visit, the bride's parents are likely to raise the issue of where the young couple will live. According to social convention, the responsibility for providing housing lies with the groom or his parents, and owning a property, even if only a small one, is considered a strong point in favor of a young man.

Anthropologists call the custom of women moving to the men's family, village, or town *patrilocality*. Two generations ago this custom usually resulted in the bride being given a room in the groom's paternal home and sharing the common areas. This practice was predicated on the existence of traditional houses with a large number of rooms built

around a central courtyard. Nowadays, at least in cities, where old houses have largely been replaced by apartments, many of them small to be affordable, young couples tend to live on their own. However, the principle of patrilocality remains, at least in social parlance, as evidenced in popular phrases such as, "She was twenty when she moved to her husband's house," even if that "house" is a 645 square feet (60 square meters) rented apartment. When a brother and a sister have married out of the same family, people say, "We have given one [the daughter] and have taken one [the daughter-in-law]."

EXCHANGE OF "PROMISE TO MARRY" (*BALE-BORUN*)

When the young couple and their families have agreed to the marriage in principle, they arrange an evening for the formal proposal visit, which is attended by grandparents, all siblings of the couple and their families, and possibly the eldest uncles and aunts on both sides. This assembly of the two families' "white beards" (elders), although only a formality, has to take place in order to work out the details, such as the very important detail of the amount of the *mehriyeh*.

The *mehriyeh*, or *mehr*, is a gift of money or property that the groom makes to the bride. According to Islamic law, half of it is payable upon signature of the marriage contract and the other half before the marriage is consummated, so the bride is well within her rights to refuse to move into the groom's house before the *mehr* is paid. However, because many Iranians feel that a harmonious life is more important than money, in practice no money or property changes hands as long as the couple live together.

Nevertheless, brides' families usually insist on a substantial amount of *mehr* as an insurance in case of divorce, when, if the husband initiates divorce proceedings, the whole *mehr* is payable. Grooms' families are usually reluctant to agree to such demands, because legally the wife has the right to demand her *mehr* even when there is no question of divorce. These two different perspectives often lead to bartering between the families, each of which tries to secure the best terms. In principle, the amount

of *mehr* agreed upon should be well within the financial capabilities of the groom, who may be asked to pay it at any time, and not only in case of divorce.

In recent years the amount of *mehr* has become something of a status object among families who want to keep up with other families who have agreed on a large amount. For example, I was at a marriage negotiation meeting in which the bride's father asked for 700 golden Azadi coins[2] (worth about $200/£150 each in June 2009) for his daughter's *mehr* because her maternal cousin had just agreed to marry for this amount of *mehr*. The groom's father bartered for a while, saying that money does not bring happiness and that harmony between the spouses is more important. After a bit of negotiation, the elders agreed on 500 Azadi coins—the equivalent of 41 years of the groom's current salary! This "keeping up with the Joneses" is currently being discouraged as a likely cause of problems for both partners later on, but it still remains a thorny issue.[3]

When an agreement is finally reached, the groom's mother usually makes a small gift of gold, for example, a bangle and a length of fabric, to the bride.

SIGNING THE MARRIAGE CONTRACT (*AQD*)

When the families have agreed on the match and all its details, the young people are still *nâmahram* to each other (see chapter 2). Conservative and pious families normally prefer to have the marriage contract signed as soon as possible, even if the couple isn't going to be married right away. The contract is authorized by an official who solemnizes marriages, either at the bride's home or in a special registry office. Strictly speaking, marriage in Islam is not a sacrament, as in Christianity, but a social contract, so the actual ceremony in the registry office is very simple and usually only attended by the couple and perhaps a few close relatives, much like a wedding conducted by a Justice of the Peace (but see the section about wedding receptions). This process concludes the legal side of the marriage, after which the young people are legally wed and have their spouse's name registered in their identity document. However, the cou-

ple continues to live in their own parents' homes until their new house is ready, and then they hold the "social" wedding reception (*arusi*).

PREPARATIONS

If the families have agreed to hold the *arusi* soon after the marriage contract has been signed, a hectic period begins immediately after the *aqd* for both families. As mentioned earlier, social convention requires that the groom's family provide the young couple's accommodation. If the family owns a property that is rented out, they will need to give notice to the tenants and after it is vacated will refurbish the residence. If they do not have a flat or a house already, a property hunt begins. The other major area of responsibility—with serious budget implications for the groom's family—is finding a suitable hall for the wedding reception.

Social conventions dictate that the bride's family provide a dowry that consists of everything that a new household needs, ranging from furniture, bedding, a sewing machine, and curtains, to all pots, pans, and dishes, right down to the cutlery. Some social circles correlate the amount of the bridal gift to the amount of the dowry, although everything the bride brings to the groom's house remains her own personal property, and in case of divorce, goes back with her to her parents' house. Over the years the bride's mother will normally have collected certain items for her daughter's dowry, but many more will need to be bought in preparation for the wedding. A number of outfits need to be ordered for all the family and for the different occasions in the process, including the wedding gown, which is ordered by the bride but paid for by the groom.

WEDDING SHOPPING

The other considerable expense for the groom's family is the wedding shopping. According to Iranian custom, the groom must buy the bride a mirror and two candlesticks, which stand for a pure, sincere, and bright married life, and a copy of the Holy Quran, for God's blessings. The mirror and candlesticks are usually bought in special shops, and nowadays they come with a matching table.

Other compulsory wedding shopping items include a jewelry set (an elaborate necklace with matching earrings and a bracelet), a complete make-up set, nightgowns, undergarments, two pairs of shoes, two hand-bags, two formal outfits or lengths of fabric to have those made to measure, and two sugar–loaves (*kalleh ghand*, symbolizing sweetness and compatibility).

All these items are kept at the groom's parental home until the day of the *arusi*, when the mirror, candlesticks, and sugar–loaves will be used on the wedding spread. The rest will be giftwrapped and placed with the other wedding presents.

BRINGING THE DOWRY TO THE NEW HOUSE (*JAHÂZ BARUN*)

Once the bridal home has been refurbished or arranged for and is sparkling clean, the dowry is brought to the new house a few days before the *arusi*. This is a joyful social occasion for the close female relatives of both families, and they get to know each other better as they help set up the new home. The kitchen, considered the woman's kingdom, is equipped down to the minutest details in coordinated colors for the kitchen towels, oven mitts, spice jars, containers for legumes, pots and pans, tea kettle, and teapot. Visitors go around the house admiring the bride's new things, wishing her a long and happy life, and congratulating her mother on her good taste. On this day the couple's bed is made, and flowers and money are scattered on it to attract happiness and prosperity.

Less affluent families may buy only the necessaries, but all items must be new. Charitable people sometimes take the initiative of collecting money or new things from among their acquaintances on behalf of a needy young woman who is about to marry.

THE WEDDING RECEPTION (*ARUSI*)

Printed wedding invitations are usually distributed by hand—not mailed—a couple of weeks before the wedding. Sometimes the cards for

an extended family are given to one person, who is then responsible for distributing them or letting the rest of the family know that they are invited to a wedding.

Wedding receptions are always held in the late evening, usually from 7:00–11:00. Fruit, pastries, tea, and chocolate milk are served throughout the evening, and the reception concludes with dinner. Some reception halls serve dinner buffet style, while others have it served family style to every table.

Aqd for the Second Time—For the Photos

As mentioned earlier, the official marriage ceremony usually takes place in a marriage registry office. However, whether this has happened or whether the couple is officially getting married on the day of the *arusi*, they will usually hold a wedding ceremony just before the reception in a special room adjacent to the reception hall, the "Wedding Room" (*Otâq-e Aqd*).

An elaborate spread is placed on the floor in the middle of the room, which has been decorated with the couple's new mirror, candlesticks, and Holy Quran. The spread includes honey and two small sugar–loaves, symbols for a sweet married life; eggs for fertility; wholegrain bread, white cheese, and herbs for prosperity; and wild rue (the dried seeds of a pungent plant with yellow flowers) against the evil eye. The couple sits on chairs at the head of the spread, surrounded by their female relatives and the male *mahrams* of the bride (her father, brothers, and uncles). The official conducting the marriage stands or sits just outside the room, so that his voice can be heard inside. While he reads the marriage formula, which includes the bride's and the groom's names and the amount of the *mehr*, two happily married female relatives hold a square of white fabric over the couple's heads, and a third one rubs together the two small sugar–loaves on the fabric. The official asks the bride whether she allows him to act as her representative to finalize the marriage. One of her female relatives answers, "The bride has gone to pick roses." The question is asked again and a female relative responds, "The bride has gone to press rosewater." When asked a third time, the bride answers, "With my parents' and all the elders' permission, I do."

Then the relatives clap and congratulate the couple, and one by one stand next to them to offer them their presents, usually gold or money, and take photos and video recordings. The wedding guests have been arriving during this ceremony, and the reception is about to begin.

MUSIC AND ENTERTAINMENT

As mentioned earlier in the book, men and women celebrate the wedding in separate rooms. In the men's hall a male entertainer tells jokes, sings, and tries to make them dance; these ongoings are sometimes shown on a large monitor screen in the women's hall. Women usually prefer to talk, dance (the younger ones and the couple's close relatives) to particularly loud Iranian pop music, and observe the proceedings. At some point the groom comes into the women's hall to greet the guests and possibly to have dinner with his bride. His arrival is announced at the door by one of his *mahrams* and is followed by a flurry of activity, as women, at least those who observe the *hijab* rules, put on patterned *chadors* and scarves.

With the end of dinner the reception is over. Close relatives first escort the new couple to the bride's paternal home, where she formally asks for her parents' permission to leave and bids farewell to them, and then again to their new home, honking their car horns through the streets on the way.

On the following afternoon the female guests bring their presents to the bride's house, where one of the bride's relatives opens them one by one and shows them to the guests. She also shows the presents, including the money, the bride received the night before at the wedding reception, so that everyone can be thanked personally and publicly.

Over the following months close relatives of the groom will invite the young couple and both sets of parents to dinner. This dinner party (*pâgoshâ-ye arus*), during which a small present of gold or a length of fabric is given to the bride, is meant to make the bride feel comfortable in visiting her husband's relatives in the future.

BIRTH

Generally, young couples decide to have a baby soon after they get married, although there is a recent trend among urban couples to delay this decision, but not for too long. Iranians consider healthy children a necessary component of a happy marriage, and the ideal is a boy and a girl. A couple not blessed with at least two children is seen as lacking in fulfillment, while a conscious choice not to have any is unusual.

When a woman gets pregnant, she becomes the object of attention of everybody in the family, especially the women, who shower her with well-meant advice and look after her in practical ways. During the pregnancy the woman's mother puts together the baby's layette (*sismuni*), which includes a cot, baby outfits, underwear, and toys appropriate for both baby boys and girls, the expectation being that sooner or later the couple will have both. A couple of months before the baby is due, the grandmother will take the layette to the new parents' house. This is an occasion for a family gathering, and the paternal grandparents, any unmarried siblings, and possibly one or two older aunts will be invited.

After the baby is born, the new parents and the baby usually stay at the maternal grandparents' house for ten days. This gives the new mother the opportunity to rest and regain her strength through the fortifying meals her mother cooks for her, as well as learn the basics of babycare. After ten days they go back to their home, ready to begin a new chapter in their shared life.

A CAMEL THAT STOPS BY ANY HOUSE: DEATH

As in many cultures, family and friends gather for a funeral. In Iran, a death in the family disrupts all normal life routines for at least seven days after the funeral.

Close relatives are informed immediately after a death. Muslims believe that the soul cannot find peace until the body is buried (similar to ancient Greek beliefs, as in Sophocles' *Antigone*), so the recommended

practice is to hold the funeral as soon as possible. However, if the death takes place in the afternoon or evening, the body is kept in the house overnight, and relatives come to offer prayers for the departed and to comfort the bereaved until the following morning.

If the body of the departed stays in the home overnight, relatives who attend the wake recite Imam Hossein's prayer (*Ziârat-e Âshurâ*) and read extracts from the Holy Quran, especially *sura* 55 (*Ar-Rahmân*, The Compassionate). If the death takes place in hospital, the body of the deceased is usually taken back to the house, so that relatives can offer prayers over it and escort it to the cemetery for the funeral.

Funeral announcements just like the one shown here are posted around the neighborhood, on relatives' cars, and on the windows of a family's shop, which remains closed and hung with black drapes until the third day after the memorial ceremony.

A FUNERAL ANNOUNCEMENT

Unto Him We Shall All Return

Mother, I cannot believe you are gone and your light's out
You've left us and embraced the soil
Our house was lit up by your face
Oh, you light of our hearts! What put you out?

With great sadness and sorrow we announce the passing of the
kind mother
Hâjiyeh Khânum Zahrâ Kamâli
(Wife of the late Hâj Ahmad Jamâlipur)
To all respected friends and acquaintances

On this occasion, a third-day memorial service will be held on
Thursday 23 Mehr 1388
From 4:00–5:30 P.M.
At the Hosseiniyeh Fâtemiyeh,
Shahr-e-Rey, Shrine Avenue, Key Cutter Alley

Please also note that the seventh-day ceremony
for the departed will take place on
Monday 27 Mehr 1388
From 4:00–5:30 P.M.
At the above mentioned venue
The honor of your venerable and respected presence will bring joy to
the soul of the departed and comfort to her family.
On behalf of the Kamâli and Jamâlipur families and the rest of her
respected relatives and acquaintances.

There aren't hearses in Iran, so the body is transported to the cemetery in an ambulance. When the ambulance arrives at the home, the male relatives of the deceased lift and lower the body three times with invocations to the Holy Prophet's daughter Fatemeh (or sometimes called Fatimah Zahra) and her martyred son Hossein (*"Ya Hossein! Ya Zahrâ!"*) and then carry it through the streets in the neighborhood on their shoulders.

A crier ahead of the procession calls out the profession of the faith, *"La Ilaha Illa-Allah"* (There is no other God except Allah), and the mourners echo him. The close male relatives—sons, sons-in-law, nephews, and grandsons—take turns carrying the bier on their shoulders, while from the houses along the street women step out of their front doors and whisper *"La Ilaha Illa-Allah"* in a final farewell for their neighbor. The procession stops at the first crossroad, where the bier is placed on the ground for the recitation of supplications. The mourners repeat the same ritual at two more crossroads, a symbolic reenactment of life in the mother's womb, earthly life, and afterlife, and an echo of the same ritual of a pilgrim's return from the *Hajj* (pilgrimage), as a reborn, sinless Muslim.

Everything has been organized with remarkable speed: the family will have hired a minibus to transport mourners to the cemetery, and those with their own cars give others rides.

At the cemetery, the mourners assemble in front of the washing house, where the body will receive a ritual wash and be prepared for burial. The building where the bodies are washed has separate sections

for men and women, into which only only mourners of the same gender as the deceased are allowed. The main washing area is a wide corridor lined with glass screens on both sides, beyond which lie three marble slabs and three large marble bathtubs. On the other side of the glass screens, the washers of the dead work: green-clad, rubber-gloved, their Wellington boots squelching on the wet floor.

After the ritual washing and preparation, the body is covered in white and taken outside, and then the men lift the bier again onto their shoulders and take it to the prayer area. The mourners line up behind a cleric and say the prayers for the dead. Then the men, who stand in front, squat around the coffin and, touching it with one hand, recite two short *suras* of the Holy Quran, *Fatiha* and *Ikhlâs*, praying for the departed soul to find forgiveness. When the men have moved away, the women carry out the same rite, and the body is taken to the grave.

The Behesht-e Zahra cemetery, beyond Tehran's southern suburbs at the beginning of the Qom desert, is a city in itself: the blocks of graves are numbered sequentially and each block contains numbered rows. Thus, the location of a grave is given as, for example, Block 224, Row 15. The professional mourner (*rozeh-khân*) hired to take charge of the proceedings, microphone in hand, clears his throat and begins reciting a supplication, at the end of which the face of the deceased is revealed. He then asks those gathered to forgive everything that the deceased may have done to them: any cross words, display of bad temper, and unkind remarks need to be forgiven, so that God will forgive him or her and every one of us ("And forgive us our trespasses, as we forgive those who trespass against us.").

A male relative climbs down inside the grave, lies down on the soil, and whispers supplications, and then he stands up to receive the body as it is being lowered from above. He guides it gently, places it on the right side with the face toward the Qiblah (the direction of Mecca), and bends over it, tapping it gently on the shoulder and reciting the names of Imam Ali and the other eleven infallible Imams: the departed must be able to answer correctly to the angels that will visit on the first night in the grave. This is considered a night of unimaginable terrors: just like the mother's body threatens to suffocate a baby before it opens its eyes to the light of the world, the grave will press upon the dead on all sides. But

a person's good deeds during their lifetime and the mourners' supplications will help on the deceased's way to God's presence.

The *rozeh-khan* now begins a dirge about a jasmine bush that was planted by a woman who is now dead. Even though she is no longer here, whenever the bush flowers, the scent ascends to the soul, like the memory of her good deeds and those of her good offspring. The refrain "Where is she now?" moves mourners to new tears. Without a break, the *rozeh-khan* changes harmony and sings of people's transience in this world and of the good memories they leave behind.

Relatives and friends cast a fistful of soil into the grave, and the gravedigger takes over. All the while, the *rozeh-khan* addresses the group: he reminds them that the deceased has just moved into a new house and asks them to say the Terror of the Grave prayer that night as a housewarming present. He then thanks everyone for taking the trouble to come to the funeral, and offers condolences to the family on their behalf. Again, on behalf of the family he thanks those present, and invites them for lunch, either at the family's home or, more customarily now, at a restaurant; their presence will give joy to the departed soul and comfort to the family.

At the end of the speech, the men squat by the grave and read a Fatiha once more, before giving way to let the women do the same. Some people tap the soil with a small stone while whispering the prayer. At one funeral I attended, a woman got up, took seven steps away, and returned and then repeated the same ritual twice more, "so that she [the departed] won't feel we've left her alone too soon," she explained.

During the lunch, men sit on one side of the hall, women on the other, with close relatives serving water, making conversation, and serving salad dishes to guests—tasks that take their minds away from their feelings of loss. At the end of the lunch, the close relatives of the deceased greet every guest individually and thank them for taking the trouble to come.

Because of the speed with which the funeral and burial take place, only neighbors and immediate family are contacted. Those who miss the funeral but would nonetheless like to offer condolences to the family and prayers for the dead can attend the third-day and the seventh-day ceremonies held in a local mosque, and they can visit the deceased's family until the seventh day after the funeral. The word used in Persian

for these ceremonies is *khatm* (closure), which indicates a sense of finality both for the bereaved and the departed soul, who should be allowed to find rest after these ceremonies.

THE MOURNING PERIOD

From the funeral until the seventh day after it, the house of the departed will be full of relatives and friends, who also stay for meals and to help the family through those difficult first days. Traditionally no cooking was done in the house of the bereaved until the seventh day, and relatives and neighbors took turns providing cooked food. The custom has since changed, at least in Tehran, and relatives now cook food in the house. A light should remain on in the house for forty days, because the soul will be visiting. This light is also a sign that life goes on for the departed and the family. This custom reminds me of a childhood memory and underlines the similarities between two apparently unrelated cultures. After my grandfather's death in Athens over thirty-five years ago, my grandmother kept an oil lamp lit day and night "for grandpa's soul," she said.

On the third day after the funeral, the family visits the grave and spreads flower petals and sprinkles rosewater on the soil. A child goes around offering fruit and dates to guests and to people visiting other graves in exchange for a Fatiha prayer. Mourners read a chapter from the Quran, intending that the divine reward reach the departed soul. Every Thursday evening until the fortieth day they visit the grave and repeat this same ritual.

The third-day ceremony takes place in the evening at a mosque or prayer hall (*Hosseiniyeh*). It starts with a recitation from the Quran and continues with a sermon intended for the congregation to contemplate the transience of this world, and of how good deeds and the prayers and donations to charity by others come to a person's aid in the afterlife. Then the preacher moves the congregation to tears with a dirge and concludes by thanking everyone for coming on behalf of the family.

If the departed owned a shop, or if close relatives own one in the area, it usually remains closed from when the person died until the third-day

or the seven-day ceremony, The mourners walk with the sons or the brothers to the shop and, reciting salutations to the Holy Prophet and his family, older kinsmen pull up the shutters and unlock the shop, symbolically granting the family permission to reopen it.

If some of the bereaved are civil servants or teachers, they are granted compassionate leave for at least seven days. For example, my sister-in-law was a schoolteacher when Mâmân-jun passed away. Even though schools don't usually have substitute teachers, she wasn't expected to report to work until the first working day after the seven-day ceremony. In her absence, her colleagues, the principal, and the vice-principal covered her class as best as they could by splitting classes for a couple of days until a retired colleague of hers volunteered to help out without remuneration. Her colleagues also attended at least one of the memorial services, even though they did not personally know the deceased, to show their compassion and their respect for my sister-in-law. On the day she was due to return to work, the principal and one of her colleagues came over to her house early in the morning to escort her to the school, where a fabric banner with all the colleague's condolences written on it was hung over the main gate. The graveside ritual has a private, spiritual nature, just like a visit to a loved one, whereas the mosque or prayer hall gathering takes on a social feeling. Both private and social memorial customs are based on the beliefs that the soul has access to the physical world and derives pleasure from the actions of the living, and that the living can help the soul in the afterlife through prayers and good deeds, for which they are also given divine reward.

THE END OF MOURNING

Forty days after the funeral another ceremony takes place, after which the mourning period is over. An older female relative usually invites other women family members to the house of the deceased in order to "bring the bereaved out of mourning." She may also bring along a hairdresser or arrange for the party to escort the bereaved to a hair salon.

The house is prepared for visitors. On the coffee table the best fruit is displayed in a colorful pyramid, and pastries are arranged on a flat

dish. A plate of halva sprinkled with pistachio and almond slivers sits alongside dark, shiny dates stuffed with walnuts.

The women make small talk while drinking tea. At some point the eldest relative may say that wearing black for too long brings bad luck, so now is the time to change into colored clothes. Doing so does not mean that they will forget the departed; in fact, the deceased would want them to come out of mourning for the sake of their husbands and their children. The eldest relative has bought lengths of colorful fabric or ready-made clothes and offers these to the mourning relatives, as an encouragement to change their black outfits.

The bereaved thank her for her kindness: may God preserve her shadow over their heads and keep her family in health and happiness, and may she taste only joys from now on.

Then the hairdresser gets to work, plucking eyebrows, removing facial hair from cheeks and upper lips with a twisted thread, and tinting hair, all of which are usually left untouched during the forty days of mourning. By the end of the day, life returns to normal once again.

NINE

The Food of Love

On my very first day in Iran I had my first experience of a traditional Iranian meal in Hossein's parents' house. In preparation for lunch, a large piece of fabric was laid on the floor with an oilcloth over it. Places were set with a spoon and a fork. Spoons were used for eating rice and either forks or spoons served as knives on the rare occasions when a knife was needed.

Five of us—Mâmân-jun, Hâj Nâsser, Hossein's younger sister and brother, and I—sat down to what seemed to me a veritable feast: a thick, nourishing potage-type barley soup containing chicken, mixed vegetables, and parsley; yogurt with mint and grated cucumber, like the Greek tzatziki; white rice with a stew of lamb, yellow lentils and thin strips of French fries.

Despite my refusals, Mâmân-jun kept refilling my plate, concerned that I was too shy to eat my fill as an Iranian might do. I finally remembered the magic words that gave her the signal to stop. "May your hand not be tired, it was very tasty," I said.

THE CENTRALITY OF FOOD IN IRANIAN CULTURE

"Love passes through the stomach," the French say. This is no less true for Iranians, for whom food, apart from satisfying physical hunger and helping keep the body healthy, is also invested with spiritual meaning.

To Iranians, the preparation and cooking of food is a prime expression of a woman's loving care, which transforms even the simplest of meals into nourishment for body and soul.

Domestic and food-related work requires a substantial investment of time, effort, and love, and it is therefore ascribed high status in Iranian culture. Women's considerable power and authority derives from such work. Traditionally, when parents' sons and their wives and children shared a large house, the mother-in-law, as the oldest female, had the overall responsibility for meals, controlling supplies and mealtimes. While large families no longer live together, the pattern continues by relatives eating meals together, a practice central to Iranian culture.

Eating on one's own is considered undesirable, even quite sad, and TV dinners inconceivable. Even if the television plays in the background, these shared meals reaffirm and strengthen family ties. As far as everyone's commitments allow, families have meals together on a daily basis, and if not for lunch, at least for dinner. Parents expect their married offspring and grandchildren to have a meal with them at least once a week, and married siblings often invite each other and their parents for dinner. Entertaining relatives and friends is one of Iranians' favorite leisure activities, with weekend evenings (Thursday and Friday) the preferred times for visiting and inviting people over.

The centrality of food in the culture is underscored by the use of the "spread" (*sofreh*), a symbolic collection of objects used on certain occasions. We have already discussed the New Year spread (*Sofreh Haft Sin*) in chapter 4, and the objects symbolizing abundance in nature, good luck, and prosperity for the new year. In chapter 8 we saw how the objects on the wedding spread (*Sofreh Aqd*) are used to attract happiness, marital harmony, and prosperity for the new couple. The use of the spread itself draws people around it and functions as a focus of unity that binds Iranians together.

DOMESTIC GODDESSES

Fruit and vegetables are transported daily from the country to central fruit markets in cities, and from there to small greengrocers, which

abound in every neighborhood. Once bought, fresh produce must be kept refrigerated or stored in a cool place because it goes bad faster than fruit and vegetables in the West, possibly because it is not treated with many preservatives.

Until quite recently, the availability of fruit and vegetables used to be dictated by the seasons, so the fruit bowl and the vegetable basket become visual anchors of Iranians' close connection with nature. Women especially, who are in charge of food preparation, are experts on which fruit and vegetables are in season. They know the best times to buy produce for preserving them (by freezing, dehydrating, or other methods) in order to have adequate supplies all year round. As recently as one generation ago housewives even made their own tomato paste.

Before the advent of freezers, Iranians preserved many foods by dehydrating (sun drying) them in the yard or on the rooftop. The traditional housewife's year was dotted with food preservation tasks. In the spring, women shell and dehydrate green peas and broad (fava) beans, the latter for *bâghâli polo* (see Recipe 2), and wash and dehydrate all the different herbs needed for many Iranian dishes: dill for *bâghâli polo*; tarragon and marjoram for meatballs; fenugreek, parsley, and coriander for a mixed herb stew (*ghormeh sabzi*); and thyme, mint, sweet basil, spring onions, and whole limes to be crushed or cooked whole in stews.

Summer was the height of domestic activity for stocking up on winter food supplies: drying tomatoes and making tomato puree, pressing unripe grapes for verjuice, juicing lemons for salad dressing and adding a tang to stews, and dehydrating and making jams and preserves from a wide variety of summer fruit such as apricots, plums, peaches, and cherries, that would be consumed in the long nights of the winter when there was scarcity of fresh fruit.

[Recipes courtesy of Hayedeh Mashayekh.]

RICE

When the new rice crop is harvested in early autumn, many Iranians buy their yearly provision of rice. In the past rice was only eaten on special occasions, but in recent years consumption of rice has risen together

with the population and living standards. Some Iranians feel that they have not eaten at all unless they have had rice for dinner. And they are quite justified: anyone who has ever tasted Iranian-style rice admires the aroma, flavor, and fluffiness of a satisfying yet unbelievably light and versatile dish that can be combined with kebabs, Iranian stews, and even Indian curries.

RECIPE 1: *CHELO* (IRANIAN-STYLE RICE)

This rice, an essential part of Iranian cuisine, is served with kebabs and a variety of Iranian stew-like dishes (*khoresh*).

1 cup of rice serves two people.
Cooking time: 1 hour

Soak the rice overnight, or at least 2 hours before cooking, in tepid water, adding 2 tablespoons of salt for every cup of rice. This salty water is drained before putting the rice into the boiling water.

Preparation:

1. Bring the water to a boil in a large pot.
2. Put rice in the boiling water and boil for 3–4 minutes.
3. Add a cup of water and bring to a boil again for another 2–3 minutes.
4. Strain. Pour a little cold water over the rice while still in the strainer.
5. (Optional) For an extra treat of *tah-dig* (bottom of the pot), which Iranians enjoy, pour a little oil in the pot and heat, then arrange thin slices of potatoes or a layer of *lavâsh* bread, sieved tomatoes (fresh tomatoes cut in half and grated), or onion (or a combination) before arranging the rice back in the pot in the shape of a mound. After steaming the rice, the *tah-dig* becomes crunchy and delicious.
6. Pour half a cup of water in the pot, put the lid on, and set on medium heat.
7. After 5 minutes, the steam that rises from the rice forms droplets on the inside of the lid. Lift the lid off the pot and shake it over the sink in order to get rid of the droplets of water.
8. Pour one or two tablespoons of oil over the rice. If you prefer, don't use oil now and serve the rice with butter.
9. Wrap the lid in a clean tea towel and cover the rice. Lower the heat and steam for 30 minutes.

10. In a very small bowl or tea-glass, dissolve a pinch of ground saffron with two or three teaspoonfuls of hot water and let stand for a few minutes.
11. When the rice is ready, mix 2 tablespoons of cooked rice with the saffron liquid and use it to decorate the rice on a serving dish.

RECIPE 2: *BÂGHÂLI POLO* (RICE WITH BROAD BEANS AND DILL, SERVED WITH LAMB KNUCKLE)

Broad (fava) beans are available from greengrocers in the spring. They need to be double peeled, boiled for three minutes, and then cooled down, and then can be stored in the freezer for future use. This dish used to be served with plain yogurt only, but nowadays it is usually accompanied with meat or chicken.

Serves 4

Cooking time: About three hours, including the meat cooking time and provided that broad beans and dill are already in the freezer or dehydrated dill is used. If serving with meat or chicken, start cooking those before starting the rice.

Ingredients for the rice:

2 cups of rice soaked in tepid water with salt for at least two hours
1 lb. (½ kg). peeled broad beans
2 lbs. (1 kg) of common dill
Cooking oil (corn or other vegetable oil)
Saffron

Ingredients for the meat:

4 lamb knuckles or chicken quarters
1 medium onion
Pinch of turmeric, ground cumin, ground cinnamon
4–6 garlic cloves
Salt and pepper to taste

Preparing the rice:

1. Bring water to boil, put broad beans (unthawed if frozen) and rice in boiling water and boil for 4–5 minutes.

2. Add one cup of cold water, boil for 3–4 minutes more.
3. Strain and pour one cup of cold water over the rice.
4. Pour one cup of water in the pot. Layer the rice and broad beans with the dill.
5. Put the pot back on medium heat for 5 minutes with the lid on until beads of steam form on the inside of the lid.
6. Pour in 3–4 tablespoons of cooking oil and a cup of water, wrap the lid in a clean tea towel, and lower the heat. Let stand for at least 45 minutes. This improves the taste and consistency of the rice by absorbing the extra moisture and by not letting the droplets formed by the steam drip back into the rice.
7. In a small bowl, dissolve a small amount of ground saffron with a little hot water and leave to stand. Mix 2 tablespoons of cooked rice with the saffron water and use it to decorate the rice on a serving dish.

Preparing the meat:

1. Put knuckles, onion, garlic and spices in a cooking pot.
2. Fill with enough water to cover the meat and bring to boil.
3. Lower heat and let cook slowly until tender (lamb takes approximately 2.5 to 3 hours, chicken 1.5 to 2 hours to cook thoroughly).

Around the middle of autumn, many housewives still make pickles by preserving many different vegetables in vinegar or brine, including cauliflower, eggplant (aubergines), celery, shallots, onions, carrots, and cabbage. After a few weeks they are ready, and families eat these as food accompaniment instead of fresh vegetables, which in the past were not available in the colder months.

Over the last three decades or so important changes have taken place in food preservation. The availability of freezers means that vegetables such as eggplant, zucchini (courgettes), and green beans needed for Iranian recipes, which could not be preserved any other way for such use, are now available all year round. Similarly, fresh herbs are often frozen instead of being dehydrated.

Although in recent years companies that produce food have expanded into every area that has traditionally been every housewife's responsibility and pride, homemade preserves are still considered supe-

rior, and conjure old-world images of mothers and grandmothers sitting on a carpet in the yard chatting and picking herbs for dehydrating, with children milling around the ornamental pool.

In Iran, meat has always been scarce and expensive. The Iranian climate doesn't support extensive raising of cattle, and Islam prohibits the consumption of pork and fish without scales[1] and recommends moderate meat consumption. As a result, many Iranian dishes use small amounts of lamb and chicken, often combined with legumes, herbs, and vegetables, making balanced, one-dish meals. Nowadays meat is more plentiful though still quite expensive, and Iranians continue to use it sparingly in recipes. A leg of lamb for an English family's Sunday lunch provides enough meat for at least four or five Iranian stews for an Iranian family of the same size, giving a new meaning to the expression "to make a meal out of it." Many households buy half a lamb, separate the different parts that are appropriate for each dish, and freeze it. For example, they use marrow bones for *âb-gusht* (see Recipe 3) and soups, leg meat cut in cubes for various stews, and mince some of the lamb meat with beef. This amount of meat, used judiciously for a family of four, usually lasts about two months.

RECIPE 3: *ÂB-GUSHT* (MEAT BROTH WITH LEGUMES)

The name *âb-gusht* comes from *âb* (water) and *gusht* (meat).

There are about ten kinds of different *âb-gushts*, the most common being *âb-gusht* with chickpeas and white beans. In the past, when meat was not eaten very often, lots of vegetable and legume dishes were common. *Âb-gusht*, eaten preferably with fresh *sangak* bread, mixed pickles and raw onion, is still a favorite lunch both at home and at traditional restaurants, where it is called *dizi* and is cooked in individual clay crocks.

Serves 4

Cooking time: 5 hours

Ingredients:

    1 lb. (½ kilo.) lamb (loin is best), including some bones
    ½ cup of chickpeas, soaked for at least 2 hours or overnight

---

1 cup white beans, soaked for at least 2 hours or overnight

2 medium potatoes

1 onion,

2–3 cloves of garlic

6–8 dried limes (available from Iranian groceries)

2 tablespoons tomato puree or 4–5 fresh tomatoes

Salt, pepper, turmeric, cinnamon, and cumin

Preparation:

1. Wash meat, put in a pot, and bring to boil. Using a slotted spoon, take the froth out.
2. Add peeled and cut onion, garlic, salt, pepper, turmeric, cinnamon and cumin.
3. Boil for an hour.
4. Add chickpeas and beans and boil for 3 hours on low heat.
5. Peel and cut potatoes into squares and add to the pot.
6. Pierce dried lemons with a knife and add.
7. Add tomato puree, or scald fresh tomatoes, peel the skin, cut into pieces, and add to the pot.
8. Bring to the boil and let simmer for another half hour until the liquid reduces and thickens.

The traditional way of serving *âb-gusht* is to drain the liquid in a bowl and soak pieces of bread in it as a first course. Then the meat is separated from the bones, mashed with the other solid ingredients to a paste and eaten with bread, pickles and onion.

YOU ARE WHAT YOU EAT

As we saw in chapter 7, many Iranians believe illnesses are caused by an imbalance in the body, and since every food is classified chemically as either "hot" or "cold," illnesses can be treated by consuming foods that counter the imbalance. Every Iranian dish is put together as a balanced whole. Lamb, mutton, and chicken are "hot," so they are balanced with

barberries (as in chicken with barberries—*zereshk polo*), tomato paste, and dried limes, and served with rice, all of which are "cold."

OUR DAILY BREAD (*NÂN*)

Even though rice is now consumed at least once a day, usually for dinner, bread remains Iranians' staple food. The first thing one notices about Iranian bread is that it is flat, quite unlike American and European loaves, and that it is usually baked while you wait. There are four main types of Iranian bread, with variations, each type appropriate to different dishes, and each bakery (*nân-vâ'i*) bakes only one kind. In the past bread dough was rolled out by hand and baked individually, but now, at least in big cities, machines do this to meet the increased demand. Handmade bread is still preferred and much sought after by urban dwellers whenever they visit the provinces, where handmade bread is more commonly found.

TYPES OF IRANIAN BREAD

- *Barbari*: The ultimate breakfast bread. Thick and long, ideal for breakfast with feta cheese or eggs.
- *Tâftoon*: Round with rows of holes that are made in the dough with a wooden implement resembling a very wide-toothed comb. This is a versatile, filling bread good for breakfast, kebabs, and meals eaten without rice.
- *Lavâsh*: The thinnest of all breads. Oblong and wide, and flexible enough to make wraps of fresh herbs and white cheese or any other filling. This bread is also used for making samosas.
- *Sangak*: The only wholegrain bread. Lightly salted, thinner than *barbari*, and baked on a bed of hot pebbles, it is especially compatible with the traditional dish of *âb-gusht*. Mind your teeth, though; sometimes little pebbles may be embedded in the bread.

QUEUING FOR BREAD

Men and women line up separately to buy bread. The long lines are for large orders (three or more breads per customer), so those needing just one or two breads form another two, faster moving lines between the two long ones. The baker serves one large order and then two small ones.

In relation to other food, bread is surprisingly cheap, because the government subsidizes flour. For example, in June 2009 prices, one *lavâsh* bread costs 2.6 cents/1.7 pence, and a *barbari* about 21 cents/14 pence.

Apart from the traditional bakeries, French-style bakeries (*nân fântezi*) provide other bakery products such as baguettes, cakes, biscuits (sold by weight), doughnuts, and anything else that the baker dreams up. Supermarkets and corner shops also stock packaged bread, both Iranian and sliced, but nothing can rival a freshly baked traditional bread of any kind.

TEA

On every social or business visit, the absolute minimum a visitor is offered is tea, traditionally served in small, hourglass-shaped golden-rimmed tea glasses standing on deep saucers. Clear glasses are preferred to china cups so the drinker can appreciate the color as well as the flavor of the tea. Many households are now replacing tea glasses with china cups, at least when entertaining guests. Iranians view the teacups as more formal and genteel, but in the privacy of one's own home, I have yet to meet an Iranian who doesn't prefer drinking tea from a tea glass.

A bowl of irregularly shaped cubes of sugar are served with the tea, but without tongs or a teaspoon. You are meant to put the sugar lump, called *ghand*, in your mouth between your teeth and tongue and let the tea wash over it until it dissolves. As you can imagine, the first mouthful is much sweeter than the later ones. The reason behind this practice

is that the sweetness of the *ghand* distorts the tea flavor, so one can only appreciate it by the gradual decrease in the sweet taste. Speaking is a little difficult while the sugar lump is in one's mouth, but experienced tea-drinkers have a way of trapping the sugar lump between teeth and cheek, or between tongue and palate while they speak.

Ghand

Ghand is not the usual cube sugar found in the West, which isn't good for drinking tea like this because it dissolves too fast. *Ghand* is made from sugar beets, not sugar cane, and is considered healthier. It comes in large cones (sugar loaves) about 20 inches (50 cm.) tall, and has to be broken into small pieces using a wedge-shaped utensil, an activity usually undertaken by older members of the family who have more time. One or two sugar loaves are broken at one time and stored, so that the broken *ghand* lasts for a few months.

All young Iranians learn how to brew and serve tea as they grow up. Young women are said to be ready for marriage when they are able to serve the perfect cup of tea, and they brew and serve the tea when a young man and his family come with a marriage proposal.

HOW TO MAKE IRANIAN TEA

Traditionally, tea is brewed (no teabag cop-outs for Iranians!) in an electric or gas-powered samovar, or from hot water heated in an electric or stove-top tea kettle. Iranian stove-top tea kettles have a special flat, metallic lid with holes, on top of which the teapot can sit securely.

1. Put the empty teapot on top of the samovar or the kettle to warm and bring the water to boil.
2. Measure three or four scoops of good quality tea leaves (the coarser the better) and fill the teapot with freshly boiled water.
3. Put on top of samovar or stove-top kettle and reduce the heat.

---

4. Let the tea brew for 15 minutes.
5. Fill a tea glass about halfway with tea and top up with hot water, depending on the strength preferred. (Iranians don't add milk because they think it spoils the flavor.) Nowadays tea glasses can withstand hot liquids without cracking, but in older times when their quality was not as good as now, they were warmed with a little hot water before having the tea poured into them.
6. Replace teapot on top of samovar while waiting for the second (and third) round of tea.

BREAKFAST

A typical Iranian breakfast consists of flat bread with white goat's cheese, similar to the Greek feta, and walnuts, butter and jam, or honey, washed down with tea sweetened with sugar, the only time when Iranians take sugar with tea. Glasses slightly larger than wine glasses can have three or four heaped spoonfuls of sugar.

A favorite winter breakfast, especially on Friday mornings, is a type of porridge made of barley oats or wheat and turkey or lamb (*haleem*) and decorated with cinnamon, ground sesame seeds, with sugar being added upon serving. This fortifying dish is prepared in special takeout outlets overnight for breakfast and also during the day for the breaking of the fast (*iftâr*) during the month of Ramadan.

THICK SOUPS

Iranian soups are much thicker and more substantial than Western broths and soups that are usually served as a first course. Closer to French *potages*, they can be family's lunch, accompanied only by fresh bread. They usually contain a wide variety of legumes and herbs. Some of them are vegetarian, others contain a bit of meat, and they are sometimes garnished with fried onions, chopped and fried garlic, dehydrated and fired mint and whey, but the overall consideration is the achievement of balance between the "hot" and "cold" ingredients described ear-

lier. If a recipe contains legumes, the recipe is usually called *âsh*; otherwise, the word *soup* is used in Persian.

RECIPE 4: *ÂSH-E RESHTEH* (NOODLES AND LEGUMES SOUP)

There are more than ten different types of *âsh* cooked all over Iran, and some recipes are specific to certain provinces. Cooking a good *âsh* requires considerable skill, hence the word *cook* in Persian is *âshpaz*, (literally, *âsh*-cook), while *âshpazi* means *cooking* in general. This *âsh* is probably the most famous and most popular of all *âshes*.

Serves 4

Cooking time: 5 hours (using canned beans reduces the cooking time to 3 hours)

Ingredients:

    2 lbs. (1 kilo.) *âsh* herbs: chives, parsley, coriander, and spinach, and beet greens if in season
    ½ cup chick-peas
    ¾ cup red kidney beans
    1 cup lentils
    1 onion, chopped and fried
    Salt, pepper, and turmeric
    1 lb. (½ kilo.) *reshteh* (Persian noodles), available from Iranian grocery shops
    Dried mint fried in oil for decoration
    Whey (a dairy product) both in the recipe and for decoration
    3–4 cloves of chopped and fried garlic for decoration

Preparation:

1. Soak legumes for two hours or overnight.
2. Clean, wash, and drain herbs and greens.
3. Boil the chickpeas. After an hour, add kidney beans; after another half hour add lentils or boil them separately. (Modify time as needed if using canned beans.)
4. Bring water to a boil in a large pot.
5. Chop the herbs and greens and put in pot to boil for half an hour.

6. Add half-cooked legumes, salt, pepper, and turmeric and stir regularly for 1½ hours.
7. Add *reshteh* and fried onion, simmer on low heat, and keep stirring for another hour.
8. In a small skillet, fry onion slivers and chopped garlic and set aside.
9. In a small skillet, fry dried mint adding a pinch of turmeric, and set aside.
10. Serve *âsh* in a deep bowl and decorate the top with patterns of fried onion and garlic, fried mint, and whey.

RECIPE 5: *SABZI POLO BÂ MÂHI, KUKU SABZI*
(FRIED FISH WITH RICE AND HERBS
AND HERB OMELET)

This is the traditional New Year (*Noruz*) dish. Just like the Noruz spread, it contains elements with symbolic meaning: herbs, representing growth and renewal; rice, for the bounty of the earth; eggs, for birth and new life; and fish, for freshness and the bounty of the sea.

Serves 4

Cooking time: 2 hours (provided that the herbs are washed already)

Rice

Ingredients

2 lbs. (1 kilo) of mixed green herbs: 200 grams chives, 8 oz. (250 gr.) parsley, 8 oz. (250 gr.) coriander, 8 oz. (250 gr.) dill, 2–3 oz. (50–100 gr.) fenugreek, 1 head of leaf lettuce, 2–3 fresh garlic stalks if in season or 1–3 cloves of dried garlic)
2 cups of rice (in Iran, rashti or gilani; abroad use basmati)
Salt
Cooking oil
1 tsp. ground saffron

Preparing the rice:

1. Wash and soak the rice with tepid water in a bowl adding 2 tbsp. of salt at least 2 hours before cooking.
2. Wash, drain, and chop the herbs except lettuce.
3. Bring water to a boil in a pot, add the rice, and boil for 3–4 minutes until it softens a little.
4. Drain the rice and rinse with a cup of cold water.
5. Put ½ cup each of water and cooking oil in the pot. Lay some lettuce leaves in the bottom of the pot.
6. Arrange rice, chopped herbs, and 2–3 stalks or cloves of garlic in layers in the pot.
7. Let rice steam for some 5 minutes, drain excess water from lid.
8. Pour another ½ cup each of water and cooking oil over the rice.
9. Wrap the lid of the pot with a teacloth.
10. Steam for 10 minutes on medium heat, then lower heat and steam for another 30 minutes.

Kuku sabzi (herb omelet)

Make this while the rice is steaming.

Ingredients

1 lb. (½ kilo.) in total of the above mentioned herbs (3–4 oz. (100 gr.) chives, 5 oz. (150 gr.) parsley, 5 oz. (150 gr.) coriander, 1–2 oz. (50 gr.) fenugreek and the rest of the lettuce, finely chopped
2 eggs
1 tbsp. dried *zereshk* (barberries)
½ cup walnuts, cut into small pieces
Cooking oil

Preparation:

Mix the ingredients in a bowl and stir well.

Pour some oil in a nonstick pan and spread the mixture in it. Put the lid semi-open and cook on medium heat for 20 minutes until it sets and looks like a cake. Cut into segments, turn over and cook the other side for 20 minutes.

Fried Fish

Make this while the rice and *kuku* are cooking.

Fry four pieces of any kind of fish fillets in oil on a low heat until golden brown.

To serve:

In a small bowl, pour 1–2 tbsp. of warm water on ground saffron until the water is a rich, golden color. Mix with a serving spoon of rice in a bowl and use the saffron rice to decorate the rest of the rice on the serving dish. Arrange fish and *kuku* on a serving platter and sprinkle some saffron rice over them. Optionally, for added visual appeal, also sprinkle fresh pomegranate seeds. The lettuce *tah-dig* can be separated in one piece from the cooking pot by cooling the bottom of the rice pot under running water.

Nush-e-jân! (Enjoy it!)

DRINKS

Meals are usually accompanied by drinking yogurt (*dugh*). This is sometimes prepared at home using sour yogurt, but can now be bought in plastic bottles like ones for family size soft drinks. It comes in two varieties, fizzy or still and is sometimes served with dried mint mixed in it.

Soft drinks produced in Iran have become more common in recent years. These include Coke and Coke Light, Pepsi, Fanta, Seven-Up and more recently Coke Zero and Red Bull.

As already mentioned (chapter 1 "Customs" and chapter 5), trading and public consumption of alcohol is strictly forbidden in Iran, so visitors should not attempt to bring any into the country or expect to be offered alcoholic drinks, at least in public settings.

DESSERTS

Iranian candy stores are filled with irresistible temptations: French-style cream cakes, Danish pastries, cream éclairs, *mille-feuilles*, and teacakes are next to traditional Iranian sweets like pistachio nougat (*gaz*), saffron

brittle (*sohan*), baklava, little parcels of shortbread pastry enclosing crushed almonds (*ghotâb*), and all sorts of salted nuts and dry fruit mixes.

Apart from store-bought delicacies, some candies and desserts are made at home on special occasions. These include a rice and saffron dessert (*shollezard*) either during Ramadan or as a pledge for a wish fulfilled to be distributed in the neighborhood, as well as halva, a candy known all over the Middle East in various guises. Rosewater, saffron, and sometimes cardamom give traditional Iranian candies and desserts a distinct flavor.

RECIPE 6: HALVA

This traditional refreshment, along with tea and dates, is also offered at funerals and memorial services. After eating it at a service, one is supposed to offer a *Fatiha* prayer for the departed soul (see chapter 8).

Ingredients:

4 cups. finely cut whole wheat flour

3 cups sugar

3 cups cooking or corn oil

1 tbsp. ground saffron

4 cups of water

½ cup of rose water

Instructions:

1. Mix sugar, rosewater, liquid saffron (as described in previous recipes) in a bowl and stir to dissolve.
2. Heat a deep cooking pot and stir in flour.
3. Keep stirring on low until flour turns the color of dry dates.
4. Remove the pot with the fried flour from the heat, add oil and stir.
5. Then stir the syrup into the pot with the flour until it is completely absorbed by the flour mixture and the mixture has the consistency of cake mixture.

If the mixture is too thin, heat on low for a couple of minutes (be careful, because the syrup can burn easily and the halva can turn dry very quickly).

Pour mixture into a flat dish and decorate with pistachio and almond slivers.

In business meetings candies or pastries may be offered, but in social visits fresh fruit is considered obligatory. The size, shape, and quality are paramount, with bigger equaling better, at least as far as oranges are concerned.

Greengrocers designate such fruit as *majlesi* ("formal," i.e., appropriate for entertaining), and raise the prices accordingly. Unpeeled fruit is neatly arranged on a platter and placed on the large coffee table in the middle of the room, from where three or four different pieces of fruit are put on a dessert plate and set in front of every visitor, with a fruit knife and fork. The accepted convention is to wait for the hostess to repeatedly press you into eating, but be forewarned that if you appear too reluctant, she may peel the fruit for you herself.

INVITATIONS TO DINNER

If you meet any Iranians during your visit, they are very likely to invite you to their house for a meal. A typical invitation between Iranians usually goes like this:

> A: I say, on Thursday evening, if you are not doing anything else, give us the honor of coming for dinner.
> B: It'll be trouble for you. (Meaning: "Yes, I'd like to.")
> A: It's no trouble—we'll just have whatever there is around. (Meaning "We will be prepared for you.")
> B: We didn't want to give you this trouble. (This is the clincher/acceptance).
> A: We will be pleased to have you.

This mode of communication, called *ta'ârof*, or ritual courtesy, is described in chapter 3. The rules of *ta'ârof* require that an offer be declined at least once, usually twice, before acceptance, out of consideration for the person making the offer. The person continues to repeat the offer to ensure that the invitee is not refusing out of concern that this is an ostensible invitation. The clues that this invitation is a "real" one is the mention of the day and the activity.

Dinner times are not set in advance. Generally dinner is not served before 8:00 in the evening, and in the summer much later than that, well

after the evening call to prayer. Even if you ask what time you should be there, the answer you are likely to receive is "any time you like we will be expecting you," indicating that the guest's comfort is more important than practical considerations. Interestingly, the quality of Iranian dishes is not affected by any delay, possibly in keeping with this relaxed attitude toward timekeeping.

A present of flowers or candies is always welcome, although the host will protest that you should not have taken the trouble. If you take any other present, it may or may not be opened in your presence, depending on the habits of different families or by the habits from the area of the country your host comes from. If the present isn't opened, the intention is that irrespective of what the gift is, your gesture is appreciated; if it is opened, it provides the opportunity for the host to show her appreciation of your taste.

SEATING AND TABLE MANNERS

As a foreigner, you occupy the position of an honored guest, so you will be seated "high up" at the place farthest from the door, a position accorded to elders as a sign of respect because they are less likely to be disturbed there by others and because they are not expected to help with the preparation and serving of the food. Other than this, there are no specific rules on who should sit where.

MINDING YOUR PPPS
(PERSIAN POLITENESS PRINCIPLES)

Whenever a newcomer enters a room, those present rise as a sign of respect. The newcomer will probably beg them to remain seated, as a show of concern for their comfort, but the request will be ignored to show that no trouble is too much. The safe rule is to follow what others your age are doing.

If other visitors rise when you enter the room, you can ask them to remain seated by saying, "*Befarmâ'id, khâhesh mikonam*" (Do sit down, please).

A small family usually sits at the kitchen table for meals. When they have guests for dinner, though, they lay a spread on the floor if there is not enough space at the table. Unlike in the West, where the size of a formal dinner party may be dictated by the size of the dining table, in Iran there are no such limitations: the more, the merrier! The dinner cloth can always be spread from one side of the room to the other so that everyone can be accommodated.

All courses are placed on the table or the spread at the beginning of the meal rather than being served individually. The hostess ensures that there are multiple serving dishes of every course so each guest can easily access all of them. In less traditional families, the meal may be served buffet style.

Because meat in Iranian recipes comes in bite-size pieces, knives are not usually included in the cutlery set. If the need to cut something arises, a tablespoon is usually used. A tablespoon rather than a fork is also used for eating rice. Usually there are no fabric or paper napkins with place settings, but boxed tissues will be around. Don't be offended if some guests begin to eat before everyone is seated, or if somebody speaks with their mouth full. You need to understand that Iranian meals are not as formal as you may be accustomed to back home. But one thing is sure: while in Iran, you will taste exquisite food, and you will feel that, even for a few days, you will have found a home away from home.

TEN

Going Places, Doing Things

Crossing a busy Iranian road is a feat only underestimated by innocent foreigners, like me when I first arrived in Tehran. After walking along the road I wanted to cross for what seemed like ages and not spotting any traffic lights, I came to a zebra crossing.

"Eureka!" I thought, and positioned myself on the edge of the curb. Cars zoomed by, oblivious of the zebra crosswalk and my presence. After a while, a car stopped, but not to let me cross; he thought I wanted to flag down a private transport car (I will return to this later in the chapter).

If you are with an Iranian trying to cross a road, you are in luck. They will encourage you to walk close to them and may even pull you by the sleeve as they thread their way among the moving cars. You will probably feel faint as the tires of oncoming cars screech to a halt, but pay no attention. Close your eyes, if you must, and put your trust in your guide. If you are alone, do what I did when I first arrived in Tehran: I made a point of standing next to other pedestrians and crossed the road with them, hoping they knew what they were doing. (Apparently this works: I'm still here to tell the tale.) In most cases you will make it to the opposite curb thanks to two things: the Tehran traffic, which makes it impossible for cars to drive very fast, and the fact that drivers expect pedestrians to do something like that; there is nothing else they can do.

GETTING AROUND IN CITIES

The car that stopped for me at the zebra crossing was one of the thousands of taxis that do a set itinerary, for example, Seyed Khandân Bridge to Haft-e Tir Square (*tâxi khatti*) in Tehran. The beginning and the end of the lines for these taxis are usually marked with small yellow signs in Persian. The number of taxis working on every itinerary is set by a central authority, who ensures that as soon as the car at the beginning of the line is full and ready to go, at least one empty one car is right behind and ready to board passengers. The system usually works, unless there is exceptional traffic or adverse weather conditions, and it provides relatively inexpensive transportation.

The arrangement is quite simple: if you haven't boarded a *khatti* at the beginning of the line, you can stand near a crossroads en route and hail one as you would a taxi. If a *khatti* can take you, it will stop. *Khattis* can carry three passengers in the back and one in the front. If you don't feel like squeezing in with two other people in the back, you can offer to pay double the fare so the driver won't pick up another passenger. In any case, the fare is usually 4,000 rials for an average ride (about 42 cents or 28 pence in June 2009 prices). If you are heading to the taxi's final destination, fine; if not, you ride until getting to the appropriate crossroad, where you get out and hail another car that goes along the intersecting road, and repeat this procedure until you arrive at your desired destination.

Every *khatti* can pick up both men and women, so a woman often ends up sitting next to a stranger in the back seat. Out of consideration for the female passengers' comfort, sometimes male passengers change places to let a woman sit next to a window or in the passenger seat. In Iran there are no limitations for women traveling alone within cities and from one city to another. Conversation between a female passenger and the (usually male) driver is acceptable, but is usually limited to practical matters, such as travel information. Male passengers and male drivers may chat about a variety of topics, from their finances to their children.

You may be thinking that only Iranians can work the *khatti* system, which requires knowing the layout of a city. That is true, but Iranians

will often go out of their way to help a foreigner, since foreigners are still, even in Tehran, a rare sight. And if you have learned a few Persian phrases, you might make some friends along the way or even get invited to their house.

MAILING ADDRESSES

Mailing addresses in Iran are written the opposite from what you may be used to: they start with the country or city and end with the addressee. The address sounds like physical directions to the mail carrier. The following is the address of a famous candy shop, Sohani and Sons, that sells traditional brittle (*sohan*) in a central spot in Tehran:

Iran,
Tehran
No. 966 opposite the Mokhâberat [telecom building]
Before Seyed Khandân Bridge
Shariati Avenue
Sohani and Sons

Other forms of transportation are licensed taxis, which are painted orange, white with an orange stripe, lettuce green, or gray with a check stripe. Some of these also travel on set routes, but they can also be hired by one person at a fare equivalent to four fares to that destination. If your destination is out of the set route, you should say "*darbast*" (closed door) and the name of your destination, and ask how much this would cost (there are no taximeters in Iran, although I am told there are plans to introduce them). It is a good idea to agree on the fare beforehand because if you get stuck in traffic or lost, the driver is not entitled to charge a higher fare. However, if you feel your journey has taken longer than usual, you may consider leaving a small tip, which is usually accepted, but unusual.

TIPPING ETIQUETTE

A small tip is normally expected by restaurant waiters, hotel staff (chambermaids, bellhops), hospital staff (nurses, auxiliaries), drivers that make large deliveries of furniture, for example, or materials at a building site, but not taxi drivers. Other regular service providers (mail carrier, street sweeper, park warden, flat caretaker) normally expect a larger bonus before Noruz.

The form of individual transportation most similar to Western cabs is called *azhans* (from the French *agence*). *Azhanses* work from an office in a residential area and the drivers own their own cars. They usually charge slightly less than a taxi you would hail down in the street, and the drivers are theoretically vetted for character and marital status. (A sign advertising for drivers in the window of our local *azhans* office reads, "We require a number of married drivers.") If a woman hires an *azhans*, she invariably sits in the back seat, whereas a man would most likely sit next to the driver.

Motor vehicle regulations are similar to those in the West, at least in theory. New drivers now have to take a written test before the driving test, but in practice drivers break quite a few rules. Drivers run red lights when they are in a hurry, don't stop at crosswalks to let pedestrians cross, disregard passing line markings, and park anywhere they can physically fit unless there's a traffic officer in sight. If they are in the wrong place and they can't do a three-point turn because it is a one-way street, they reverse the whole length of the road, because if they spot a traffic officer they can stop and pretend they are going with the flow. Drivers even do this on freeways if they have missed their turn, and they don't worry about other drivers because everyone knows how to cope with this driving behavior. New drivers can drive as soon as they get their driving licence, but are not allowed on motorways until a year later. Women also commonly drive in Iran and they can be taught by either male and female instructors.

Motorbikes seem to follow their own rules. They rarely stop at a red light and they feel able to go against the flow of traffic even on busy expressways. Families of four can ride on a motorbike in this order: older child on the handlebars; father; younger child; then the mother perched at the end of the seat, miraculously holding on to the man's waist and securing the sandwiched child in her precarious hold. Such practices are obviously dangerous, but Iranians place their trust in God and the good wishes of their family. My favorite stickers on back windshields and bumpers of vehicles include: "Insured by My Mother's Prayers," "Insured by Imam Mahdi," and "Dad, don't go too fast."

To be fair, traffic authorities try to enforce rules, improve traffic conditions in big cities, and clamp down on parking and driving offenses. At the time of writing this book, a program to trade in old vehicles for new ones, much like the "clunker" program in the U.S., is in its final stages. This has resulted in the replacement of thousands of old, mainly (Iranian-made) passenger cars, resulting in a positive environmental impact. In addition, a new system of annual inspections for cars is currently being introduced to ensure that standards of roadworthiness are maintained.

GAS/PETROL STATION ETIQUETTE

In Iran, male drivers pump gas themselves, while female drivers hand the gas tank keys to the attendant, who fills the tank for them. I've been told that this practice is to ensure women's comfort.

Rental cars are almost nonexistent in Iran, so you don't have to worry about trying your skills and adhering to the Iranian Highway Code. If you need to rent a car, you will hire the driver too.

You might prefer to use buses, which run along main routes. You buy a ticket, usually sold in multiples, from a special booth at the beginning and end of the routes. If you don't have one, don't worry; you can always offer to buy one from a fellow passenger, who will almost certainly

give it to you for free. Fares are heavily subsidized by the government, so they are almost free anyway. The standard bus and subway fare is 1,000 rials (about 10 cents or 7 pence), although some busy bus routes are also served by private buses that charge a slightly higher fare. Women board the back of the bus and males the front, and the two parts are separated by a rail, so, unlike shared taxis, a woman never shares a seat with a man and is spared the inconvenience of being squashed between unrelated males. A couple traveling together board through different doors and sit separately.

A subway is a recent welcome addition to Tehran's public transportation system. It can get quite crowded during rush hours: most schools and civil service jobs start at 7:30 A.M. and end by early afternoon. I like three things about the Tehran subway system. First, it helped me realize that distances in Tehran are actually not as large as I had thought. Shahr-e Rey, Hossein's home town in the south of Tehran, to Abbâs-âbâd, where we live north of the center of Tehran, takes just over half an hour on the metro even though in heavy traffic it can take up to two hours to drive this distance. Secondly, I love the air-conditioned stations. In the summer I am often tempted to decamp to a subway station until I feel brave enough to emerge into the pollution and the heat of central Tehran. Thirdly, women once again receive preferential treatment: although they can board any car, the first and the last car of every train is designated "Women only." This means that these cars can sometimes be used as an "inside" or informal space, where women can laugh or talk loudly, eat fruit, or chat with each other, out of men's earshot. This is a paradise for nosy people (like me), who can use the women's car to observe and strike up conversations with virtual strangers.

WEEKEND AND SHORT BREAKS

Much like Western urban dwellers, Iranians who live in cities like to get away from the pollution and noise on weekends and short vacations, and they head for the countryside to enjoy the quiet and spend time outdoors. Those Tehranis lucky enough to own a summer home in the

north (Shomâl) or in the foothills of the Alborz mountain range north-east of Tehran often leave on Thursday afternoon and return on Friday night.

But even if an overnight break is not possible, many people, especially young adults and families with young children, drive to the foothills of the Alborz to hike, choosing as demanding or as easy a trail the climbers prefer, and then have breakfast at a traditional tea shop. From early spring until autumn Iranians also like to drive to the mountains and picnic by a stream, or gather firewood to cook kebabs and brew tea over a campfire.

In the winter months Tehranis enjoy playing in the snow and skiing on the Alborz mountain slopes around Tehran (e.g., Âb-ali, Dizin) and riding on the Tochâl telecabin (a cable car), which affords panoramic views of the mountains below and the whole of Tehran sprawling toward the south.

FAVORITE DOMESTIC DESTINATIONS

Iranian families travel mostly during Noruz (the New Year holiday) between March 20–April 2 or 3, and during the school holidays (June 15–September 22). Even if you manage to get tickets and accommodations during Noruz, everywhere is bound to be much more expensive and crowded, so if possible avoid traveling during those two weeks. I think the best times to visit Iran are in the spring (after the Noruz holiday) and late autumn, when the weather is pleasantly mild in most areas. At the height of summer southern areas can get unpleasantly hot, but some parts in the West (e.g., Ardebil, Sar'ein) and the North (e.g., Klâr-dasht) are cool throughout the summer.

Highlights of any trip to Iran are bound to include Isfahan, for Safavid glory; Shiraz, the city of poets (Hafez and Sa'adi are buried there) and which is close to Persepolis; and the Caspian littoral in the north for its natural beauty. There are many other interesting and beautiful places to visit in Iran. Refer to travel guides (e.g. Bradt Guide or Lonely Planet) for detailed information.

WHEN TO VISIT WHAT

City/Area	Location	Best Times to Visit
Tehran	North, to the south of the Alborz mountain range	Autumn and spring.
The North	Far north of Iran, north of the Alborz mountain range, along the Caspian littoral	This is the most humid area in Iran and can be very sticky in the summer. Its high-altitude areas may be inaccessible in winter. Visit in the spring and autumn.
Iranian Azerbaijan	Northwestern Iran	Avoid it at the height of winter, when snowfall may cause transportation problems.
Qom	South of Tehran, in the desert	Too hot from May to October.
Isfahan	Central Iran	All year.

FOREIGN TRAVEL

Although foreign travel for leisure has become much more common in recent decades, traveling abroad still remains mostly the privilege of affluent Iranians. Turkey and Cyprus are favorite destinations because Iranians don't need visas to travel there, but European and Far East destinations are also popular. Others travel for business or to visit relatives living or studying abroad.

Pious Iranians try to visit Mecca at least once, and more often if they can afford it. The Pilgrimage Organization offers pilgrimage trips at sub-

sidized prices, but there is usually a long waiting list of those who have paid a deposit toward the journey. Priority is given to older people, but sometimes names are pulled out of a hat, so some lucky people don't have to wait for too long. Other pilgrimage trips from Iran go to Iraq, where six of the Holy Imams are buried (see appendix C), and to Damascus in Syria, where Imam Hossein's sister Zeinab is buried.

THE TRAVELING RITUALS

In the distant past, traveling was fraught with dangers: highway robbers, damage to carriages, and unpredictable adverse weather conditions. Today the dangers are different but no less present in every trip. Iranians recognize and accept the possibility that one may not return; they believe that life and death are in the hands of God alone, and only He knows when everyone is destined to die.

This awareness, even if not explicitly acknowledged, is at the back of every Iranian's mind when preparing for a journey. Especially before long trips, Iranians make sure they bid farewell to their close relatives, preferably in person, but if this is not possible, by phone. Near the end of the visit or the conversation, the traveler usually says, "Well, if you don't see me again, give me your forgiveness (*halâl-kon*)." The traveler says this because God will forgive sins or injustices committed against other people on the condition that they are prepared to forgive those who wronged them (see the discussion of funeral ceremonies in chapter 8). Of concern are not only great injustices, which we all aim to avoid, but also seemingly small acts that constitute grave sins, such as anger or backbiting, which must be forgiven for the soul to find peace. The usual response to this entreaty is good wishes for a safe journey and a prompt return.

Just before departure, a relative holds the Holy Quran aloft by the front door of the traveler's house. The traveler walks through the door under the Quran, comes in, then goes back outside and kisses the Quran, crossing the threshold for a third time, in a symbolic enactment of the whole journey and its return under God's protection and guidance. After the traveler leaves from the front gate, a relative pours a bowl of water on the ground to ensure the traveler's safe return.

Incidentally, similar rituals take place at schools and in the army. On the first day of school, a senior teacher holds the Quran high up for the students to file under it into the school building. During the Iran-Iraq war, footage from the war front shows soldiers kissing the Quran and walking under it just before leaving for battle, from which they knew many would not return. (For more on the war and the culture of martyrdom, see chapter 11.)

THE THRONE VERSE (ÂYAT-UL-KURSI)

Iranians usually recite this Quranic prayer to invoke God's protection before setting off on a trip.

In the Name of Allah, the Compassionate, the Merciful

God! There is no deity except Him, the Living, the Eternal. Slumber does not overtake Him, nor does sleep. What the Heavens hold and what the Earth holds [belongs] to Him. Who is there to intercede with Him except by His permission? He knows what lies before [His creatures] and what's behind them, while they embrace nothing of His knowledge except whatever He may wish. His Seat extends far over Heaven and Earth; preserving them both does not overburden Him. He is the Sublime, the Almighty![1]

On the third day after the traveler's departure, close relatives usually cook a thick potage-type soup (*âsh*) and distribute it among neighbors in exchange for their good wishes for the traveler's safe return.

OTHER LEISURE PURSUITS

TV and Radio

State television runs five general channels broadcast all over Iran and some local stations: the national channels include one news channel; one foreign network (Sahar), which broadcasts in Arabic, English, and

occasionally other languages; a Quran network; Channel 3, popularly known as the young people's channel because it often broadcasts comedies and sports; and Channel 4, which often broadcasts literary and cultural shows as well as documentaries and films in English and other languages.

Very popular especially with women are daytime and evening TV magazine shows, which have programs on cooking, family health, raising children, and current issues. Experts on health, nutrition, psychology, and safety make frequent appearances on these shows, which often influence behavior and habits. For example, a government campaign currently underway focuses on conserving energy and water. This promotion is being carried out on several fronts, including on TV. Experts on programs stress public responsibility in energy use ("Let's use energy wisely, so that every citizen can have access to it.") and give practical advice on how to save energy by sealing windows, insulating hot water pipes, or simply by turning down the heat and wearing an extra layer of clothing.

Iranian television produces a number of family comedy and drama serials every year, and their plots are based on current social concerns, such as marriage, infidelity, money and family problems, and crime. Two or three 30-episode serials are specially commissioned and broadcast for the first time during the month of Ramadan, and these attract large audiences. Iranian television also produces one or two long-running serials each year about the life of a religious or a historical figure, such as the hugely successful series *Imam Ali*, about the first Imam, *Imam Rezâ*, about the eighth Imam, *Holy Mariam*, about the life of Virgin Mary, and *Yusuf [Joseph] the Prophet*, which ran for ten months from 2008 to 2009. The movie version of *Holy Mariam* was screened in Austria in Christmas 2008, and *Yusuf the Prophet* has been exported to other Muslim countries, such as Iraq and Afghanistan.

Iranian television games are usually called "competitions." The luck element is minimal, because any contestants' gains resulting from luck would be considered gambling, which is strongly proscribed in Islam. In games where contestants compete individually, they are rewarded for their answers to general knowledge questions, which often include questions on religious history, the Quran, and prophetic traditions. Other

games are played in pairs, teams, couples, or family groups, and these reward players for showing harmony and cooperation.

On weekends and public holidays television channels screen popular Iranian and foreign films, mostly action and adventure, the latter almost always dubbed in Persian, except for some on Channel 4.

About twenty nationwide radio stations play a wide variety of shows. These include Radio *Javân* (for young people), *Salamat* (health), *Varzesh* (sports), *Farhang* (culture), *Ma'âref* (religious knowledge), *Quran* and *Goftegu* (dialogue and discussion), and *Payâm* (driving information). There are local radio stations as well.

Going to the Park, Picnics, and Eating Out

Families who don't get out of the city on weekends will often arrange with another family to have a picnic in a city park. Favorite picnic foods are cold meat sandwiches, boiled eggs, fresh tomatoes and cucumbers, potato and chicken salad (called Olivier salad), baguettes, and fruit, tea, and any nuts or candies people have at home. During the picnic the younger members of the families play ball games or play in the park's playground.

Eating out at elegant, possibly foreign, restaurants, for example, Indian or Chinese, of which there are only a few in big cities, is only common among the urban affluent classes who may have tasted such food during their travels abroad. Traditional and expensive Iranian restaurants can be found in Tehran and in cities visited by foreign tourists. These restaurants are decorated with Iranian handicrafts, rugs, and other traditional objects such as *hookah* (water pipe) bottles, copper jugs, and sometimes even an ornamental fountain in the center. Some may also have live Iranian music. Hosts are likely to entertain foreign guests at such a place.

The majority of Iranians may occasionally eat out at an inexpensive *kabâbi*, a restaurant offering hearty meals of kebabs with rice or freshly baked bread accompanied by yogurt and cucumber as a side dish, or may take the kebab home as takeout.

Similar restaurants, although more expensive and offering a wider variety of kebabs, side dishes, and cooked dishes, can be found at the

foothills of mountains, at Evin and Darband in Tehran, and at Zoshk and Shandiz near Mashhad. These restaurants are decorated with traditional paintings and have no tables and chairs; instead, diners eat on large wooden platforms with rails on three sides and covered with carpets, much like a traditional room. After the meal many Iranians like to smoke a *hookah* (water pipe) with fruit-flavored tobacco.

Other types of places for eating out are traditional restaurants, called *Dizi-sârâ*, and Western-style eateries. *Dizi-sârâs* only offer *âb-gusht* (see chapter 9 for the recipe) at lunchtime, served with *sangak* bread, fresh onion, and pickles. A number of fast-food restaurants and chains provide the usual fast-food fare—pizzas, hamburgers, and fried chicken, as well as fresh hot and cold sandwiches, roast chicken, and Turkish-style doner kebab, an upright, revolving spit of lamb or chicken meat made into a sandwich or wrapped in pitta bread—and are popular mostly with young people and families. Falafel stands are also popular in busy areas.

Visits and Entertaining

As mentioned earlier, a main leisure pastime for Iranians is visiting with their parents and siblings and eating meals together. In response to a question in the World Values Survey (2000), almost seventy percent of respondents of both genders said that they spend time with parents or relatives once a week.

Cultural Activities

Many Westerners are familiar with serious, artistic Iranian movies, such as the work of Abbas Kiarostami and Mohsen Makhmalbaf, who have received international prizes. Such films are not usually shown in theaters in Iran, although they can be purchased on DVD. The majority of theaters show Iranian-made dramas and comic films that feature popular television actors. Iranians can purchase DVDs of Iranian films that had previously been shown in theaters, as well as bootleg foreign films, usually of the more action and violent ilk.

In Tehran there are only about a dozen theaters that perform plays, the most notable being the City Theatre in the center of Tehran. The-

aters usually perform works by Iranian playwrights, or foreign ones in translation. Mostly urban, Western-educated artistic people, intellectuals, and literati go to plays; the vast majority of Iranians have never been to a live theater performance.

There are two main halls where concerts of classical Iranian and European music are performed: the Vahdat (Unity) Hall (formerly Rudaki Hall) on Hafez Avenue and the Niavaran Palace, both in Tehran. Events are advertised in the daily papers, and tickets for most plays and concerts can be bought in person at the box office or on the Internet, but tickets can be difficult to get for popular shows. Your hotel or tour guide should be able to help. The website *www.tehranavenue.com* has useful information on current cultural events in Tehran. Popular shows may sometimes travel to other large cities.

Large cities and towns have a variety of fine museums, galleries, and temporary art exhibitions that attract mainly young and foreign visitors, and those with special interests. Mansions and palaces formerly belonging to the royalty and the aristocracy have generally been converted into museums, such as the Golestân, Niâvarân, and Sa'adâbâd Palaces in Tehran. Museums and landmarks often have different hours, so check before going there.

Shopping

As in other countries, shopping used to be an activity undertaken in response to a specific need. Traditional bazaars and shopping precincts were laid out with this principle in mind, so shops selling similar merchandise are grouped together in the Tehran bazaar. Such shopping trips are usually tiring and therefore not normally classified as leisure activities by Iranians.

However, the Western cultural concept of shopping as a pastime is now becoming popular, at least in Tehran and other cities. Western-style shopping centers or malls that could be anywhere from Hong Kong to Seattle to Athens promote the concept of the "shopping experience" and sell mostly imported, luxury goods at high prices. These malls also have coffee shops, restaurants, and areas for children to play.

Reading

In modern Iranian culture, reading is not generally regarded as a leisure activity, although daily newspapers have a wide circulation and there are a number of "family" magazines, similar to women's magazines in the West, which contain advice on family relationships, children's upbringing and education, cooking, general interest, some celebrity news, and astrological predictions. There are numerous specialty magazines geared for specific markets, including soccer and sports fans, jokes and cartoons, crosswords, and sudokus. On the more serious end of the spectrum, there are business, political, architecture and interior design, and literary and philosophy journals. Foreign magazines such as *National Geographic* and *Time* can be found at international hotels and some central spots, such as in Enghelab Street around the main building of Tehran University. This, by the way, is the place to locate any book, from study aids to foreign language materials, and art and photographic books, as well as educational CDs. Almost every Iranian publisher has a central outlet, and some foreign publishers have representatives here.

However, book reading for enjoyment is by no means widespread among Iranians in the way it is elsewhere. Very few Iranians read at home for pure enjoyment. I believe there are two main reasons for this. The first is that reading is intrinsically a solitary pastime and is incompatible with the warm gregariousness of Iranians, who prefer companionship over any solitary activity. Secondly, as a result of the educational system, many Iranians have generally come to regard reading only as a means of rote learning, at least for literature and the humanities (history, geography, religious education), and they have not learned to derive pleasure from it. Students have to learn the meanings of difficult words in poems and to identify literary features (e.g. metaphors, similes) without being asked to analyze their function/effect on the text or to offer a personal response. In history, geography, and RE, they have to learn the lessons by heart and reproduce them, without exercising any critical thinking.

When an Iranian relative of ours traveled on the London Underground for the first time, he was surprised by the number of people

reading, especially because the subway car was quite crowded. As mentioned earlier, the English value privacy, independence, and freedom from imposition, and any genuine interest in reading aside, the English often use reading in public as a kind of shield protecting them from outside disturbances and helping them avoid making unwitting eye contact with strangers.

In Iran, habits are very different. More people travel in pairs or in small groups, and even if they are traveling alone, they don't hesitate to look at other passengers, and often start a conversation with the person sitting next to them. If you decide to read on public transportation, be prepared to attract the stares of other passengers. An Iranian friend explained that reading in public gives the impression that there is something important in the reading material and makes bystanders curious.

Certain groups of people read for pleasure or as part of their jobs: academics, lawyers, clerics, writers, and people who have grown up in a family where reading and literature were important. But such people are in the minority, although most households own at least one copy of the Holy Quran, a prayer book (*Mafâtih al-Jinân*—see chapter 4), and a copy of the *Divân* (collection of lyrics) by Hafez. The Quran and the *Mafâtih* are often read for devotional purposes by many people. (See the discussion of Hafez and the extensive poetic tradition in the next chapter.)

ELEVEN

The Soul of the Nation

Scene: A women's hairdressing salon during my first visit to that hair salon. By now I have become used to people asking me questions about how I ended up in Iran, whether I like it here, whether I had to embrace Islam in order to marry. The conversation turns to the Islamic Republic and its rules. The young hairdresser takes the opportunity to rant and rave because of high prices, unemployment, even the compulsory hijab. God looks into people's hearts, she says, not at their appearance. Eventually she asks how I would like my hair cut. She picks up the scissors and before she makes the first cut, she whispers, "In the name of God, the Compassionate, the Merciful."

The preceding chapters have explored some common themes found throughout many aspects of Iranian life. These themes blend together like the warp and the weft in a multicolored, intricate Persian carpet. But we'll pull the strands apart now and delve deeper in search of the Iranian psyche.

I've observed many seemingly paradoxical behaviors—concepts and character traits that seem to contradict each other—in Iran, and have

discussed these topics with numerous Iranians. In this chapter I share what I've learned.

PARADOXES

At first glance Iranian everyday life features numerous paradoxes relating to behavior. The reasons behind them may seem to be at odds with other expectations, but a closer look often reveals the principles in operation, as in the following examples.

Paradox: Keeping Children Safe

Parents are often anxious about their young children catching a cold, picking up infections, or getting a stomachache from eating too many "cold" foods (see chapter 9). And yet these same parents will let a small child sit on an adult's lap in the car's passenger seat instead of in a secure baby car seat.

Explanation

Parents, and especially mothers, try to shield children from harmful environmental influences. Similarly, they feel it is their responsibility to ensure that the child is safe while in the car, which to them means holding the child rather than leaving the child alone in the back seat. This behavior is also linked to a mother's special bond with her small child: the child feels safer sitting on the mother's lap, even though if an accident were to happen, this is a potentially dangerous place for the child to be.

Paradox: Giving Way

In chapter 2 we saw how Iranians give way at doorways and often insist that a companion go first. This practice seems to be at odds with another very common practice on the road: that of very rarely yielding to others while driving. Every driver wants to go first, so intersections not policed by a traffic officer are sometimes gridlocked during rush hour because no one will give way.

Explanation

This instance of apparently paradoxical behavior may be explained by two cultural realities:

- The status of politeness rules
- The in-group/out-group distinction

Politeness rules hold more weight than traffic regulations because the former have developed as a result of cultural social conditions over hundreds of years. Traffic regulations have been imposed by the government to address safety issues and have nothing to do with interpersonal considerations, which, as we have seen throughout the book, are extremely important.

Iranians give way as an expression of respect to others who belong to their circle of acquaintances, that is, their in-group, within which they have to uphold face and maintain the social obligation to uphold others' face. While driving, which is usually anonymous behavior, such considerations are irrelevant, so it's everyone for himself (and the wish of a kind God for everybody else). This is where safety campaigns play a part. To encourage people to drive safely and to take safety precautions, governmental agencies use cultural realities such as *shakhsiat* in their messages (as we saw in chapter 2).

POSITIVE TRAITS

Many positive character traits are linked to the collectivism prevalent in Iranian culture. Even though they are not always present in every individual, they are seen as ideals to strive toward. Among those mentioned frequently are forbearance (*gozasht*), foregoing one's rights in the interests of the group, overlooking the shortcomings of others, going along with the wishes of the group (*tâbe'e ye jam' budan*), helping in any way one can, and showing concern for others' feelings and compassion to the point of self-sacrifice.

Margaret Bateson et al.[1] in their extensive study of Iranian national character identify the following positive traits that Iranians value in themselves: kindness (*mehrabâni*), modesty and unpretentiousness (*forutani, tavâzo'*), sensitiveness (*hassâs budan*), commitment to and involvement with others (*bâ-âtefeh budan*), emotional responsiveness (*delsuzi, khun-garmi*), generosity (*dast-o delbâz budan*), loyalty (*vafâdari*), and awareness of a spiritual sphere (*e'teqâd be âlam-e rohani*). Again, as we saw with face considerations, these traits mostly pertain to the in-group (*khodi*) and contribute to the preservation of group unity.

The common denominator of most of these positive character traits is a correspondence of thought and action, a unity between what is professed and what is felt, with its opposite, *riyâ* (hypocrisy), constituting a cardinal sin.

THE VIRTUE OF PATIENCE AND "KEEPING THE PEACE"

In addition to the preceding characteristics, many Iranians display two prominent character traits that are also linked to the importance of the in-group in Iranian life and which have their roots in the nation's past: the virtues of patience and "keeping the peace." Throughout its long history, the Iranian nation has suffered waves of foreign conquests and natural disasters but has always managed to spring back. Until well into the twentieth century it was a predominantly agricultural nation, schooled in patience for both manmade and natural adversities, and in placing its trust in God (*tavakkol be Khodâ*) for a good harvest and a better future. Iran's pre-Islamic religions and, later, Islam encouraged the Iranians' innate patience with the promises that a Messiah will come to dispense justice and of the reward of paradise (a Persian word that came into the English language through Greek).

Despite, or perhaps because of, having suffered violence throughout history, Iranians love peace and friendship, and try to minimize differences and avoid confrontation in their personal relationships. Thus, extreme expressions of violent feelings are normally restrained and swearing is never heard in mixed company. This patient restraint is visible among strangers too: although large socioeconomic gaps exist between

people in big cities, instances of violent crime are very rare. Also, despite the often chaotic driving conditions in cities, drivers are generally patient, even to the point of stoicism.

PATRIOTISM

Unlike other states in the Middle East, Iran's borders were not arbitrarily drawn by colonial powers. As a result of their pre-Islamic heritage, Shi'a religious identity, and the political and historical experiences shared in the recent past, and despite their diverse ethnic backgrounds, Iranians have a very strong sense of national identity.[2] In response to the 2000 World Values Survey question "How proud are you to be Iranian?" 91.9 percent of males and 92.5 percent of females answered "very proud," and 3.5 percent of males and 2.7 percent of females said "quite proud."

In practical terms, this sense of belonging and pride in their national identity means that Iranians will put aside any differences in the face of a common enemy. This opinion was expressed during my private conversations with Iranians. And, in a public forum, the journalist Mashallah Shamsolvaezin[3] expressed the view that Western powers shouldn't make the mistake of assuming that groups currently opposing the government or the Islamic Republic itself will automatically side with Iran's enemies: throughout history love for the motherland has always united the Iranian nation against external threats.

NEGATIVE TRAITS

In the same study by Bateson et al. cited earlier,[4] Iranian respondents also identified a cluster of negative character traits that pertain mostly to Iranian merchants and politicians as well as to the middle- and upper-class of the large cities, such as Tehran and Isfahan. These traits include shrewdness (*zerangi*), being calculating (*hessâbgari*) and opportunistic (*forsat-talabi*), hypocritical (*motazâher/doru*), obsequious and insincere (*charb-zabân*), and glibly dishonest (*châkhân*). Unlike the positive traits mentioned earlier in this chapter, these traits have one thing in common:

the disjunction between action and purpose, diametrically opposite to the ideal of sincerity, which may be justifiable in one's behavior toward members of the out-group (*qarib*). In the same way, one may be suspicious (*badbin*) of members of the out-group and expect the worst from unfamiliar persons. This pessimism toward strangers is likely to be related to instances of foreign intervention that the Iranian nation experienced in the nineteenth and twentieth centuries. Many Iranians initially perceived the Great Powers (Britain, France, Imperial Russia and then the Soviet Union), and later the United States, as a "friend," but later felt manipulated by what they perceived as self-serving, ulterior motives behind these countries' actions.

DUALISM

The ancient Iranian religion of Zoroastrianism was based on the struggle of two equally powerful gods striving for supremacy in the world—Ahura Mazda, the god of Truth and Light, and Ahriman, the god of Lies and Darkness. Humans could choose to join the battle on either side, but their actions would have consequences in their afterlife, where they would be punished or rewarded accordingly. This ongoing struggle between the embodiments of all that is good and all that is evil upsets the world's balance and has colored Iranians' worldview ever since.[5]

With the advent of Islam, this dualism was adapted to the Quran's strict monotheism: God is all-powerful and Satan is a fallen archangel who refused to prostrate before Adam and was punished by God. Then he deceived Adam and Eve with his wiles and caused their ejection from paradise. After the Fall, he was granted permission by God to try and win as many followers as he could until the end of the world. And so the struggle between God's good and Satan's evil continues in the world and in every one of us, who, by undertaking our Greater *Jihad* (struggle—see chapter 4), have to try to fight against our lowly instincts and desires that Satan still uses to deceive humans.[6]

Iranians are on a constant quest for equilibrium. Too much (*efrat*) or too little (*tafrit*) of something can easily upset the balance in one's

body or psychological make-up, in the family, and in society at large. We will now look at how this dualism permeates much of Iranian life.

BLACK OR WHITE?

Chapter 2 discussed three of Hofstede's classification axes—collectivism vs. individualism, quantity vs. quality of life, and hierarchy vs. equality—in Iranian society. Now let's consider another one of his axes, uncertainty avoidance, which refers to the extent a society conditions its members to tolerate uncertainty and ambiguity. Societies with a high uncertainty avoidance score show a tendency toward rules and regulations through which they attempt to minimize uncertainty and impose structure on social situations. Members of such societies are used to laws and rules that regulate aspects of their lives and usually feel uncomfortable in unfamiliar, unusual, or surprising situations. Such societies do not accept change readily and are usually risk-averse. Conversely, societies with a low uncertainty avoidance score have few social rules, their members are at ease in unfamiliar situations, and they are more prepared to take risks.

On a philosophical level, uncertainty avoidance also relates to the human search for the ultimate truth. According to Hofstede, high uncertainty avoidance cultures are absolutist: there is a tendency for absolute truths in the form "there can only be one Truth and we have it." By contrast, cultures with a low uncertainty avoidance score accept and possibly celebrate diverse, even conflicting ideas. People in the former type of culture express emotions openly and their actions are characterized by nervous energy, whereas members of the latter type cultures are not socialized in expressing emotions openly and tend to be more contemplative.

In Hofstede's study (1972), Iranian society scored at fifty-nine on the uncertainty avoidance scale.[7] Various aspects of Iranian life can provide relevant evidence: in earlier chapters we came across numerous rules that regulate social relationships and religious beliefs that distinguish right from wrong. On the other hand, it can also plausibly be argued that Iranian social life allows a much higher uncertainty threshold than an American one. Let us now look at these apparently conflicting views in more detail.

The Iranian educational system, predicated on the principle of one right answer, socializes the young into "certainty" by lowering marks for wrong answers. The system does not reward initiative, creativity, original thought, imagination, critical thinking, or research skills. Even the highly competitive university entrance examination (*concour*) consists of a series of multiple-choice (objective) questions that test everything from physics to Persian literature. Humanities classes (e.g., history, sociology, and religious studies) are taught from set textbooks that present "knowledge" to be learned, but offer little scope for discussion and debate.[8] Rote learning and memorizing are therefore a student's most important skills.

One of the main reasons behind Iranians' difficulty in mastering foreign languages lies precisely here. Learning a foreign language demands creativity, imagination and, above all, the courage to make mistakes, or in a sense, high uncertainty tolerance. Because the educational system penalizes wrong answers, Iranian students generally avoid running the risk of getting something wrong.

However, on the social level Iranians can tolerate a high level of uncertainty. We saw in chapter 3 how Abbas asked Reza for information on bank loans, which Reza interpreted as an indirect request for a loan. Whether Abbas' intention was nothing more than the surface meaning of his question or what Reza understood from it may never be ascertained. Beeman writes that in the United States the successful completion of a communicative event depends on the participants' "knowing the score" and "arriv[ing] at a single set of interpretive criteria for understanding the relationship between form and message content," which he glosses as "certainty."[9]

In Iranian communication such certainty is not always expected or even actively pursued. Interpersonal considerations, adherence to politeness rules, attention to interlocutors' face needs may often supersede the need for certainty or clarity. We also saw how timekeeping and deadlines are flexible (chapter 5) and of how unexpected events and delays beyond one's control are seen as unavoidable, a state of affairs that Iranians are socialized in expecting and participating in. This expectation also contributes to the overall uncertainty (from a foreigner's point of view) which may be disorientating to foreigners, but which Iranians see as a fact of life.

BALANCE

Iranians consider the achievement of balance an ideal to be strived for in all aspects of human existence, and this belief is evident in a variety of practices. In the domestic sphere, this desire for balance is visible in the arrangement of objects. Carpets are often sold in pairs, and they cost more than if sold individually; ornaments, for example, vases, are also bought in pairs and arranged symmetrically. As we saw in chapter 9, the same principle is followed in food combinations and recipes, ensuring bodily health and correct nutrition through the balance of "hot" and "cold" foods.

A similar desire is seen in parents' choice of children's names in a family. Names beginning with the same letter (e.g., Mojgan and Mojdeh), deriving from the same root (e.g., Hassan and Mohsen, from the Arabic triliteral root h-s-n), having the same number of syllables and rhyme (e.g., Majid and Hamid), or being linked in some other way (e.g., Fatemeh and Ali, after the daughter and son-in-law of the Holy Prophet) are all attempts at recreating perfection and reflecting balance.

In speech and writing, binomial expressions are used much more extensively than in English: the collocation of two near synonyms to express a single idea (e.g., "patience and fortitude" and "mercy and kindness") lends a sense of completion to a sentence and creates a pleasing feeling of balance in the mind of speakers and listeners.

BODY VS. SPIRIT

Throughout this book we have seen that Iranian culture has been strongly influenced by Islam. A view derived from Islamic teachings is that body and spirit are complementary and not in opposition to each other. The satisfaction of physical needs should be subject to moderation because the body and its life in the physical world are seen as the means of contributing toward humans' spiritual progress and eventual reunion with God. Thus, activities that could be seen as satisfying bodily needs, for example, eating, drinking, and physical love (the latter always within the framework of marriage) have a spiritual dimension too.

As mentioned in earlier chapters, a visit not culminating in a meal is somehow seen as incomplete, so sharing a meal with relatives becomes a reenactment of close ties, a parallel to the Holy Communion. The act of drinking water, apart from quenching thirst, reminds a believer to offer thanks to God for his blessings and to remember Imam Hossein's suffering. This remembrance connects the drinker with other believers who remember the Imam at that moment, and with the Imam himself and his followers, who, being martyrs are not dead, although they are beyond our view.[10] Iranians find a similar connection in the love between a man and a woman, viewing this as a pale foreshadowing of the love between humans and God and a fleeting foretaste of paradise.

WEALTH VS. PIETY

Based on Islamic teachings and according to the Iranian worldview, there is no incompatibility between piety and wealth.[11] As long as wealth does not lead to waste, extravagance, or ostentation, it is seen as necessary for the smooth functioning of society: a wealthy person can create job opportunities for others and give to charity. In fact, as we saw in chapter 4, paying levies on agricultural produce (*zakât*) and the tithe on one's surplus income (*khoms*) is obligatory for those meeting certain criteria. The payments are based on precise calculations and are spent helping fellow humans. The payment of *zakât* and *khoms* is seen as a debt due to God in return for the material blessings He provides and is made with the intention of worshipping Him.

ZÂHER VS. BÂTEN (EXTERNAL VS. INTERNAL)

The symbolic contrast between the "external" (*zâher/birun*) and "internal" (*bâten/andarun*) aspects of human existence is a potent one in Iranian culture. The two poles exist as physical locations in traditional houses: the *biruni* was the area where guests were entertained and where the family met with others from the outside world, whereas the *andaruni* was the

women's quarters, out of bounds to strangers and *nâmahrams* and only open to the family's men and other women.

In addition, the contrast between *birun/andarun* not only refers to spatial points but also to states of mind. The *zâher* is the external, public aspect of one's existence: the arena of materialism, a space of controlled behavior, correct expression, and politeness, and a mode in which social relationships are delineated and established, where manipulation and *ta'ârof* take place and corrupting influences can take effect. In contrast, the *bâten* is the source of purity and an individual's internal, private world, where one assumes one's own integrity and sincere, true self and the seat of the deepest, sometimes uncontrollable, emotions.[12]

The dominant theme of *zâher* and *bâten* has its roots in mystic practice and poetic expression. In both these areas, the external (*zâher*) is the instrument one has to use to access the deep, internal meanings. Since the *bâten* of individuals is inaccessible, "a deep, dark and secret well," music, poetry, and religious ritual provide a way to express the emotions that lie below the surface.[13]

MYSTICISM (SUFISM, *IRFÂN*)

Wherever you turn, there is the face of God.
　　—The Holy Quran, *sura 2, Baqarah* (The Heifer), verse 115

Mysticism or Sufism (*irfân*) is the mystical branch of Islam that places the emphasis on achieving closeness to God through the purification of the believer's heart, which is the focus of one's existence and understanding and the means of spiritual progress. Since the moment that God blew soul into a lifeless lump of clay to create Adam, every incarnated soul yearns to return to its source, God, and be reunited with Him.

Many people do not understand this yearning for what it is: they seek power, wealth, beauty, and enjoyment as ends in themselves, but when they attain their goals they realize that they haven't found happiness. Others discern earthly life's true purpose as a preparation for the eternal life in the other world and make the Major Struggle (*Jihad –e Akbar*) or

follow the path of spiritual perfection (*soluk*). Their lives' goals are to overcome their moral defects and their attachment to the world. By worshipping God and cleansing their hearts of faults of character, such as arrogance, envy, hypocrisy, backbiting, and anger, their hearts become clear as a polished mirror in which God is reflected.

The mystic, or *âref*, is moved by Divine Love (*eshq*), the desire to be united with God, the Beloved (*ma'shuq*), not by the fear of hell or the hope of paradise. For the mystic, the seeker or lover (*âsheq*) of God, hell's torment lies in the eternal separation from the Beloved and paradise's bliss and the eternal union with Him.[14]

PERSIAN POETRY

Iranian culture is closely linked to classical Persian poetry, which in turn is related to mysticism; in fact, many poets who composed in Persian were practicing mystics themselves. Between the twelfth and the fifteenth centuries, an illustrious line of poets, including Sana'i, Omar Khayyam, Attar, Rumi (*Mowlânâ* or *Mowlavi* in Persian), Hafez, Sa'adi and Jami, created poetic masterpieces that transcend their time and place.

Sa'adi's collections *Bustân* (The Orchard) and *Golestân* (The Rose Garden) contain didactic tales aimed at inculcating virtues such as humility, kindness, wisdom, and common sense. Iranians often use his verses to substantiate an argument, such as "If you don't work hard, you can't find a treasure" (*Naborde ranj, ganj moyasar nemishavad*)—in other words, "No pain, no gain." His famous quatrain beginning "Human beings are members of a whole/ In creation of one essence and soul . . . ," adorns the main entrance of the United Nations headquarters in New York.[15]

Over the years Westerners have related to Persian poets in response to the concerns and literary sensibilities of their times rather than for the intrinsic qualities of the poems themselves. In the nineteenth century Hafez seemed to speak to the romantic mood of the time; in the twentieth century Omar Khayyam's musings were in tune with the aesthetic movement; and now, at the beginning of the third millennium, Rumi's

universality and love for all humanity holds out the hope of spirituality and inner peace to a fragmented world.[16]

OMAR KHAYYAM ON MORTALITY

In kuzeh cho man âseq-e zâri bude ast
Dar band-e sar-e zolf negâri bude ast
In dasteh ke bar gardan-e u mibini
Dast ast ke bar gardan-e yâri bude ast.

This clay jug was once a moaning lover, just like me
Entangled in his lover's tresses, just like me
The handle you can see around the jug's neck
Was once an arm around a lover's neck, just like mine.[17]

But of all the poets who composed in Persian, the one who occupies a special place in every Iranian's heart is Hafez, the thirteenth century mystic who knew the whole Quran by heart (hence his name, which literally means "memorizer of the Quran") and whose works came to be known as the "Quran in the Persian language." A collection of his lyrical poems is found in every Iranian home, and Iranians often turn to it for daily auguries or for seeking advice to problems.

HAFEZ ON A LOVE QUEST

Dard-e eshqi keshide-am ke mapors
Zahr-e hejri cheshide-am ke mapors
Gashte-am dar jahân o âkher kâr
Delbari bargozide-am ke mapors.

The pains of Love that I have suffered, do not ask
The bitter poison that I have tasted, do not ask
I've wandered through the world and in the end
I've chosen a Beloved of whom do not ask.

HOW IRANIANS TAKE A HAFEZ AUGURY

There are different ways of asking Hafez for an augury, but here's a common method.

1. Hold the collection of Hafez's lyrics in your hands.
2. Invoke the name of God ("In the Name of God, the Compassionate, the Merciful") and say a salutation (*salavât*) to the Holy Prophet and his infallible household.
3. Recite a Fatiha prayer (see chapter 4).
4. Address Hafez with the verses, *O Hafez of Shiraz/You who reveal all secrets/I seek an augury/Look down upon me/For the sake of Shâkh-e Nabât*/(name your problem or intention here)/In your kindness/From behind the dark veils of the future/Reveal my good or bad destiny.*
5. Close your eyes and, using your fingernail, select three pages. Your augury is on the previous page of the third page you selected.

Some books contain a page with a grid of numbers corresponding to the numbers of the poems. In this case, close your eyes and let your finger hover over the numbers before choosing one.

*Shâkh-e Nabât was the woman Hafez loved but never married. Thus, her name symbolizes the lover one strives to be united with but who is always out of one's reach.

On a superficial level Persian poetry may seem to be nothing more than endless talk about wine, the state of inebriation, carnal desire, and hopelessness, but layers of multiple meanings lie beneath the words.

For example, in Persian poetry "wine," which is strictly forbidden to Muslims, stands for the ecstasy found in Divine Love. "Drunkard" refers to the mystic who has reached the state of ecstasy, and the "tavern" represents the heart.[17] The ambiguous symbolism of "face of the Beloved" is compounded by the absence of grammatical gender in Persian. In an initial reading the poems may seem to refer to a woman, but they are really referring to the Face of God; "strands of hair," "tresses," "curtains," and "veils" denote worldly objects and ideas that hide, or veil, the face of God, and "perfume" means God's blessing.[19] The cycle of water—with

water evaporating from the ocean, becoming a cloud, falling on the ground as rain and again flowing down to the ocean—is used as an extended metaphor of the soul's journey from separation from God, incarnation, spiritual path, and return to its source.

Classical Iranian poetry as an expression of the *bâten* speaks to all Iranians, regardless of their level of education. It resonates with the depths of their souls, even when the significance cannot be articulated or understood, because it expresses unspoken or indescribable feelings.

One person I spoke with described the Iranian psyche as tender and delicate (*latif*), and felt that this sensitivity was best expressed through figures of speech (metaphors and similes) and symbolism in poetry. Because of its wide appeal, poetry is used extensively: on gravestones, at the very beginning of TV shows and speeches, in daily planners, and in wedding invitations. Poetic themes, images, and allusions find their way into prose, the visual arts, advertising, and everyday speech.

Schooled in the idea that external appearances hide a deeper level of meaning, Iranians tend to look for hidden significance everywhere, from a verse of classical poetry to a politician's speech to a friend's casual remark. In this same way, they also tend to use indirectness when talking and verses of classical poetry or figures of speech to make a point in a roundabout way.

THE CULTURE OF MARTYRDOM

In the Iranian collective consciousness, Imam Hossein's martyrdom at the hands of his enemy's army commander, Yazid, has come to represent the perennial struggle between Yazid's evil (*zâher*) and Imam Hossein's good (*bâten*). In deciding to stand up to Yazid, Imam Hossein not only refused to recognize Yazid's unlawful claim to the Caliphate of the Muslims, but asserted the inner truth of the spiritual leadership that fell to him by virtue of his ancestry as the son of Imam Ali and as the grandson of the Holy Prophet.[20]

Thus, the chest-beating and self-flagellation mourning rituals to the rhythm of a throbbing heart beating in unison with others becomes an assertion of the *bâten's* moral superiority over the oppression of the *zâher*,

opens a pathway to the bâten, and establishes a connection with the Imam, the symbol of the purity of faith.

Imam Hossein's standing up for the truth even though it meant certain death has served as a model that Iranians have emulated during times of suffering, and encourages many to embrace martyrdom in defense of their homeland. During the eight years of the war with Iraq, Imam Hossein's sacrifice was a constant inspiration for the thousands of soldiers who left for the front lines prepared for the ultimate sacrifice.

SPIRITUALITY AND BELIEF IN FATE

Mâ râzi hastim be rezâ-ye Khodâ.

(We are content with whatever God is content with.)
—Iranian saying

Peter Avery writes that the Iranians' remarkable ability to recover after disasters and social turmoil is largely due to their remarkable tolerance and their deep spirituality. He argues that although not every Iranian is a practicing Sufi, every Iranian has some characteristics of a Sufi— forbearance, forgiveness, and love—which provide protection against the adversities of a hostile world.[21] Even those Iranians who don't observe the religious rules to the letter have a deep, unshakable faith in God and show resilience and fortitude. According to the World Values Survey in 2000, Iranian respondents gave the following positive responses to these questions:

Do you believe in God? 99.2 percent (male), 99.7 percent (female)
Do you believe in life after death? 97.3 percent (male), 98 percent (female)
Do you believe that people have a soul? 98.6 percent (male and female)
Do you believe in hell? 98.1 percent (male and female)
Do you believe in heaven? 98.3 percent (male), 98.6 percent (female)

Closely linked to Iranians' belief in God is their belief in fate. Humans know how God wants them to live their lives and they have the choice of

obedience or disobedience. To the extent of exercising their free will, they can determine whether through their actions they will be rewarded with paradise or whether they will taste hell. But certain events in people's lives are clearly beyond their control. A chance encounter with a person who changes one's life, or missing a plane that then crashes into the mountains are all expressions of God's will and fit into the master plan He has for every human. Perhaps the total submission (*tasleem*, from the same root as *Islam*) to God's will is the achievement of balance in a person's character, when his/her *zâher* and *bâten* become the same.[22] It is then that a believer reaches the point of utmost sincerity or unity of thought and action that ultimately leads to a union with God.

EPILOGUE

As we saw in the introduction and throughout the book, Iranian society is now in a transitional phase, so among different social strata, traditional customs and modern practices may be witnessed. Similar to other parts of the world, tradition tends to remain alive for longer in the provinces and among the poorer/working-class urban areas, whereas Western-imported practices first appear among the affluent urban strata and spread elsewhere from there. In the last ten years or so the appearance of the internet and satellite channels has also had a huge influence on popular culture.

After the privations of the Iran–Iraq war and the post-war period, material comfort has increased, sometimes at the expense of human relationships, a change that often becomes the object of regret among middle-aged and older Iranians. They look back at a time only a generation ago when life was simpler.

Twenty years ago not every household, even in Tehran, had a telephone connection; today the landline network covers almost every point in the country and mobile phones are everywhere. Houses were simply furnished with only the essentials, with bedding folded away during the day, so homes were easy to keep clean and tidy (in less affluent urban areas and in the provinces many houses are still organized this way). People owned only essential items, and these were replaced only when they were worn out. Without telephones to help keep in touch, relatives visited each other often and were always prepared to receive visitors with whom they shared their food, whatever it was, without pretensions. Nuclear families spent most of their time together in a large sitting room

where different activities took place side by side: children doing homework, father doing accounts or resting, mother preparing meals or doing handiwork. That was a time when nuclear families were embedded within extended families, their children playing, fighting, and growing up together with their cousins and with other neighborhood children, acquiring life skills for their future adult life. The adults benefited from the elders' life experience, who offered practical help within the extended family. The pressure caused by any problems between spouses was relieved in the presence of relatives and peers and relative harmony was maintained.

In the space of one generation life has become more complicated. Nuclear families, especially in the cities, live on their own, often far from their relatives. As a result, children are deprived of extended contact with their grandparents and cousins, and of the life skills opportunities that such contact afforded them in the past, while adults are sometimes denied the "cushioning" that an elderly presence can provide when relationships become stressed.

Consequently, over the last decade or so the role of family and marriage counselors and psychologists has increased significantly, as old, traditional ways become inadequate in dealing with new realities. These professionals use both Western psychological models and extensive input from religious sources (e.g., The Holy Quran, traditions of the Holy Prophet and the Imams) in offering practical solutions to life's problems. A positive development in this area is the gradual weakening of an older taboo against consulting such professionals, which was often seen as a weakness in one's character, mental health, or degree of piety.

Increased affluence and higher quality of life among some segments of the population have in turn led to raised expectations. House interiors now increasingly resemble Western ones, with display units for china and crystal ornaments, natural and artificial flowers, and all sorts of electrical appliances and media systems. Many children and youngsters own PlayStations, electronic games, and personal computers, which increasingly occupy the time previously filled with human contact. For youngsters, these pastimes provide more entertainment than spending time with the rest of the family.

To meet these new material needs the family's main income needs to be supplemented by the husband taking on a second job, which limits the free time that can be spent with the children and with other relatives. As a result, contact with relatives has become less frequent.

Increased affluence among some groups has given rise to wasteful use of resources, which is often seen as an indication of status. Shared meals with relatives and friends are arranged in advance and tend to be elaborate. This practice, combined with lack of time, makes contact among relatives infrequent and sometimes limits it to a short visit during Noruz (New Year). At a time when the world adjusts its consumption in response to diminishing natural reserves, in Iran a rise in consumerism and often outright waste of energy, fuel, and water that were unknown one generation ago exert increased pressure on already overstretched resources. To educate the public on the optimum use of resources, the Supreme Leader Ayatollah Ali Khamene'i, declared the year 1388 (2009–2010) the Year of Adjustment of Consumption Patterns, and the government has launched a countrywide campaign against wasteful practices.

Technological progress has also had a strong impact on Iranian culture. Two important factors in the last decade have been the widespread use of satellite receivers and Internet usage, which, according to one estimate, is the highest in the Middle East. Just like every new technology can prove both beneficial and harmful, these two new technologies are used inappropriately by many. The term *mâhvâreh* (satellite) has come to connote corrupt influence, especially on the young, for bringing images of Western lifestyles to Iranian families from the most Westernized to the most conservative.

Satellite dishes, although technically forbidden, are everywhere, but instead of being used to access educational programs and reliable news channels, they are generally used to tune in to music, foreign movies, fashion, and commercial channels, and end up influencing fashion, make-up, and hairstyles, and promoting behaviors alien to the Iranian culture.

As in other parts of the world, despite the fact that the Internet can be put to harmful use by unscrupulous people, it provides easy access to information and services: from ayatollahs' websites, through which one

can ask for clarification on religious rulings, to hotel and railway databases that offer online booking facilities. Students can use the Internet to register for the national university entrance examination, and householders can pay bills and manage their bank accounts online, thus alleviating street traffic and congestion in banks and other places.

But among all these shifts, certain aspects of the culture remain constant. Iranians' love for and loyalty to their homeland and pride in their ancient and Islamic cultural and artistic heritage was tested in recent history, when Iran's national sovereignty was compromised by foreign interference, first by Britain and Russia, and then after the Second World War by the United States, which inherited their colonial mantle.[4] This interference, which went on until the victory of the Islamic Revolution and continues still among its neighbors, has engendered distrust of Western powers and continues to color Iran's relationships with them. Iranians resent the negative stereotypes of themselves and their country that are painted by some Western media and governments, and view them with the same distrust.

Iranians also share a strong aspiration for Iran to take its rightful place in the world. During the celebrations for the thirtieth anniversary of the victory of the Islamic Revolution in February 2009, Ayatollah Khamene'i and President Ahmadinejad, in their numerous speeches, spelled out their vision for Iran's future. Iran's achievements in the medical, technological, and scientific fields that took place despite, or possibly because of, the economic sanctions imposed on Iran for the last three decades have given the Iranian nation a strong sense of self-reliance, confidence, and national pride. Iran is on course to become a model for showing the way of progress by sharing its scientific and technological achievements with others and aspires to be a force for the good.[5]

President Ahmadinejad announced that Iran is also a force to be reckoned with in the Middle East,[6] but, he pointed out, Iran sees its role not as a superpower bent on advancing its own interests, but as a leader for peace, friendship, and progress in its neighborhood and the world at large. Iran has now become a key player in promoting just, dignified, and peaceful solutions to the challenges the Middle East faces, not least by making earnest efforts to foster unity among all Muslim peoples.

The Iranian nation has been shaped by history, successive occupations, domestic crises, and foreign intervention, only to rise from the ashes.[7] My prediction is that Iranians will deal with the present challenges as they have done throughout their history and that they will come through as winners. Patience, fortitude, self-reliance, and self-belief, together with their spirituality and resilience, will once again stand them in good stead. Iranian culture will, in time, assimilate external influences and make them its own as it has done many times throughout its long and turbulent history.

Over twenty years ago, as an awkward foreign bride, I needed someone to explain the behaviors I have written about here. As we come to the end of our short journey together, I hope that some of you who picked up this book may become if not warm admirers, then at least better-informed observers of Iran's complex and intriguing culture. Even if we haven't yet touched all the parts of the elephant, at least we now know that they exist.

APPENDIX A

Iran: A Brief History

There is evidence of human settlement in Iran as early as the Neolithic period (about 7,000 B.C.). By 3,000 B.C. the Elamites, who were settled in the east of the country, maintained trade links with the neighboring Sumerians. In the seventh century B.C., extensive military campaigns by the Assyrians put an end to these eastern settlements, but with the decline of Assyrian control, western Iran was dominated by two groups, the Medes and the Persians. These two groups became linked by marriage, and eventually the Persian commander Cyrus II (Cyrus the Great) prevailed over the alliance and extended his control of the west, establishing the Achaemenid dynasty and the first world empire.

THE ACHAEMENID EMPIRE (550–330 B.C.)

This was a time of gradual expansion of Iranian borders westward into Lydian Anatolia, Babylon, and Syria, to Egypt and Ethiopia, into the Balkans and the north of Greece, and eastward into Central Asia— almost to the borders of present-day China. During the reign of Darius the Great (Darius I, who died in 486 B.C.), many architectural and infrastructure projects took place, including the building of the palace

complex in Persepolis. This extensive network of roads linked the regions of the vast empire, and a canal project connecting the Mediterranean and the Red Sea anticipated the Suez Canal by about twenty-four centuries.

Iranians of all persuasions take pride in Cyrus' attitude of religious tolerance and justice shown toward the conquered peoples, who weren't forced to adopt the Zoroastrianism beliefs of the Iranians and continued to be governed mostly by their own rulers.

ALEXANDER OF MACEDON

As the vast empire expanded, some of the conquered lands rose in revolt, gradually weakening Achaemenid power. Realizing his father's Philippus' dream of expanding eastward into Asia, Alexander (*Megas*, "The Great," according to the Greeks), who ruled from 336–323, took Persepolis in 330 B.C. The burning of Persepolis, whether carried out as a deliberate act by Alexander's orders or in a moment of drunken irresponsibility, has remained indelible in collective Iranian memory and has earned Alexander the less-than-coveted title, "accursed" (*guzastag*), which he shares with Ahriman, the embodiment of evil, in later Zoroastrian writings.[1]

AFTER ALEXANDER (323–C. 240 B.C.)

After Alexander's early death, his empire was divided among his successors, with Seleucus I assuming control of Iranian territory and establishing his capital at Ctesiphon, south of Baghdad in today's Iraq, after which the army gradually loosened its grip over the eastern provinces.

THE PARTHIANS (C. 238 B.C.–A.D. 224)

This gave the Parthians, a tribe moving down from the northeast, the opportunity to bid for power over the region. The Parthians went as far as challenging Rome's power by proceeding toward Syria and the Caucasus. An uneasy and delicate balance was established between them,

with sometimes one and sometimes the other side enjoying a short-lived victory. Eventually a new power emerged in the region, the dynasty of the Sassanids, which put an end to Parthian rule.

THE SASSANIDS (A.D. 224–658)

This dynasty, which ruled over Iran for four centuries, was characterized by efficient administration, elaborate court practices, and a concerted effort to salvage what was left of Zoroastrian writings after the destruction of the royal archives by Alexander's army. In an effort to reassert Persian superiority and to formalize Zoroastrianism, the Sassanids undertook persecution of other religious minorities, such as the Jews, Manicheans, Mazdakites, and Christians. This persecution would later play an important role in the expansion of Islam in Iranian lands.

THE ADVENT OF ISLAM

With the Arab conquest between 637–641 A.D., Iranian lands began to be Islamized gradually. This Islamization was a result of several factors. The long-term persecution of non-Orthodox Christians by the Byzantines and of non-Zoroastrians by the Sassanids, as well as heavy taxation imposed on religious minorities,[2] had created resentment among these minorities and prepared the ground for acceptance of the new religion that preached equality among all people and accorded a position of respect to "People of the Book," that is, Jews, Christians, and, later, Zoroastrians.

Persian society at the time had rigid class distinctions with an established aristocracy, which in the mind of the populace contrasted unfavorably with Islam's egalitarianism and simplicity of lifestyle. Another favorable factor was that the Arab conquerors only replaced local rulers with ones of their choice and didn't engage in large-scale forced conversions or mass murder. In addition, numerous elements of Zoroastrianism, Iranians' pre-Islamic religion, such as righteous thought and action, the final judgment, and heaven and hell, were consistent with Islamic beliefs.[3]

THE UMAYYADS AND THE ABBASIDS

For a time Iranian lands were under Arab domination by the Umayyad dynasty (661–750) before giving way to the Abbasids (750–1258). Both dynasties traced their ancestry back to the Holy Prophet's relatives. However, the Iranians resented this rule and during the Abbasid reign, several Iranian local rulers and dynasties reigned over different parts of Iran: the Tahirids (821–872), the Saffarids (861–1003), the Samanids (875–999), the Ziyarids (c. 929–1078), and the Buyids (932–1056).

Despite the political domination by Arab rulers, Iranian presence in the arts and the central administration of the empire ensured that Persian art and culture developed in new ways and in turn influenced newly developing Islamic artistic endeavors.

IRAN'S TURKIC RULERS AND THE
MONGOL INVASIONS

Persian cultural and artistic activities flourished during this period, a blossoming that continued during the rule of the Turkic dynasties of the Ghaznavids (977–1041) and the Seljuks (c. 1035–1194).

It was during this time that the Persian language enjoyed a revival too: it was adopted as the second language of Islamic civilization and was used as the court language as far away as India and in some parts of Asia Minor. Probably the most important literary work of this period is Ferdowsi's *Shâh-nâmeh*, *The Book of Kings*, which contains traditional stories and passages about the lives of Iranian heroes and kings preserved in classical Persian. This book used very few Arabic words, which by Ferdowsi's time had entered the Persian language to a considerable extent.

The 150 years of Seljuk rule was a time of central efficient administration and a strong army. This stability provided fertile ground for the blossoming of architecture and artistic expression, but these were cut short by the Mongol invasion in 1219. There followed a short period of peace during the rule of the Il-Khanids (1258–c. 1350), the name the Mongols adopted in Iran. The Mongols' rule was interrupted by Tamerlane's invasion (1380), which brought widespread death and destruction throughout Iran. His successors proved committed champions of Iranian

culture and art, however, and prepared the ground for the great achievements of the Safavid era.

THE SAFAVIDS (1500–1735)

After the political fragmentation and repeated invasions, the Safavid period is generally considered the beginning of Iran as a state. The glory of the era can be clearly seen in the historic city of Isfahan, where the Safavids had their capital for most of their rule. Under the Safavids, the adoption of the Shi'a branch of Islam as the official state religion proved a potent factor in the political unification of Iran.

NADER SHAH AND THE ZAND DYNASTY (C. 1750–C. 1794)

The Afghan invasion in 1722 brought about a short period of instability in the eastern provinces of Iran until Nader Afshar, an army officer, crowned himself king (1736) and proceeded to conquer parts of Afghanistan and as far as Delhi, but this success was not to last. He was replaced by the Zand dynasty, which ushered in a short-lived period of stability, economic security, and another renaissance of art and architecture.

THE QAJARS (1795–1925)

The Qajar period is generally regarded as a time of large territorial losses, a weakening of the traditional monarchical model, and the introduction of technology and education from the West.

Iranian territory shrank as the early Qajars lost the Caucasus, northern Azerbaijan, and Turkmenistan to Russia and the province of Herat to Afghanistan. Sons of courtiers and other nobility were sent to Europe for their education, and under the influence of the French Revolution returned with ideas that challenged established beliefs that the Shahs derived their power from God. Debate raged until 1906, when Mozaffar od-Din Shah reluctantly agreed to grant a constitution modeled on the Belgian one, but his successor, Mohammad Ali Shah was hostile. After

nationalist forces deposed him, his son Ahmad, then only twelve years old, succeeded to the throne but proved to be a weak monarch.

Eventually he left for Paris, ostensibly for medical treatment, but he was effectively encouraged to abdicate, thus putting an end to the Qajar dynasty. This provided an opportunity for Reza Khan, a brigade commander in the Cossack regiment who had risen through the ranks to the post of Prime Minister, to declare himself Shah and to found a new monarchical line, the Pahlavi dynasty.

THE PAHLAVIS (1925–1979)

Reza Khan sought to unify the various Iranian peoples into one coherent nation. He set out to achieve this by making education in Persian universal and compulsory, introducing reforms in dress, and carrying out infrastructure projects such as all-weather roads, and Iran's first railway line, which established easier links between the capital and the provinces.

He perhaps became too ambitious, seeing racial affinity between the German race and the Iranians, who both descended from Aryan peoples, and adopted a pro-German stance during the Second World War. As a result, under British and Soviet pressure, he decided to abdicate (1941) in order to pass the crown on to his son Mohammad Reza and ensure the continuation of the Pahlavi dynasty.

After the end of the Second World War, British influence and control of the important Iranian oil and petroleum resources, which had begun in the nineteenth century, gradually lessened, and was gradually replaced by influence from the United States. When the nationalist Prime Minister Mossadeq, in charge of the only democratically elected government in Iran before the Islamic Revolution, took the bold step of nationalizing Iran's oil and petroleum industry, the U.S.'s Central Intelligence Agency (CIA) and the British Secret Intelligence Service (SIS) planned his fall and consolidated Mohammad Reza's power. This event remains alive in Iranian collective memory as a prime example of foreign intervention in the fortunes of the country and as justification of the doubt and skepticism with which Iranians still view Western powers.

The Shah then launched a "White Revolution," which involved land redistribution. This should, in principle, have benefited peasants, but it

resulted in more hardship for them while granting more privileges to the rich. Gradually the Shah became dictatorial, repressing opposition from religious circles and leftist organizations, while spending the ever-increasing revenue from oil sales on armament programs and on supporting a luxurious lifestyle, while maintaining that he worked toward Iran's modernization. Iranians feel that his delusion and megalomania reached its peak in 1971, when he organized a so-called celebration of 2,500 years of continuous Persian rule in Iran, starting the reckoning from the ascension of Cyrus the Great to the throne. According to this calculation, the Iranian solar year 1355 became 2535, in effect dismissing the nation's Muslim heritage and according more importance to its pre-Islamic, imperial history.

As the years went by the Shah increasingly targeted the clergy and religious institutions and gradually lost popular support. In the last years of his reign public unrest grew, and despite desperate efforts to bring the country under control by declaring martial law and indiscriminate killing of demonstrators, he left Iran on January 16, 1979 and died in exile in Egypt the following year.

THE ISLAMIC REPUBLIC (EST. 1979)

On February 1, 1979, after 15 years in exile, Imam Khomeini (often called Ayatollah Khomeini in the West) returned to Iran. With general popular backing he began work toward establishing the world's first Islamic republic, based on the doctrine of *velâyat-e faqih* (regency of the jurist, Islamic government; see chapter 4).

Since the victory of the Islamic Revolution, Iran and the United States have been locked in a position of mistrust that continues to the present. The roots of this mistrust run deep and are more extensive than many think,[4] but certain events stand out in Iranian collective memory. In October 1979 a group of revolutionaries and students took over the American Embassy in Tehran and held the staff hostage for 444 days, an event that according to some analysts brought about the fall of President Carter's administration.

A year-and-a-half later Saddam Hussein, taking advantage of the political change in Iran, attacked Iran in an attempt to claim oil-rich

southwestern Iran. During the war, referred to as "The Imposed War" by Iranians, who were simply defending their country, Western powers supplied Saddam Hussein with modern weaponry, including chemical weapons, while the Iranian army equipped with American weapons purchased by the Shah had no access to spare parts under the U.S. embargo.[5]

In July 1988, the USS *Vincennes* shot down an Iran Air passenger aircraft killing all 250 people on board, a traumatic event for which the U.S. not only did not apologize, but responded with self-justifications and inaccuracies, later conferring a campaign medal on the *Vincennes* commander.[6]

After eight years of heavy material losses and human casualties, Imam Khomeini was persuaded to accept a ceasefire in August 1988. Ten months later, in June 1989, the Imam passed away and a new period in the life of the Islamic Republic began, with the election of Ali Khamene'i, who held the presidency at the time, to succeed the Imam in the position of the Supreme Leader. Ali Hashemi Rafsanjani, a veteran of the Islamic Revolution was then elected president, a post he held for two terms (1989–1997). A shrewd politician and a pragmatist, Rafsanjani attempted a shake-up of the economy and favored more open relations with the West, but his reforms were not a successful as he anticipated. In 1997 in a landslide victory Seyed Mohammad Khatami, another progressive, urbane and Western–educated cleric, was elected president on a platform of domestic reform and conciliation with the West.

In Chapter 1 it was mentioned that the 1979 Constitution which was voted after the Islamic Revolution instituted the division of power among different bodies in order to ensure that no individual or body would ever be able to seize absolute power. In practice, this means that a fine balance must always be struck between progressive and conservative elements within the system, and that this safety valve of the Islamic Republic has often led to the blocking of initiatives from one governmental body, e.g. the parliament, by another, e.g. the Assembly of Experts.

By the end of the second term of Khatami's presidency (1997–2005), the promised reforms had not come. Then, in a similar landslide victory, Mahmoud Ahmadinejad, the then mayor of Tehran, was elected president in 2005, and again in 2009.[7]

The Solar and Lunar Calendars and Public Holidays

THE SOLAR CALENDAR AND PUBLIC HOLIDAYS

The Islamic solar year *anno Persico* (A.P.) is used for governmental and administrative purposes in Iran. The solar year 1389 begins on March 21, 2010.

Spring

> *Farvardin* (March 21–April 20): March 21–April 2, New Year holiday (*Noruz*); April 1, Islamic Revolution Day (*Ruz-e Jomhuri-ye Eslâmi-ye Irân*); April 2, Nature Day (*Sizdeh Be Dar*)
> *Ordibehesht* (April 21–May 21): May 21, end of school year
> *Khordâd* (May 22–June 21): end-of-school year examinations in all schools; June 4, Anniversary of Imam Khomeini's death (*Rehlat-e Hazrat-e Imâm Khomeini*).

Summer

Tir (June 22–July 22)
Mordâd (July 23–August 22)
Shahrivar (August 23–September 22)

Autumn

Mehr (September 23–October 22): September 23, schools reopen
Âbân (October 23–November 21)
Âzar (November 22–December 20)

Winter

Dey (December 21–January 19)
Bahman (January 20–February 21): February 2, anniversary of the
   Islamic Revolution (*Piruzi Enghelâb Eslâmi*)
Esfand (February 22–March 20): March 20, nationalization of the oil
   industry (*Melli-shodan-e san'at-e naft-e Irân*)

THE LUNAR CALENDAR AND PUBLIC HOLIDAYS

Iran uses the Islamic lunar calendar (*anno Hegirae*) for observing religious holidays. The Islamic lunar year 1431 begins on December 18, 2009
and 11 days earlier every year thereafter. The usual Arabic spelling for
each month is given below in parentheses if it differs from the Persian
spelling.

Moharram (*Muharram*): 9 and 10, martyrdom of Imam Hossein
Safar: 20, forty-day ceremony of Imam Hossein's martyrdom; 28,
   death of the Holy Prophet and martyrdom of Imam Hassan; 30,
   martyrdom of Imam Reza
Rabi ol-avval (*Rabi ul-awwal*)
Rabi os-sâni (*Rabi uth-thâni*)
Jamadi ol-avval (*Jumadi ul-awwal*): 17, Holy Prophet's birthday
Jamadi os-sâni (*Jumadi uth-thâni*): 3, martyrdom of the Holy Fatima

Rajab: 13, Imam Ali's Birthday; 27, beginning of the Holy Prophet's mission

Sha'bân: 15, birthday of the twelfth Imam, Imam Mahdi

Ramezân (*Ramadân*): the month of fasting; 21, martyrdom of Imam Ali

Shavvâl (*Shawwâl*): 1, Eid Fitr (Feast of the end of Ramadan) I spell the name of the month as 'Ramadan' here, because it is the standard form in English.

Zil Qadeh (*Dhu'l Qa'dah*): 25, martyrdom of Imam Ja'afar Sadeq

Zil Hajjeh (*Dhu'l Hijjah*): the month of the annual pilgrimage to Mecca; 10, Eid Qorbân (Feast of Sacrifice); 18, Eid Ghadir Khom (Feast of Ghadir Khom [a location in today's Saudi Arabia; the story is explained in chapter 4)

APPENDIX C

The Holy Imams

	Name	Title(s)	Died	Buried in
1	Ali	Al-Mortezâ	A.H.* 40 (A.D. 662)	Najaf, Iraq
2	Hassan	Al-Mojtabâ	A.H. 50 (A.D. 672)	Jannat-ul-Baqi cemetery, Medina, Saudi Arabia
3	Hossein	Sayed-ush-Shohadâ	A.H. 61 (A.D. 683)	Karbala, Iraq
4	Ali	Zain-ul-Âbedin	A.H. 95 (A.D. 717)	Jannat-ul-Baqi cemetery, Medina, Saudi Arabia
5	Mohammad	Al-Bâqer	A.H. 116 (A.D. 738)	Jannat-ul-Baqi cemetery, Medina, Saudi Arabia
6	Ja'afar	As-Sâdeq	A.H. 148 (A.D. 770)	Jannat-ul-Baqi cemetery, Medina, Saudi Arabia

	Name	Title(s)	Died	Buried in
7	Musâ	Al-Kâzem	A.H. 183 (A.D. 805)	Kazemain, Baghdad, Iraq
8	Ali	Ar-Rezâ	A.H. 203 (A.D. 825)	Mashhad, Iran
9	Mohammad	Taqi, Al-Javâd	A.H. 220 (A.D. 842)	Kazemain, Baghdad, Iraq
10	Ali	An-Naqi, Al-Hâdi	A.H. 254 (A.D. 876)	Samarra, Iraq
11	Hassan	Al-Askari	A.H. 260 (A.D. 882)	Samarra, Iraq
12	Mohammad	Al-Mahdi, Imam Zamân, Sâheb-ul Amr, Al-Hojjat	Still living	First heavenly concealment: A.H. 260 (A.D. 882) Final heavenly concealment: A.H. 328 (A.D. 950)

*A.H. (*anno Hegirae*) is the Islamic lunar year.
Based on information from *Know Your Islam* by Yusuf N. Laljee.

Although all twelve Imams form an unbroken chain of divine guidance until the end of time, the lives of some of them are better known and have become part of Shi'a collective consciousness. Here follows selected information on some Imams whose presence has an impact on Iranian everyday life and culture.

The Imams Ali, Hassan, and Hossein
The first Imam, Ali, was a live repository of divine knowledge and wisdom, but his right to the leadership of the Muslims was bypassed in favor of other companions of the Holy Prophet. For a long time he chose not to assert his right in order to avoid a breach among the nascent Muslim community, until he was chosen as the Fourth Caliph. He was assassinated in the month of Ramadan by a former supporter; the day of his

martyrdom coincides with one of the three "Nights of Power," the odd-numbered nights near the end of Ramadan, on which the first Quranic revelation may have descended. His son Hassan chose a conciliatory stance towards Mu'awiyah, the unjust ruler who usurped power after Imam Ali's death, but only temporarily and in order to avoid a civil war among the young Islamic community.

Hassan's brother Hossein, the third Imam, chose a different approach: military confrontation with Yazid, Mu'awiyah's son, which resulted in a massacre in the desert of Karbala, now near the city by the same name in Iraq. This event, in which Imam Hossein, along with 72 members of his family and loyal companions were cut off from water supplies for three days before being killed in battle on the 10th of Moharram 61 A.H. (A.D. 683), is one of the most significant events in the Shi'a calendar. The martyrdom on the day of Âshurâ (meaning "tenth") embodies the perennial battle between good and evil and the eventual triumph of good. Even though the Imam and his followers were martyred, they gained entrance to paradise, and their message of standing up to oppression is immortalized in believers' hearts. Although their enemies enjoyed a temporary triumph in Karbala, their abominable actions of killing the Holy Prophet's grandson earned them hell's punishment and the abomination of believers for evermore (see chapter 11).

The memory of Imam Hossein's martyrdom is kept alive every year in the month of Moharram. For the first ten days of the month believers gather in prayer halls, mosques, and makeshift tents in the streets where they participate in mourning ceremonies, ritual chest-beating, and lamentations, as well as processions that march through the streets carrying battle standards. At the end of every ceremony, cooked food that has been offered as a pledge (*nazr*) to Imam Hossein is distributed to participants and to the poor. Shi'as believe that Imam Hossein is the host of this ceremony and undertake the preparations in his name, and that consuming this food has healing properties. They feel that by mourning for the martyred Imam, feeding mourners in his name, or slaking their thirst, they receive blessings and divine reward.

But remembering Imam Hossein is not confined to one month in the year: he is also recognized through everyday acts. Drinking fountains on pavements are dedicated to Imam Hossein's memory, and passersby

who quench their thirst remember Imam Hossein's suffering and send salutations to him, with some of the heavenly reward (*savâb; thawâb* in Arabic) being apportioned to the person who provided the drinking fountain. Many cars carry stickers with invocations to Hossein, such as, "Peace be upon you, Prince of the Martyrs" and "All my life belongs to Hossein."

Imam Reza

Imam Reza, the eighth Imam, is the only one buried in Iran, in the eastern city of Mashhad. The extensive complex of his shrine, comprising several mosques and courtyards, museum, bookshop, religious seminary, and bazaar, is the object of a minor pilgrimage that many Iranians undertake. Visiting the Imam's grave (*ziârat*) and facilitating a pilgrim's visit are both acts of piety attracting divine reward.

Imam Mahdi

The last of the spiritual leaders, Imam Mahdi or Imam Zamân (The Imam of Time), is believed to be still alive but hidden, having gone into occultation in 939 A.D., similar to Jesus Christ's bodily ascension to heaven. When God decides that the time has come, Imam Mahdi (and Jesus Christ) will return to dispense justice before the Day of Judgment. The expectation of the Imam's return and the beginning of his just government is a potent feeling among Muslims, with many of their supplications asking God to hasten his reappearance, which, it is believed, will happen on a Friday. This expectation is a source of hope for many. A sticker on a car's back window muses, "He might come this Friday . . . he might . . ." (*Shâyad in jom'e biayad, shâyad . . .*).

Even though Imam Mahdi is hidden does not mean he is out of touch with his community. He is believed to listen to the supplications of believers and to extend his protection over them. Another sign on a back windshield reads: "Insured by Imam Zamân."

NOTES

INTRODUCTION

1. The story is quoted in Imam Khomeini's *Forty Hadith Collection*, Hadith 19. An English translation can be found at *www.al-islam.org/fortyhadith*
2. Ervand Abrahamian, *A History of Modern Iran* (Cambridge: Cambridge University Press, 2008: p. 180 (hereafter cited as Abrahamian 2008).

CHAPTER 1

1. For a brief introduction to Iranian flora and fauna see *Iran: The Bradt Guide* by Patricia L. Baker, pp. 4–6. (hereafter cited as Baker 2005)
2. Abrahamian 2008: p. 86.
3. Page 221 of *The Persian Sea* by Manouchehr Tayyab (Tehran: Ketab-e Khorshid Publications, 2007) mentions that the name "Persian Gulf" (*Sinus Persicus*) appears in a map by Claudius Ptolemaeus (second century A.D.). The name "Sinus Arabicus" (Arabic Gulf) is used for the Red Sea on that map.
4. For more detailed treatment, see Abrahamian 2008, pp. 162–169; Beeman 2005, pp. 194–203.

CHAPTER 2

1. In response to the question "How important is service to others?" Sixty percent of Iranian males and sixty-five percent of females said "very important," while another thirty-five percent of males and thirty percent of females said, "rather important." (Source: World Values Survey 2000.)
2. This is a complex concept simplified for the purposes of this book. See, for example, Bateson, Margaret et al., "Safâ-yi Bâtin: A Study of the Interrelations of a Set of Iranian Ideal Character Types" in *Psychological Dimensions of Near Eastern Studies*, edited by L. C. Brown and J. Itzkowitz, Princeton, NJ: Darwin Press, 1977, p. 263 (hereafter cited as Bateson et al 1977).
3. The Holy Quran, sura 4 *Nisâ* (Women), verses 22–24.

4. Hofstede's Model of Cultural Dimensions has been used extensively in the analysis of cultures, but, as with all studies of culture that draw generalizations, a few reservations should be borne in mind. As I pointed out in the Introduction, every analysis of culture identifies tendencies, not absolutes, and should be used as a general guide and not as a statement with the application of natural law. Cultural differences exist even within very small communities, many more across large nations, and within those there are individuals who do not fit into the pattern.

   Another general reservation relates to the use of questionnaires as a method a data collection. As mentioned in my Ph.D. thesis (*The Persian system of politeness and the Persian folk concept of face, with some reference to EFL teaching to Iranian native speakers*, University of Wales College of Cardiff, 1997, chapter 3, hereafter cited as Koutlaki 1997), despite the obvious advantage of questionnaires in gathering a large body of data in a short time, studies have documented that reported and actual behavior often diverge, with responses reflecting prescribed rather than actual behavior.

   Thirdly, in Hofstede's specific study of Iranian culture, data were collected in 1972 and although I do not wish to argue against the general validity of the study's results, the time lapse is nonetheless significant.

5. Koutlaki, Sofia A. 1997; "Offers and Expressions of Thanks as Face Enhancing Acts: Ta'ârof in Persian," in *Journal of Pragmatics* 34: 2002, pps. 1733–1756, (hereafter cited as Koutlaki 2002); "Two Sides of the Same Coin: How the Notion of 'Face' is Encoded in Persian Communication," in *Face, Communication and Social Interaction*, edited by F. Bargiela-Chiappini and M. Haugh, London: Equinox Press., 2009 (hereafter cited as Koutlaki 2009).

6. In fact, an abundance of stories from the lives of the Holy Prophet and Imam Ali relate how they gladly took on such tasks, thereby setting an example for all believers.

7. The Iranian year 1388 (2009–2010) has been named Year of Adjustment of Consumption Patterns in an attempt to address waste and to promote responsible use of resources.

8. Beeman, William O., "Emotion and Sincerity in Persian Discourse: Accomplishing the Representation of Inner States." *The International Journal of the Sociology of Language* 148, 2001, p. 40 (hereafter cited as Beeman 2001). To read more about this, see William Beeman's *The "Great Satan" vs. the "Mad Mullahs": How the United States and Iran Demonize Each Other*, Westport, Connecticut and London: Praeger, 2005, pp. 52, 101, 121, and passim, (hereafter cited as Beeman 2005).

9. Erving Goffman has written extensively on face. See, e.g., *The Presentation of Self in Everyday Life*. New York: Doubleday, 1959 (hereafter cited as Goffman 1959); *Interaction Ritual: Essays on Face-to-Face Behavior*. New York: Doubleday, 1967, pp. 7–10, 14 (hereafter cited as Goffman 1967); "On Face-work: an Analysis of Ritual Elements in Social Interaction." In *Communication in Face-to-Face Interaction*, edited by J. Laver and S. Hutcheson. Harmondsworth: Penguin, 1972, p. 322, (hereafter cited as Goffman 1972).

10. See my 1997, 2002, 2009.

11. For an English translation of Imam Khomeini's *Forty Hadith*, see *www.al-islam .org/fortyhadith*. Hadith number 19 deals with backbiting.

12. Sales blurb on *www.boomcat.com*, accessed on March 10, 2009.

13. Mir-Hosseini Ziba, *Islam and Gender: The Religious Debate in Contemporary Iran.* London: I. B. Tauris 1999, p. xviii.

CHAPTER 3

1. World Values Survey 2000.
2. In fact, historically, English had a familiar second person pronoun too. Remember *thee, thou,* and *thine* when you studied Shakespeare at school or in the King James' Bible? This was the English familiar pronoun with a similar distribution, respectively, to children, servants, and God, which has now disappeared.
3. Keshavarz Mohammad Hossein, "Forms of address in post-revolutionary Iranian Persian: A sociolinguistic analysis," in *Language in Society* 17, 1988, p. 570; Beeman 1986, pp. 147–151.
4. Sura 50, *Qaf* ([The Letter] Qaf) verse 16.
5. Malinowski, Bronislaw, "The Problem of Meaning in Primitive Languages." in *The Meaning of Meaning*, edited by C. K. Ogden and I. A. Richards. London: Routledge & Kegan Paul 1923; "Phatic Communion," in *Communication in Face-to-Face Interaction*, edited by J. Laver and S. Hutcheson. Harmondsworth: Penguin 1972; Laver, John, "Communicative Functions of Phatic Communion." In *Organization of Behavior in Face-to-Face Interaction*, edited by A. Kendon, R. M. Harris, and M. Ritchey Key. The Hague & Paris: Mouton Publishers, 1975.
6. Beeman 1986, pp. 176–177.
7. Until very recently Iranians did not depend on the telephone to communicate with government offices. Instead, they would go there in person, even just to request information. This practice is slowly changing as a result of a governmental drive to reduce traffic, gas consumption, and, consequently, pollution.
8. For a comparison between American and Iranian telephone sequences, see Beeman 1986, pp. 180–181.
9. Beeman 1986, pp. 185–186.
10. Ibid., p. 56.
11. Rafiee Abdorreza, *Variables of Communicative Incompetence in the Performance of Iranian Learners of English and English Learners of Persian.* Unpublished Ph.D. thesis, University of London, 1992, pp. 85–86.

CHAPTER 4

1. It is customary among pious Muslims to say salutations after every mention of the names of the Holy Prophet, the prophets that preceded him (e.g., Moses, David, Jesus), his daughter Fatemeh Zahra, and the Holy Imams. In English texts this salutation may appear as *pbuh* (Peace Be Upon Him/Her) or *s*, from the first letter of the salutation in Arabic. To avoid repetition here, the salutation is implied if not actually present throughout this text.
2. This book includes a necessarily brief treatment of a vast subject and touches only upon points that are helpful in understanding Iranian culture. There are many introductory books on Islam, including Haeri Shaykh Fadhlallah, *The Elements of Islam.*

Shaftesbury: Element Books, 1993 (hereafter cited as Haeri 1993); Ruthven, Malise, *Islam: A Very Short Introduction*, Oxford: Oxford University Press, 1997, (hereafter cited as Ruthven 1997); Tabataba'i Ayatollah Sayyid Muhammad Husayn, *Islamic Teachings In Brief*, translated by Muzhgan Jalali. Qom: Ansariyan Publications 1980.
3. Indicatively, see Haeri 1993, chapter 3; Ruthven 1997, chapter 3, and Baldock John, *The Essence of Sufism*. London: Arcturus, 2004, pp. 50, 113 (hereafter cited as Baldock 2004).
4. The majority of Iranian Shi'as belongs to the Ithna-'Ashari branch, or Twelver Shi'as, which acknowledges all twelve imams. Other branches of Shi'ism do not recognize all twelve Imams.
5. Haeri 1993:38.
6. Baldock 2004:55.
7. The Holy Quran, sura 5 *Al Mâ'ida* (The Table Spread), verse 32, translation by T.B. Irving.
8. Haeri 1993, 43, Catherwood Christopher, *A Brief History of the Middle East*. London: Robinson, 2006, p. 75. See also the discussion of mysticism in chapter 11. For a more detailed treatment of the basic practices of Islam, see Haeri 1993, Ruthven 1997, Baldock 2004.
9. There is a multitude of English translations (or rather interpretations, since according to orthodox belief, the Quran is untranslatable) by Muslims and non-Muslims. Abdullah Yusuf Ali's well-known version with detailed commentary follows a Biblical style, A. J. Arberry's version attempts to reproduce the rhythm and the resonance of the original in flowing English without the distraction of footnotes, while T. B. Irving's rendition is probably the most accessible, in simple, everyday language.
10. For a detailed account of the history of the Noruz festival, Shab-e Yalda, and related customs, see Shaida Margaret, *The Legendary Cuisine of Persia*. Henley-on-Thames: Lieuse Publications 1992, (hereafter cited as Shaida 1992)

CHAPTER 5

1. See my 2000 article for such an extended sequence.
2. For a detailed discussion of the Bazaar's involvement in Iranian social and political fortunes, see Hiro Dilip, *Iran Today*, London: Politico's 2005, chapter 1.
3. For more up-to-date information on such opportunities contact the Commercial Sections of Iranian Embassies abroad and go to *www.irantender.com*, which includes information on many practical issues, such as how to get a visa, Iranian embassies and consulates abroad, the banking system, airports and transportation, Free Trading Zones, and much more. The website *www.irxp.com/fairs/info* also contains information and contacts on upcoming international expositions and fairs in Iran.

CHAPTER 6

1. The Holy Quran, sura 24, *Nur* (Light), verses 30–31.
2. World Values Survey 2000.
3. Abrahamian 2008, p. 95.

CHAPTER 7

1. According to UNICEF statistics, in 2001 the literacy rate of Iranians over age six was 80.4 percent (85.1 percent for men and 75.6 percent for women). The gap between urban and rural areas has narrowed by fourteen percent (86.25 percent urban vs. 72.4 percent rural). The net school enrollment ratio is almost 98 percent and approximately equal among girls and boys. (Source: *www.unicef.org/infoby-country/iran.html.*)
2. Shaida 1992:10–11; Fani K., *Medicine and Medication, in The Splendour of Iran*, vol. 3, London: Booth-Clibborn Editions 2001.
3. The Middle Ages theory of humors showed the direct relationship to this ancient system.
4. Dabashi Hamid, *Iran: A People Interrupted*. New York, London: The New Press 2007, p. 144.
5. Baker 2005, p. 29.
6. The information presented has been compiled from various printed and online media including the daily newspapers *Iran Daily* (in English), *Siasat-e Rooz* (in Persian), the websites *www.middle-east-online.com*, *www.iran-daily.com*, *www.boston.com*, and *www.mondediplo.com/2008/04/15iran*, and a feature by Patricia Khashayar dated 27 Bahman 1387 (February 15, 2009) on the English section of the Siasat-e Rooz website.
7. *www.boston.com/news/world/middleeast/articles/2006/08/22*. Accessed March 18, 2009.
8. See Nomani Farhad and Sohrab Behdad, *Class and Labor in Iran: Did the Revolution Matter?* Syracuse, NY: Syracuse University Press, 2006, p. 66: Total population in 1976 was 33 million, in 1986 49.5 million, and 60 million in 1996.
9. Abrahamian 2008, p. 84.
10. *Iran Daily*, "Health Sector Performance Exemplary," February 7, 2009.
11. *www.mondediplo.com/2008/04/15iran*, accessed March 18, 2009.

CHAPTER 8

1. Beeman 1986, p. 47.
2. Golden Azadi coins are similar to British golden sovereigns in that converting money into Azadi coins is a way of maintaining the value of one's savings during times of inflation, as their value fluctuates only slightly according to market conditions. They come in three denominations (whole, half and quarter) and are always exchangeable for cash.
3. Once again, this is a simplified account of a controversial social issue. Indicatively, see Mir-Hosseini Ziba. 1993. *Marriage on Trial: A Study of Islamic Family Law: Iran and Morocco Compared*. London: I. B. Tauris 1993 and Mir-Hosseini 1999, the latter containing a comprehensive bibliography.

CHAPTER 9

1. Islamic dietary prohibitions bear close similarities to Jewish ones. See Douglas Mary, *Purity and Danger*. London: Routledge and Kegan Paul (1966) 2002 edition, pp. 51–71.

CHAPTER 10

1. The Holy Quran, sura 2, *Baqarah* (The Heifer), verses 255–257, translation by T.B. Irving.

CHAPTER 11

1. Bateson et al 1977, p. 262.
2. Abrahamian 2008, pp. 194–195.
3. Public meeting organized by the *Don't Attack Iran* Coalition, School of Oriental and African Studies, University of London, July 10, 2008.
4. Bateson et al. 1977, pp. 261–262.
5. For a more detailed exposition of the development of the Zoroastrian faith, see Axworthy Michael *Iran: Empire of the Mind*. New York: Basic Books, 2008, pp. 5–9.
6. See also Beeman 2005, p. 122.
7. The results can be seen at *www.geert-hofstede.com/hofstede_iran.shtml*. Again, keep in mind the significance of such results; see chapter 2, endnote 4.
8. However, it should by no means be assumed that Iranians accept everything unthinkingly. In fact, traditional learning methods in religious seminaries (*howzeh*) include *mobâheseh* (discussion) and *monâzereh* (debate, disputation), which require logical reasoning, analogies, and other analytical skills to arrive at rigorous conclusions. In fact, one of the positive effects of the Islamic Revolution has been the development of political conscience and cultural awareness among the vast majority of Iranians. Recent social and cultural changes and the effects of globalization engender lively debates on politics, globalization, the erosion of Iranian culture by Westernization, family relationships, issues relating to young people and marriage, and the interface of Islam and aspects of modernity in an attempt to reach consensus and pave the way for solutions.
9. Beeman 1986, p. 22.
10. See sura 2, *Baqarah* (The Heifer), verse 154: "And say not of those who are slain in the way of Allah: 'They are dead.' Nay, they are living, though ye perceive (it) not." and sura 3, *Âl Imrân* (The House of Imran): verse 169.
11. Compare to St. Matthew 6:24: "No man can serve two masters . . . Ye cannot serve God and mammon."
12. Beeman has written extensively on this important distinction. See, e.g., 1974, pp. 275–276; 1986, pp. 72–79; 2001, pp. 38–39; 2005, pp. 24, 27, 28, 100.
13. Beeman 1986, pp. 70.
14. Once more, this account of a vast subject is much too brief and necessarily oversimplified. For more details see two excellent introductions, Baldock 2004; Chittick C. William. *Sufism*. Oxford: Oneworld Publications, 2000. Seyed Hossein Nasr has also written extensively on Islamic mysticism.
15. For the complete poem with its English translation, see Axworthy 2008, pp. 111–112.
16. Axworthy 2008, p. 116.

17. The translation of the Khayyam and Hafez quatrains is mine. Shakespeare expressed a similar idea in *Hamlet*, V, i, 200–211, that of Alexander's or Caesar's dust being used to seal a barrel or a hole in the wall.
18. Baldock 2004, pp. 77–78.
19. Ibid., p. 79.
20. Beeman 1986, p. 71; Beeman 2005, p. 24.
21. *The Splendour of Iran*. Three volumes. 2001. London: Booth-Clibborn Editions 2001 vol. 3, p. 381.
22. Bateson et al. 1977, pp. 269–270; Beeman 2005, p. 26.

EPILOGUE

3. Beeman 2005, p. 205.
4. See the article dated February 2009 in *www.wbeeman.blogspot.com*. Also see Hiro 2005 chapters 3 and 4, Abrahamian 2008, chapters 4 and 5, and Axworthy 2008 chapter 7.
5. See the February 2009 article at *www.wbeeman.blogspot.com*.
6. See also Abrahamian 2008, p. 194.
7. Beeman 2005, pp. 50, 121.

APPENDIX A

1. Axworthy 2008, p. 32.
2. Baker 2005, p. 10.
3. Axworthy 2008, p. 77.
4. See Beeman 2005 for a very useful overview.
5. For a detailed exposition of the Iran-Iraq War, see Hiro 2005, chapter 8.
6. Axworthy 2008, pp. 273–4; Beeman 2005, p. 132
7. This historical note has been compiled using information from Abrahamian 2008, Axworthy 2008, Baker 2005, Hiro 2005, the Historical Note from *The Splendour of Iran* Volume 3.

BIBLIOGRAPHY

QURAN TRANSLATIONS

Abdullah, Yusuf Ali. 1934. *The Holy Quran: Text, Translation and Commentary*. Durban, South Africa: Islamic Propagation Centre International.

Arberry, Arthur J. 1964. *The Koran Interpreted*. Oxford: Oxford University Press.

Irving, T. B. (Al-Hajj Ta'lim Ali) 1998. *The Qur'an: Text, Translation and Commentary*. Tehran: Suhrawardi Research and Publication Center.

GENERAL BIBLIOGRAPHY

Abrahamian, Ervand. 2008. *A History of Modern Iran*. Cambridge: Cambridge University Press.

Avery, Peter. 2001. "The Shaping of Iran's Character." In *The Splendour of Iran*, vol. 3. London: Booth-Clibborn Editions.

Axworthy, Michael. 2008. *A History of Iran: Empire of the Mind*. Harmondsworth: Penguin.

Baker, Patricia L. 2005. *Iran: The Bradt Guide*, Second edition. Bradt Travel Guides, UK; The Globe Pequot Press Inc., USA.

Baldock, John. 2004. *The Essence of Sufism*. London: Arcturus.

Bateson, Margaret C., J. W. Clinton, J. B. M. Kassarjian, H. Safavi, and M. Soraya. 1977. "Safa-yi Batin: A Study of the Interrelations of a Set of Iranian Ideal Character Types." In *Psychological Dimensions of Near Eastern Studies*, edited by L. C. Brown and J. Itzkowitz. Princeton, NJ: Darwin Press.

Beeman, William O. 1974. "The Hows and Whys of Persian Styles: A Pragmatic Approach." In *Studies in Language Variation*, edited by R. W. Fasold and R. W. Shuy. Washington, DC: Georgetown University Press.

Beeman, William O. 1986. *Language, Status and Power in Iran*. Bloomington, IN: Indiana University Press.

Beeman, William O. 2001. "Emotion and Sincerity in Persian Discourse: Accomplishing the Representation of Inner States." *The International Journal of the Sociology of Language* 148 (2001): 31–57.

Beeman, William O. 2005. *The "Great Satan" vs. the "Mad Mullahs": How the United States and Iran Demonize Each Other.* Westport, CT and London: Praeger.

Catherwood, Christopher. 2006. *A Brief History of the Middle East.* London: Robinson.

Chittick, C. William. 2000. *Sufism.* Oxford: Oneworld Publications.

Dabashi, Hamid. 2007. *Iran: A People Interrupted.* New York, London: The New Press.

Douglas, Mary. 1966, reprinted 2002. Purity and Danger. London: Routledge and Kegan Paul.

Fani, K. 2001. "Medicine and Medication." In *The Splendour of Iran*, vol. 3. London: Booth-Clibborn Editions.

Goffman, Erving. 1959. *The Presentation of Self in Everyday Life.* New York: Doubleday.

Goffman, Erving. 1967. *Interaction Ritual: Essays on Face-to-Face Behavior.* New York: Doubleday.

Goffman, Erving. 1972. "On Face-work: an Analysis of Ritual Elements in Social Interaction." In *Communication in Face-to-Face Interaction*, edited by J. Laver and S. Hutcheson. Harmondsworth: Penguin

Haeri, Shaykh Fadhlallah. 1993. *The Elements of Islam.* Shaftesbury: Element Books.

Hiro, Dilip. 2005. *Iran Today.* London: Politico's.

Hofstede, Geert. 2001. *Culture's Consequences: Comparing Values, Behaviors, Institutions and Organisations across Nations*, 2nd ed. London: Sage Publications.

Keshavarz, Mohammad Hossein. 1988. "Forms of address in post-revolutionary Iranian Persian: A sociolinguistic analysis." *Language in Society* 17:565–575.

Koutlaki, Sofia A. 1997. *The Persian system of politeness and the Persian folk concept of face, with some reference to EFL teaching to Iranian native speakers.* Unpublished Ph.D. thesis, University of Wales College of Cardiff.

Koutlaki, Sofia A. 2002. "Offers and Expressions of Thanks as Face Enhancing Acts: Tae'arof in Persian." *Journal of Pragmatics* 34 (2002), 1733–1756.

Koutlaki, Sofia A. 2009. "Two Sides of the Same Coin: How the Notion of 'Face' is Encoded in Persian Communication." In *Face, Communication and Social Interaction*, edited by F. Bargiela-Chiappini and M. Haugh. London: Equinox Press.

Laljee, Yusuf N. (undated). *Know Your Islam.* Qom: Ansariyan Publications.

Laver, John. 1975. "Communicative Functions of Phatic Communion." In *Organization of Behavior in Face-to-Face Interaction*, edited by A. Kendon, R. M. Harris, and M. Ritchey Key. The Hague & Paris: Mouton Publishers.

Malinowski, Bronislaw. 1923. "The Problem of Meaning in Primitive Languages." In *The Meaning of Meaning*, edited by C. K. Ogden and I. A. Richards. London: Routledge & Kegan Paul.

Malinowski, Bronislaw. 1972. "Phatic Communion." In *Communication in Face to Face Interaction*, edited by J. Laver and S. Hutcheson. Harmondsworth: Penguin.

Mir-Hosseini, Ziba. 1993. *Marriage on Trial: A Study of Islamic Family Law: Iran and Morocco Compared.* London: I. B. Tauris.

Mir-Hosseini, Ziba. 1999. *Islam and Gender: The Religious Debate in Contemporary Iran.* London: I. B. Tauris.

Nomani, Farhad and Sohrab Behdad. 2006. *Class and Labor in Iran: Did the Revolution Matter?* Syracuse, NY: Syracuse University Press.

Rafiee, Abdorreza, 1992. *Variables of Communicative Incompetence in the Performance of Iranian Learners of English and English Learners of Persian.* Unpublished Ph.D. thesis, University of London.

Ruthven, Malise 1997. *Islam: A Very Short Introduction.* Oxford: Oxford University Press.

Shaida, Margaret. 1992. *The Legendary Cuisine of Persia.* Henley-on-Thames: Lieuse Publications.

The Splendour of Iran. Three volumes. 2001. London: Booth-Clibborn Editions.

Tabataba'i, Ayatullah Sayyid Muhammad Husayn. 1980. *Islamic Teachings In Brief.* Translated by Muzhgan Jalali. Qom: Ansariyan Publications.

Tayyab, Manouchehr. 2007. *Persian Sea.* Tehran: Ketab-e Khorshid Publications. In Persian.

INDEX

Index

Qajar dynasty, 74, 93, 205–6
Qom, 64, 65, 136, 168
Quality of life. *See* Quantity vs. Quality of life
Quantity vs. Quality of Life (Hofstede's classification axis), 27–28
Quran. *See* Holy Quran, sura

radio, 170, 172
Rafiee Abdorreza, 222, 229
Rafsanjani. *See* Hashemi Rafsanjani
rahn, 18
Ramadan (*Ramezân* in Persian), 6, 7, 43, 57, 59, 78, 102, 152, 157, 171, 213, 216, 217
reading, 175
Red Sea, 202
relationships. *See* interpersonal relationships
religious rules, 63, 64, 192; collection of (*Resâleh al-Amaliyeh*), 64. *See also* âyâtollâh, source of emulation
renting, 17 8
respect, 8, 20, 24, 29, 31, 33, 35, 36, 38, 41, 45, 50, 52, 57, 63, 64, 77, 80, 91, 102, 139, 159, 179, 203
restaurants, 22, 51, 59, 73, 86, 137, 147, 163, 172–3
Reza Khan (Pahlavi the First), 3, 69, 94, 206
rezâei'at (contentment, willing obedience), 29
rial (Iranian currency), 71, 72, 162, 165
rice 59, 141, 143–5, 160, 172; Iranian-style rice (*chelo*) recipe, 144–5, rice with broad beans (*bâghâli polo*) recipe, 145–6; rice with herbs and fried fish (*sabzi polo bâ mâhi*) recipe, 154–5
ritual impurity, 14–15
Rome (ancient city), 66, 203
Rumi (poet, *Mowlânâ* or *Mowlavi* in Persian), 2, 113, 188
Russia (Imperial), 182, 198, 205
Ruthven, Malise, 222, 229

Sa'adi (poet), 167, 188
sabzi polo bâ mâhi (rice with herbs and fried fish) recipe, 154–5
sâdât (descendant of the Holy Prophet through the imams), 68
Safavid dynasty, 167, 205
safety campaigns, 32, 171, 179
Saffarid dynasty, 204
sâl-e hejri qamari. See calendars (Islamic lunar)

sâl-e hejri shamsi. See calendars (Iranian/Islamic solar)
sâl-e Milâdi. See calendars (Western Christian calendar)
Samanid dynasty, 204
Samarra (city in Iraq), 216
Sana'i (poet), 188
Sar'ein (spa town outside Ardebil), 167
Sassanid dynasty, 203
Satan, 61, 182, 220, 228. *See also devil*
satellite: television (*mâhvâreh*), 195, 197
School of Oriental and African Studies (SOAS), University of London, 225
Scots (ethnic group), 3
Scottish (language), 106
secondary articles of Shi'a Islam (*Furu-e Din*), 54
Secret Intelligence Service (SIS), 207
Seleucus I, 202
Seljuk dynasty, 204
seminary (*howzeh*, religious school), 225
Shabdolazim. *See* Shahr-e Rey
Shab-e Yâldâ (eve of the winter solstice), 66, 68, 223
Shâh-nâmeh (*The Book of Kings* by Ferdowsi), 204
Shahr-e Rey, 1, 134, 165
Shaida, Margaret, 68, 223, 224, 229
Shakespeare, William, 221, 226
shakhsiat, 31–3, 48, 123, 179
Shamsolvaezin Mashallah, 181
Shi'ism, 8, 53, 205, 217; *Ithna-'Ashari* (Twelver Shi'as) 222
Shiraz, 9, 167, 190
shoes, 12–3, 65, 67, 73, 74, 89, 130
Shomâl (North), 166
shopping: bargaining 73–4; experience, 174; opening hours, 75; small shops 72–3
slippers, 14–5
Slovakia, 28
social groups. *See* social circles
socks, 12, 97
sofreh (spread): as a symbolic collection of objects, 142; wedding spread (*sofreh aqd*), 131, 142. *See also* Noruz, decorative spread (*sofreh Haft Sin*)
soluk (path of spiritual perfection), 188
source of emulation (*marja' taqlid*), 64. *See also* religious rules
Soviet Union, 4, 182, 206

234

PRAISE FOR *AMONG THE IRANIANS*

"Packed with fascinating insights into an ancient and widely misunderstood culture, it is part-travel guide, part-sociological analysis, part-autobiography—and a must-read for anyone who wants to know the real story about life in Iran."

—Sarah Arnott, correspondent, *The Independent*

"Sofia Koutlaki has opened a window onto ordinary Iranians and their everyday lives. She takes us inside the home, but also out into public spaces, and shows us, with love, an Iran rarely seen by outsiders and a culture whose subtleties she has penetrated with skill and understanding. Her book is essential reading for outsiders who want to understand Iran. Iranians abroad too will find much here to please—and perhaps surprise—them."

—Ziba Mir-Hosseini, author of *Islam and Gender:*
The Religious Debate in Contemporary Iran, **and co-director**
of the award-winning film *Divorce Iranian Style*

"An excellent, useful introduction to Iranian culture and customs for people who have never been to Iran, or potential visitors. . . . The fact that the author has lived in Iran herself as a member of an Iranian family, enables her to go into greater detail on Iranian customs and habits of life than has been done in most other previous books."

—Michael Axworthy, author of *A History of Iran: Empire of the Mind*

"This book provides a fascinating insight into the realities of daily life in Iran. Looking beyond the grim news headlines, the author paints a sympathetic and evocative portrait of the Iranian people, their habits, customs, and histories. It will become essential reading for anyone planning a trip to Iran, or who simply wishes to get to know the Iranian people better."

—Dr. Stephanie Cronin, Oriental Institute,
University of Oxford